THE JEWISH COMEDY CATALOG

THE JEWISH COMEDY CATALOG

☆☆☆☆☆☆☆☆☆☆☆☆☆☆☆☆☆☆☆☆

Darryl Lyman

Jonathan David Publishers, Inc.
Middle Village, New York 11379

THE JEWISH COMEDY CATALOG

Jonathan David Publishers, Inc.
68-22 Eliot Avenue
Middle Village, New York 11379

1992 1991 1990 1989
10 9 8 7 6 5 4 3 2 1

Library of Congress Cataloging-in-Publication Data

Lyman, Darryl, 1944-
The Jewish comedy catalog / by Darryl Lyman.
p. cm.
Includes index.
ISBN 0-8246-0339-7
1. Jewish comedians—United States—Biography.
2. Jews—United States—Biography. I. Title.
PN2285.L96 1989
792.7'028'0922—dc19
[B] 89-1123
CIP

BOOK DESIGN BY BERNARD SCHLEIFER AND ARLENE GOLDBERG

Printed in the United States of America

☆☆☆☆☆☆☆☆☆☆☆☆☆☆☆☆☆☆☆☆☆☆☆☆☆☆☆☆☆☆☆☆

Acknowledgments

Thanks are due to the following institutions and individuals for the photographs reproduced in this book: Larry Edmunds Bookshop (Hollywood); Jerry Ohlinger's Movie Material Store, Inc. (New York), Movie Star News (New York), the film companies ABC Motion Pictures, American International Pictures, Avco Embassy Pictures, Brooksfilms, Columbia Pictures, Gladden Entertainment Corporation, Metro-Goldwyn-Mayer, New World Pictures, Orion Pictures, Paramount Pictures, Seven-Arts Pictures, Touchstone Films, Tri-Star Pictures, Twentieth Century-Fox, United Artists, Universal City Studios, Universal Pictures, Walt Disney Productions, and Warner Brothers; the television networks ABC, CBS, NBC, PBS, and Showtime; the staffs of the American Jewish Archives, Davidson and Choy Publicity, the Garrett Company, Management Company Entertainment, Rollins and Joffe, Rollins, Morra, and Brezner, Inc., the Shefrin Company, Wilkinson/Lipsman, the William Morris Agency, and Zarem, Inc.; and the individuals Joey Adams, Gale Adler, Holly Bower, Clarence S. Bull, Christie (Columbia Pictures photo), Crosby (Columbia Pictures photo), Greg Gorman, Brian Hamill, Elmer Holloway, Rose Joseph, Judy Katz (Richard Grant & Associates), Laurel Moore, Eugene Robert Richee, Joyce Rudolph, Richard Sherman, Marc Weiner, and Lotus Weinstock.

Contents

Thumbnail Sketches

Introduction

A catalog of Jewish comedians is a virtual who's who of comedy. The names include Woody Allen, Jack Benny, Milton Berle, David Brenner, Fanny Brice, Mel Brooks, Lenny Bruce, George Burns, Sid Caeser, Eddie Cantor, Billy Crystal, Rodney Dangerfield, Buddy Hackett, Goldie Hawn, Madeline Kahn, Danny Kaye, Alan King, Jerry Lewis, the Marx Brothers, Jackie Mason, Bette Midler, Don Rickles, Joan Rivers, Peter Sellers, the Three Stooges, Gene Wilder, Ed Wynn, and Henny Youngman.

One cannot speak of a "typical" Jewish comedian. The variety is too great.

Some of them present explicitly Jewish stage personae through the use of accents or Yiddish words (Mel Brooks, Myron Cohen, Jackie Mason), or through direct references to their Jewishness (Woody Allen, Lenny Bruce, Don Rickles). Others make little or no comedic use of their ethnic background (Jack Benny, Milton Berle, Jerry Lewis).

Some of them portray schlemiels, losers, or victims (Woody Allen, Rodney Dangerfield, Joan Rivers). Others present an angry, aggressive image (Mel Brooks, Alan King, Don Rickles).

Why are there so many Jewish comedians? There are at least three principal reasons.

First, there is a long-standing comic tradition in the Jewish world. For centuries, jesters were the most popular entertainers in Jewish communities. In addition, some of those clowns were allowed to entertain the upper levels of gentile societies. Many a

☆☆☆☆☆☆☆☆☆☆☆☆☆☆☆☆☆☆☆☆☆☆☆☆☆

Jewish child must have yearned to grow up to be a clown. (See "Medieval Comedy" and "Purim Plays" below.)

The tradition of Jewish humor also reveals itself in Yiddish folk proverbs. The seeds of many familiar modern jokes can be seen in such proverbs as the following:

> Women persuade men to good as well as to evil, but they always persuade.
>
> The mother-in-law and the daughter-in-law do not ride in the same cart.
>
> If a poor man eats a chicken, either he is sick or the chicken was sick.
>
> If a Jew breaks a leg, he says, "Praised be God that I did not break both legs." If he breaks both legs, he says, "Praised be God that I did not break my neck."
>
> If the Jew be right, he is beaten all the more.
>
> Every man knows that he must die, but no one believes it.

Yiddish folklore also has comical stories about the archetypal schlemiel, Motke Habad. In one story, the eternal loser Motke, in financial trouble, appeals to community leaders for help. "If you do not support me," he tells them, "I will become a hat maker!" The elders laugh. "What if you do?" they reply. "But don't you see what that would mean?" Motke explains. "If I turn hat maker, all the infants in this town will be born without heads."

Another stock character in Yiddish folklore is the schnorrer, the professional beggar. In a certain village, it was the custom for pious householders to take wandering mendicants home on Friday evening for shelter over the Sabbath. One man was returning home from prayer service with a poor guest in tow when the householder noticed a second schnorrer trailing them. "Who is that?" the householder asked. "It's my son-in-law," the first beggar replied. "I am supporting him."

The above elements—clowns, proverbs, and folklore—reflect a strong, centuries-old comic tradition in the Jewish community. That tradition formed the historical matrix out of which evolved the great number of modern Jewish comedians.

The second reason for so many Jewish comic entertainers pertains to the nineteenth-century assimilation movement and its twentieth-century aftereffects. Jews were finally allowed into gentile society, yet full acceptance was rarely possible without completely hiding their ethnic heritage. Even today, anti-Semitism, in both overt and subtle forms, creates daily tensions in the lives of Jews. Drawing on the Jewish comic tradition and on the widespread Jewish trait of verbalizing emotions, Jewish entertainers released those tensions by exploding them in laughter.

☆☆☆☆☆☆☆☆☆☆☆☆☆☆☆☆☆☆☆☆☆☆☆☆☆

The principal technique was self-deprecation. Yet behind the mask of self-criticism lay self-preservation and even self-assertion. Jewish comedians stole their enemies' thunder: "I'll say it before you can—and better," the Jewish entertainer tacitly proclaimed.

The third principal reason for so many Jewish comedians is that show business is a readily available, and potentially lucrative, way to escape poverty and the ghetto. The ethnic stereotypes in early vaudeville (such as the dumb Swede and the Irish drunk) opened the stage door to Jewish entertainers willing to portray Jewish caricatures. Later many Jews who began their careers in other fields discovered that their quick wit (forged through centuries of Jewish intellectual tradition) could take them further in life when applied to the field of comedy. Among the countless Jewish comedians who made such switches (and their first interests in life) are Morey Amsterdam (cello), Gertrude Berg (writing), Elayne Boosler (singing), Victor Borge (piano), Sid Caesar (saxophone), Myron Cohen (sales), Norm Crosby (commercial art), Marty Feldman (trumpet), Madeline Kahn (singing), Sam Levenson (teaching), Jackie Mason (rabbinics), Zero Mostel (art), Mort Sahl (city management), and Al Schacht (baseball).

These, then, are among the contributing factors accounting for the large number of Jewish comedians: comedy as a Jewish tradition, comedy as a way of releasing tensions arising from assimilation, and comedy as a means of achieving career advancement.

The following is a brief historical review of Jews as comic entertainers.

Ancient Comedy

Jews have provided the world with comedy since ancient times. At first, however, they were mainly the butts of the jokes. During the first century B.C.E., gentile theaters were established in Palestine. By the second century of the Christian Era, the shows were dominated by coarse, ribald comedy that often ridiculed Jews and their customs.

Pious Jews refrained from all stage activity, and no Jewish theater was created in Palestine. However, some Jews did attend pagan theaters. By the first century of the Christian Era, Jews were even performing on the pagan stage. In Rome, the Jewish actor Aliturus was among Emperor Nero's favorites, and a man named Menophilus appears to have been a Jewish comedian. The third-century rabbinical scholar Resh Lakish earned his living as a circus strongman.

☆☆☆☆☆☆☆☆☆☆☆☆☆☆☆☆☆☆☆☆☆☆☆☆

Medieval Comedy

In the Middle Ages, troupes of gentile clowns, mimes, and acrobats roamed Europe. They told jokes, acted in skits, and performed feats of physical dexterity in marketplaces and in princely courts. They even livened up Christian mystery plays (religious dramas based on biblical texts). Amog those performers were nearly always some Jews.

Often Jews were singled out for enforced roles as clowns or buffoons. Beginning in the thirteenth century, or even earlier, Jews in Italian cities were compelled to participate in carnival shows as mounts for soldiers or for the general populace. Jews also clowned for the diversion of powerful men in the Christian world and, from the sixteenth century on, in the Muslim world (such as for the sultan in Constantinople).

In the Jewish community itself, clowns were routinely hired to appear at ghetto social events and at wedding parties. In fact, the earliest, and for a long time the only, professional Yiddish theatrical performers were clowns. As late as the nineteenth century, some Hasidic rabbis employed their own court jesters.

Purim Plays

From the Christian use of comedy in their mystery plays, medieval Jews derived the idea of adding humor to their own elaborate plays that celebrated the holiday of Purim. The celebration would begin with a procession led by all sorts of clowns. The clown-hero of the day rode on a wine cask pulled by schoolboys; he was the crazy Purim King, a fat Bacchus holding a wineglass. Accompanying him were assorted fools and clowns, such as one holding—and wearing—kitchen utensils and another dressed as a servant girl. Following the clowns came biblical characters, tradespeople, musicians, and others—all proceeding through the ghetto streets to the location of the play itself. Purim plays were based on Bible stories, but they always included slapstick clowning between serious plot elements.

Such plays remained the principal expression of the Yiddish theater from the late medieval period till the late nineteenth century. During that span of time, several types of Yiddish comedians evolved. A *lets* was a pure slapstick clown, as was a *nar.* A *payats* often recited the Prologue to a play and gave stage directions to actors; if audience attention seemed to be waning, he would stand on his head or spout puns. A *marshelik* was a more dignified

☆☆☆☆☆☆☆☆☆☆☆☆☆☆☆☆☆☆☆☆☆☆☆☆☆

entertainer, a kind of master of ceremonies. A *badkhen* specialized in weddings, where he used his sharp wit to comment on the festivities.

Jews in the Gentile Theater, Middle Ages to 1900

Meanwhile, Jews were seldom allowed to participate in the gentile theater. Many Jewish characters were created for the gentile repertory, but they were nearly always villainous roles (such as Shylock in Shakespeare's *The Merchant of Venice*) and they were played by non-Jews.

In the late eighteenth and early nineteenth centuries, things began to improve through the emancipation and assimilation movements.

British theaters were among the earliest to open their stages to Jews. The first notable Jewish actress in England was Hannah Norsa, who won great success in 1732 by acting and singing the comic role of Polly Peachum in *The Beggar's Opera.*

An important English comedian from the 1780s to the 1820s was Jacob de Castro (on the gentile stage his first name was often recorded as James, and his surname has gone into print as de Castro, De Castro, and Decastro). He began in Purim plays as a mimic. In the 1780s he was engaged by Philip Astley, and thereafter he performed as part of an ensemble called "Astley's Jews" in burlesques, pantomimes, and musical farces. In 1824, shortly before his death, de Castro published his memoirs, a valuable record of theatrical activities of the period.

Among later nineteenth-century Jewish comedians on the British stage were Henry Sloman (né Solomon), popular in London pantomimes; Harry Jackson (né Jacobson), well known for his Jewish stock-character roles; and David James (né Belasco), famed for his role as Perkyn Middlewick in the comedy *Our Boys* (in several productions from 1875 to 1892).

Other nineteenth-century Jewish comedians on the gentile stage included Frederick Adrianus Rosenveldt in Holland and Anton Ascher in Germany. In Italy, Claudio Leigheb specialized in comic roles, and Giuseppe Sichel helped to popularize French comedy in his native land.

☆☆☆☆☆☆☆☆☆☆☆☆☆☆☆☆☆☆☆☆☆☆☆☆☆

Yiddish Comedy

However, the Yiddish comedy tradition was still being kept alive. Hershele (or Hirsch) Ostropoler, a late-eighteenth-century court jester to various Hasidic rabbis, wander eastern Europe and uttered satiric Yiddish barbs that shocked the elite and delighted the simple folk.

Purim plays provided the seed for the modern Yiddish theater, principally fathered by Abraham Goldfaden (a playwright, composer, producer, manager, and impresario), beginning in Romania in 1876. The movement soon spread throughout Europe and the United States, a strong Yiddish theater thriving for many years in New York City.

The first great comedian of the modern Yiddish theater was Sigmund Mogulesko. Born in Bessarabia, he moved to the United States in 1886, when he was twenty-eight. A comic genius, Mogulesko could insure the success of a play solely through the power of his presence. His winks and nuances added rich meanings to songs. And in addition to handling sensitive character portrayals, he could quickly slip into brilliant, often obscene, improvisations.

Mogulesko had many outstanding successors as Yiddish clowns on the American stage. Aaron Lebedeff, with his knowing, street-wise grin, specialized in musical comedies. Ludwig Satz, billed as the man who "makes you laugh with tears and cry with a smile," had a feminine grace, a round, wide-eyed face, and a look of childlike bewilderment. Menasha Skulnik, famed for his portrayal of an inept army recruit in *Straw Soldier*, was a sad-looking comic noted for his ludicrous shrugs of helplessness. Others included Max Bozyk, Michel Rosenberg, and Molly Picon.

A decline in the American Yiddish theater set in between World Wars I and II as more and more American Jews grew up without Yiddish. In the popular theater, performers began to combine English and Yiddish into a form sometimes called "potato Yiddish."

In Poland during those years, Shimon Dzigan and Israel Schumacher developed a kind of witty, irreverent Yiddish cabaret revue. In their dialogues, Dzigan played a quick-witted ignoramus, while Schumacher was a sedate know-it-all. During World War II they went to Russia, and in the early 1950s they settled in Israel, where they poked fun at the absurdities of politics and manners in the new country.

Other post-World War II Israeli comedians included the Burstein family, consisting of father Pesach, mother Lillian (née Lux), and son Michael (or Mordecai), known in the United States as Mike Burstyn. They also performed in the United States, gaining special renown for their musical comedy *The Megilla.* Pesach issued about three hundred recordings, which made him one of the most famous and beloved personalities in the Yiddish-speaking world.

☆☆☆☆☆☆☆☆☆☆☆☆☆☆☆☆☆☆☆☆☆☆☆☆☆

Jacob Jacobs and Leo Fuchs helped to keep the comic spirit alive on the American stage after World War II. They were joined by the excellent comedienne Henrietta Jacobson.

Mickey Katz was a brilliant comedian and musician whose English-Yiddish *Borscht Capades* revue delighted audiences for decades. His English-Yiddish parodies of popular songs created some of the most hilarious comic recordings of all time.

Modern Vernacular Comedy

United States

Vaudeville and **burlesque.** Vaudeville and burlesque were popular entertainment forms that evolved to meet the needs of the masses of urban working people. A vaudeville show consisted of a variety of unconnected comedy, dancing, musical, and specialty (such as magic, juggling, and acrobatic) acts. Burlesque began as comic parodies of well-known topics or people, but soon the genre became dominated by girlie shows.

The vaudeville vogue for Jewish-dialect comedians was initiated in the late nineteenth century by non-Jewish performers. Among the most popular was Frank (originally Benjamin Franklin) Bush, who caricatured Jews with a song that included these lyrics: "Oh, my name is Solomon Moses. I'm a bully sheeny man."

An important early Jewish comedian in vaudeville was Joe Welch (originally Joseph Wolinski). He played a sad-faced Jewish character who had a pointed beard, wore oversize clothes, plopped a derby over his ears, and opened with this line: "Mebbe you t'ink I am a heppy man." Hundreds of later Jewish-dialect comedians patterned their style and delivery after Welch's. He died in 1918 at the age of only forty-five.

Other Jewish dialecticians in vaudeville included Benny Rubin, Smith and Dale, David Warfield, and Weber and Fields.

Many Jewish vaudevillians made little or no direct use of their ethnic background in their acts. Among them were Jack Benny, Milton Berle, Eddie Cantor, the Marx Brothers, and Ed Wynn.

Burlesque comics had to face some of the most difficult of all audiences—those who were waiting impatiently for the arrival of scantily clad women. Jewish entertainers forged into first-rate comics by such experiences included Fanny Brice, Bert Lahr, and Phil Silvers.

Broadway. On the Great White Way, Jewish comics have been well represented in revues, book comedies, and one-man shows. Fanny Brice and/or Eddie Cantor dominated many of the *Ziegfeld*

☆☆☆☆☆☆☆☆☆☆☆☆☆☆☆☆☆☆☆☆☆☆☆☆☆

Follies from the 1910s to the 1930s. During those same years, Willie Howard appeared in numerous revues, including nearly a dozen under the titles *The Passing Show* and *George White's Scandals.* Ed Wynn became a Broadway star in the Ziegfeld Follies of 1914 and went on to create, and head the casts of, his own series of "entertainments," including *Ed Wynn Carnival* (1920) and *Laugh, Town, Laugh* (1942).

The Marx Brothers starred in the Broadway musical comedies *The Cocoanuts* (1925) and *Animal Crackers* (1928). Judy Holliday made theatrical history as Billie Dawn in the straight comedy *Born Yesterday* (1946). Phil Silvers sparkled in the musical comedy *Top Banana* (1951). And Zero Mostel created the role of Tevye in the musical *Fiddler on the Roof* (1964).

The pianist-comedian Victor Borge starred in the one-man Broadway show *Comedy in Music* from 1953 to 1956. Jackie Mason has ruled Broadway since December 1986 in his one-man show *The World According to Me!*

Borscht Belt. The borscht belt (or circuit) is the group of theaters and nightclubs associated with the Jewish summer camps and resort hotels of the Catskill Mountains. The resorts started to develop in the early twentieth century, and entertainers became important factors there between World Wars I and II.

Besides hiring "name" performers for various periods of time, the resorts usually had on their staffs a resident entertainer called a social director or, more informally, a toomler (*toomler* is a corruption of *tumulter,* short for *tumult-maker,* that is, a "creator of comic tumult"). Among the many great comedians who had early training in the borscht belt were Joey Adams, Red Buttons, Danny Kaye, and Jerry Lewis.

Films. Jewish characters entered films early in motion-picture history. Often, however, the roles were played by non-Jews.

One of the earliest Jewish comedians on film was Max Asher, who portrayed the Jewish character Jake in a series of Mike and Jake pictures in 1913. The following year Max Davidson was the lazy Izzy in another series.

George Sidney (originally Sammy Greenfield) played a different Izzy in a series beginning with *Busy Izzy* (1915). Sidney, one of America's leading vaudeville comedians, went on to become the principal player of Jewish roles in movies of the 1920s and 1930s. Short, stocky, balding, and bug-eyed, he was known for his excitability and his hyperactive hands. Sidney played Abe Potash in a series of comedy films that included *In Hollywood with Potash and Perlmutter* (1924), and Jacob Cohen in a series that included *The Cohens and Kellys in Hollywood* (1932).

George Jessel portrayed the title role in *Private Izzy Murphy* (1926), which tried to break racial barriers by showing a successful

☆☆☆☆☆☆☆☆☆☆☆☆☆☆☆☆☆☆☆☆☆☆☆☆

romance and marriage between a Jew and a Gentile. Sammy Cohen's screen humor was often based on jokes about his large nose, as in *Why Sailors Go Wrong* (1928), where he played "Sammy Breezeroff—with a nose for money." In the late 1920s and early 1930s, one of the busiest Jewish comedians on film was Benny Rubin.

As protests against Jewish caricatures arose, opportunities for Jewish comic roles declined. In the 1960s such roles reemerged, but without the previous tendency toward harsh mockery of supposed Jewish characteristics (large nose, cowardliness, business scheming, thickly accented English). The two leads in Mel Brooks's comedy *The Producers* (1967) were Jewish characters played by Zero Mostel and Gene Wilder. Wilder portrayed a rabbi in *The Frisco Kid* (1979). Woody Allen often plays Jewish characters in his films, such as *Annie Hall* (1977), *Manhattan* (1979), and *Hannah and Her Sisters* (1986).

Many other Jewish comic performers have appeared in films without portraying overtly Jewish characters. The Marx Brothers never played Jews on-screen, but in the 1930s and 1940s they exuded the Jewish urban experience through their streetwise Lower East Side language, their ingenious (albeit eccentric) debates reminiscent of the Talmud, and especially their sense of alienation from the mainstream of society.

Other Jewish film comedians in their heyday during the 1930s and 1940s included Jack Benny, Eddie Cantor, the Ritz Brothers, and the Three Stooges. Later came Danny Kaye (1940s-50s), Judy Holliday (1950s), Jerry Lewis (1950s-60s), Peter Sellers (1950s-70s), Goldie Hawn (1970s-80s), Madeline Kahn (1970s-80s), and Bette Midler (1980s).

Radio. Jewish comedians headed many of the most popular radio programs of the medium's golden era, the 1930s and 1940s. Jack Benny reigned as king of the airways for over twenty years because of his well-defined character and his effective use of sound effects. Gertrude Berg was the lovable Molly Goldberg in *The Goldbergs*. Fanny Brice delighted audiences with her characterization of the impish Baby Snooks. George Burns and his wife, Gracie Allen, played off each other beautifully in their long-running comedy series. Eddie Cantor pioneered the use of live-audience response and introduced the country to another comedian of Jewish heritage, Harry Einstein, who performed under the Greek name of Parkyakarkus.

Television. Some radio performers made the transition to TV and retained or increased their popularity, such as Jack Benny and George Burns. Other experienced entertainers suddenly discovered the infant medium to be the perfect vehicle for them, and they rose to heights never dreamed of in their earlier careers. Milton Berle

☆☆☆☆☆☆☆☆☆☆☆☆☆☆☆☆☆☆☆☆☆☆☆☆☆

became Mr. Television, TV's first superstar, through his vaudeville-inspired buffoonery on *The Texaco Star Theater* (1948-53). Sid Caesar won fame by creating a host of zany characters and performing well-rounded skits on *Your Show of Shows* (1950-54). Red Buttons headed a similar program in the early 1950s, and the borscht-belt comedian Jan Murray struck it rich as host of *Treasure Hunt* (1956-59) and other TV game shows.

In the 1960s Bill Dana was popular on TV as the timid José Jimenez, Soupy Sales raised camp comedy to an art form, Joey Bishop updated the classic image of the sad-faced clown, and Avery Schreiber played a Jewish taxicab driver. In the 1970s Bea Arthur won fame as the comically commanding title character *Maude,* Gabe Kaplan starred as Gabe Kotter in *Welcome Back, Kotter,* Gilda Radner invented a host of characters for *NBC's Saturday Night Live,* and Andy Kaufman played Latka Gravas in *Taxi.* Since 1985 Bea Arthur and Estelle Getty have acted in the hit sitcom *The Golden Girls.*

In addition, innumerable Jewish stand-up comedians won huge followings by doing their routines on TV talk and variety shows. Among those performers were David Brenner, Rodney Dangerfield, Totie Fields, Alan King, Robert Klein, Jackie Mason, Don Rickles, Joan Rivers, and David Steinberg.

Nightclubs, cabarets, and **comedy clubs.** Nightclubs and cabarets provide the steadiest employment for modern comedians. The words *nightclub* and *cabaret* are sometimes used synonymously, but the latter term is more closely associated with artistic experimentation. Related venues include hotels, casinos, and theaters. The entertainment provided at such places tends to be fairly sophisticated and/or risqué (or downright dirty) because the audiences are typically small, adult, and well-educated. Among the Jewish stand-up comics who found their greatest success through nightclubs and related outlets were Belle Barth, Lenny Bruce, Shecky Greene, Buddy Hackett, Joe E. Lewis, and Mort Sahl.

Comedy clubs are nightclubs where the entertainment is provided mostly or solely by comedians, especially newcomers. The comedian Sammy Shore helped to initiate such clubs when he opened his Comedy Store in Los Angeles in 1972. The big boom in professional comedy clubs took place in the early 1980s. One of the featured comedians in that movement was Marc Weiner.

Other Countries

The British equivalent of American vaudeville was called music hall. In the late nineteenth century, Anna Held, after beginning her career in the Yiddish theater, became one of London's top music-hall comediennes. Later she moved to the United States, married the impresario Florenz Ziegfeld, and performed in American musical comedies and vaudeville before her death in 1918.

Bud Flanagan, beginning in the 1920s, was another major music-hall star; he also appeared in many films. Ron Moody, a master of disguises, has excelled in the theater, on TV, and in movies. The popeyed comic Marty Feldman won a cult following on British TV before turning to American films. The crumple-faced comedy character actor Sid James worked extensively in England on TV; his movies included the classic *The Lavender Hill Mob* (1951) and several pictures in the Carry On series, such as *Carry On, Cabby* (1967).

In Canada, the comedy team of Johnny Wayne (né Weingarten) and Frank Shuster entered radio just after World War II and later worked on Canadian and American TV. Their wide-ranging skits included corn, slapstick, pantomime, visual tricks, and original twists on familiar situations. Despite the lure of fame and fortune in the United States, Wayne and Shuster have remained solidly based in Canada.

However, some European-born comedians permanently moved to the United States. Victor Borge won great renown in his native Denmark before fleeing the Nazis and immigrating to America in 1940. George (originally Jiri) Voskovec was immensely popular in Czechoslovakia as part of the comedy team Voskovec and (Jan) Werich. Voskovec performed satiric sketches aimed first at Nazism and later at Communism. Both parties forced him out of his homeland, the first in 1939 and the other just after World War II. In the early 1950s he finally settled permanently in the United States, where he became a successful dramatic actor.

The German actor Max Pallenberg, a brilliant improviser, was successful in both tragicomic roles and light-comedy parts till the Nazis came to power in 1933. He died the following year in a plane crash.

Arkady Raikin became the Soviet Union's most beloved comedian by poking fun at the Soviet system under rulers from Stalin to Gorbachev. Raikin's humor mixed satire, sentimentality, and, in his younger days, slapstick. Though he ridiculed the shortages, corruption, and bureaucracy in Soviet Russia, he was appreciated even by the highest government officials. He died in 1987.

Misha Belenky, a graduate of both the Moscow Conservatory and Leningrad's Comedy Performance school, blends music and comedy in a unique kind of one-man show. He has concertized in Russia, Eastern Europe, and the United States. Another Russian comedian, Yakov Smirnoff, began his career in the Soviet Union but immigrated to the United States, where he became a naturalized citizen in 1986.

In India, David Abraham made over a hundred Hindustani films. He specialized in comedy roles.

One of Israel's most versatile entertainers is Ezra, an international singing and comedy star. He performs in English, Hebrew, Yiddish, French, Spanish, Turkish, Greek, and Arabic. Sandy Shmuely also blends vocal music and comedy. His impersonations leave audiences rolling in the aisles.

Who is a Jew? In this book, I have followed the definition established by Jewish law: a Jew is anyone who was born of a Jewish mother or who converted to Judaism. This definition forces the exclusion of performers born of a Jewish father and non-Jewish mother, as in the case of Don Adams.

The Jewish Comedy Catalog is a compendium of about one hundred major biographies supplemented by an appendix of thumbnail sketches of Jewish comedians/comediennes and comic actors/actresses. I hope that you, the reader, get as much enjoyment from reading the stories of these diverse and fascinating personalities as I did in researching and writing them.★

DARRYL LYMAN

Whittier, California

MAJOR BIOGRAPHIES

JOEY ADAMS
Catskills Comic

Joey Adams has been a nightclub, vaudeville, theater, radio, and TV comedian. But he made his greatest impact in the resorts of the Catskill Mountains, where he long reigned as the most sought-after entertainer. His own career played a major part in the history of that popular region, a story that he related in his excellent book *The Borscht Belt* (1966).

Adams was born in New York City, New York, on January 6, 1911. His original name was Joseph Abramowitz.

He entered show business in his teens. His first Catskills job was as a bellboy and assistant bookkeeper in a hotel. In his spare time he was also expected to function as a toomler (creator of comic tumult), more elegantly referred to as a social director, whose wide-ranging tasks included singing, dancing, telling jokes, arranging games, forming exercise programs, and even matchmaking.

Adams eventually headed his own troupe of performers who traveled the Catskills resorts, often performing one-night stands. As one of the most dedicated, dependable performers in the borscht belt, he found himself in big demand.

His routines included one-liners, stories, parodies on hit songs, and even condensed versions of Broadway shows, such as *The Jazz Singer.* Like all Catskills comics, he constantly had to add new material to his act because his audiences tended to be the same people over and over again each summer (as distinct from nightclub comics, who could take the same act all over the country). Buying, trading, and stealing material were accepted practices.

"In one place I found that the social director who preceded me was my old saxophone player from two summers before," Adams has recalled. "He had lifted all of the original scenes and gags I had bought from fellow comic Lou Saxon, who had stolen them direct from the gag fence Eddie Davis, who received them from Leon Fields, who had gotten them from Buddy Walker, who had copied them all down from Milton

Civic Interests

Because of his early association with Fiorello La Guardia, Adams has had a lifelong civic-mindedness. Among the many high posts he has held are chairman of a March of Dimes special-events committee, commissioner of youth for New York City, and president of the American Guild of Variety Artists.

In 1952 Adams was honored by the Israeli government for his work with the United Jewish Appeal and Israel Bond drives. He received humanitarian awards from the American Cancer Society (1952), Crusade for Freedom (1956), and the Yiddish Theatrical Alliance (1960). He was named Man of the Year by the March of Dimes (1958), the City of Hope (1959), and the New York City Police Department (1960). In 1971 he was awarded the Pope's Medal.

Berle at Loew's State when they were still warm."

Adams got a lot of mileage out of George Jessel's famous "Mama on the Telephone" routine. The toomler also had to have a good supply of one-liners, such as "Remember, it is better to have loved and lost—*much* better." One of his favorites was "Here's a song dedicated to Mae West: 'I've got the sun in the morning and the father at night.' "

While he was conquering the Catskills, Adams also had outstanding success elsewhere, including vaudeville and nightclub circuits. He frequently appeared on TV in its early days, hosting, for example, *Back That Fact* in 1953. Adams produced and starred in the movie *Singing in the Dark* (1956). Musical comedy was another vehicle for him, as in a 1960 stage production of *Guys and Dolls.* In 1961, at the request of President Kennedy, Adams headed a troupe of entertainers on a tour of Asia. In recent years he has hosted his own popular radio show in New York City.

While continuing his comedy-performing career, he has also become a prolific writer. He has written a syndicated column, *Strictly for Laughs*, for the *New York Post.* His books include volumes of collected humor as well as works on historical aspects of the entertainment industry. Among his many books are *From Gags to Riches* (1946), *Strictly for Laughs* (1955), *Joke Dictionary* (1961), *On the Road for Uncle Sam* (1963), *The Borscht Belt* (1966), *Joey Adams' Speaker's Bible of Humor* (1972), *Here's to the Friars* (1976), and *The Roast of the Town* (1986).☆

Adams Roasts Friars

Long an active member of the Friars Club, Adams especially enjoys the gatherings where one member is verbally roasted by the others. Adams was proposed for membership by Milton Berle and Henny Youngman.

La Guardia's Boy

As a small child, Joey Adams stood on a Harlem street, listening to and mimicking the campaign oratory of Fiorello La Guardia, a congressional candidate. La Guardia took a liking to the youth, who came to be known as "La Guardia's boy."

"As the 'adopted son' and protégé of the late mayor of new York City, Fiorello La Guardia," Adams has written, "I have always lived by his words to me: "Don't worry about people knowing you—make yourself worth knowing.' "

Some Favorite Jokes

From Billy Gray, Joey Adams purchased some "sock blackouts," jokes strong enough to close an act. Among Adams's favorites were these:

FIRST LADY: I'm going through agony and ecstasy with my daughter.
SECOND LADY: So what's the agony?
FIRST LADY: The agony is she's marrying a Gentile.
SECOND LADY: And the ecstasy?
FIRST LADY: The ecstasy is, thank God, he's a doctor.

WIFE: Darling, I dreamed last night that you bought me a mink coat.
HUSBAND: That's nice. Next time you dream, wear it in good health.

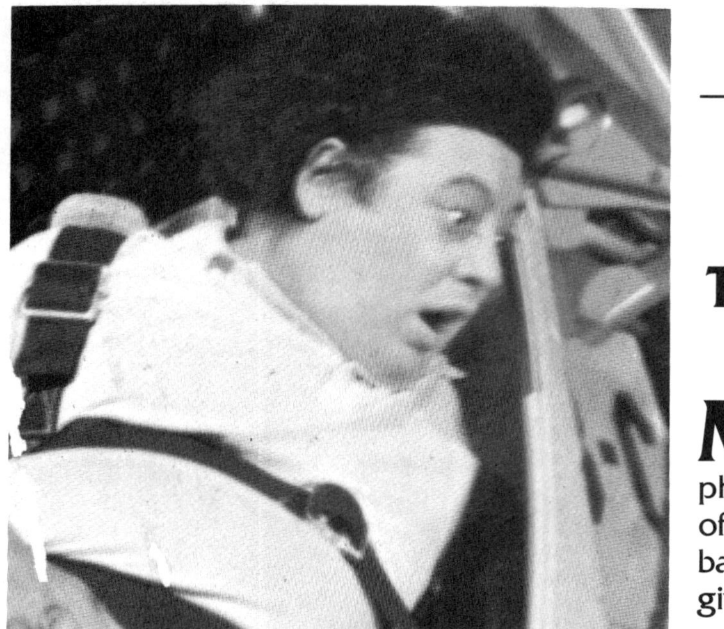

MARTY ALLEN
The "Hello Dere" Comedian

Marty Allen, with his partner Steve Rossi, was one of the hottest comedians of the 1960s. Allen's physical trademarks are his mournful nasal voice, mass of black hair, and large frightened eyes. His humor is based on an impish little-boy view of the world: "Oh, give me a home where the buffalo roam—and I'll show you a house full of dirt."

Allen was born in Pittsburgh, Pennsylvania, on March 23, 1922. After military service during World War II, he attended the University of Southern California and simultaneously began his entertainment career in local night spots.

Later he joined the singer Steve Rossi to form a duo that was seen in some quarters as successors to the comedy team of Dean Martin and Jerry Lewis. Rossi, like Martin, was the Italian singer and straight man, while Allen, like Lewis, was the Jewish childlike troublemaker.

Playing in nightclubs throughout the United States, Allen and Rossi used interview routines to break up audiences. Rossi, the interviewer, struggled in vain to control the wild answers from Allen, who played an astronaut, a mechanical man, an Oriental athlete, a Playboy bunny, and other characters.

One routine had Allen as Richard Burton's stand-in during the filming of *Cleopatra*:

> ROSSI: I hear it cost $40 million to make *Cleopatra*.
> ALLEN: Yeah, some girls are more expensive than others.
> ROSSI: Cleopatra's a mummy.
> ALLEN: No wonder, the way she fooled around.

Another routine:

> ALLEN: I feel like a dog.
> ROSSI: How long have you felt like a dog?
> ALLEN: Since I was a puppy.

The team made a tremendous impact during the early 1960s. Allen created a national catchphrase with "Hello dere," the opening line for all his characters. The team's first album, *Hello Dere*, went gold in 1962. The next, and best, album was *Too Funny for Words*, released in 1963. They performed over forty times on Ed Sullivan's popular TV variety series.

In 1968 Allen and Rossi amicably split up to pursue separate careers. For the next fifteen years Allen played a solo act in nightclubs and theaters, appeared on TV game shows, and acted in a few movies, such as *Murder Can Hurt You!* (TV, 1980).

Allen called his solo act a "comedy concert" because it consisted not only of stand-up humor but also of singing, dancing, and one-man skits. He often ended his shows with a poignant pantomime of a clown who suddenly realizes that he is growing old.

In 1983 Rossi happened to catch Allen's solo act. The audience prodded Rossi to the stage, where the pair soon discovered that they still enjoyed working to-

Marty Allen (left) with Steve Rossi.

Allen's Agility

Marty Allen, despite his short, heavyset build, is agile, as he clearly shows onstage while dancing. His physical humor would not work without his excellent body control, as in his routine as a drunk wine taster staggering about the stage, and in his drag bit singing, "Hey, Big Spender" while bumping and grinding.

Weight Control

Marty Allen has made significant efforts to control his weight and to keep generally fit, as in his frequent visits to the Harbor Island Spa in Long Branch, New Jersey.

Best Friend

One of Marty Allen's best friends is Mike Douglas, whose popular TV show Allen has cohosted many times.

Contemplated Lawsuit

While Marty Allen and Steve Rossi were separated, Rossi briefly teamed up with Bernie Allen. Marty felt that the public's confusing the two Allens could hurt the professional value of his name. He contemplated a lawsuit, but Rossi and Bernie Allen soon parted anyway.

gether. Since then Allen and Rossi have successfully performed together many times in Las Vegas and Atlantic City.

In 1988 Allen appeared on a television fund-raiser for the Chabad House drug-rehabilitation program. ★

WOODY ALLEN
Sage of Anxiety

Woody Allen, today's premier comic neurotic, typically portrays an intelligent contemporary urban man struggling feebly against the alienation and anxieties of the cold, mechanized world. In one of Allen's stand-up fantasy routines, a talking elevator turns anti-Semitic. In another, a squad from the local public library surrounds his house to retrieve books from him.

Consumed by the modern existential crisis, Allen's intellectual character forever debates with himself about the relative importance of the mind and the body, of the spiritual and the material. He frequently produces a comic effect by juxtaposing the profound with the commonplace, as in his description of his parents' values as "God and carpeting."

A classic schlemiel, whose pain is intensified through his sense of guilt, Allen's character sums up his feelings with this gem: "My one regret in life is that I'm not somebody else."

Much of Allen's humor parodies his Jewish background. "I once won two weeks at an interfaith boarding camp," he says, "where I was sadistically beaten by kids of all races and colors."

Allen directs Elaine Stritch (left) and Mia Farrow.

Suffering from Anhedonia

Allen has long suffered from anhedonia, the inability to experience happiness. When, for example, he contemplated "engulfing a slab of the world's richest cheesecake," he experienced, he said, "the guilty cholesterolish hallucination that I could hear my aorta congealing into a hockey puck." And he claims that moviemaking is "a thoroughly unpleasant experience," but "I figure if I don't make movies now, I'll regret it later on."

Playing

Allen regularly plays clarinet with a jazz group at Michael's Pub in New York City. His clarinet plays a prominent role in the jazz background score for his movie *Sleeper.*

Enjoying Diversions

Walking, buying records, sitting on park benches, and drifting in and out of revival houses—these are some of what Allen calls the "foolish things" he does for fun.

In his film *Hannah and Her Sisters* (1986) Allen's Jewish character is thinking of converting to Catholicism. In preparation he buys white bread and mayonnaise.

In *Annie Hall*, Allen's highly regarded 1977 movie, he pokes fun at the Jewish intellectual and religious tradition. He speaks of merging two Jewish intellectual magazines, *Dissent* and *Commentary*, into a periodical called *Dissentary*. In college, he says, he took courses called Truth, Beauty and Advanced Truth, and Beauty. He was expelled for cheating on the metaphysics final: he had looked into the soul of the boy sitting next to him.

Woody Allen was born of Orthodox Jewish parents in New York City, New York, on December 1, 1935. His original name was Alan Stewart Konigsberg.

In his early teens he began his career by contributing one-liners to newspaper columnists, such as Earl Wilson. Soon he was ghostwriting lines publicly attributed to celebrities, including Guy Lombardo and Arthur Murray.

At the age of seventeen Allen was hired as a full-time staff writer for Peter Lind Hayes at NBC-TV. Later Allen wrote for Sid Caesar, Buddy Hackett, Gary Moore, Jack Paar, and other TV personalities.

In 1960 Allen began to perform his own stand-up comedy act in nightclubs. Shy and painfully nervous, he was unsuccessful for more than a year. One crowd virtually heckled him off the stage.

Eventually, however, he developed an affective stage presence and perfected his fictional persona of the modern intellectual loser. By 1963, through nightclub dates and TV appearances, he had established a national reputation.

Allen's comic stage character was abused, insecure, and too civilized for the real world. "I used to steal second base," he would say, "and feel guilty and go back." And: "This is an antique pocket watch. My grandfather—on his deathbed—sold me this watch." Frustrated, Allen's character would say, "I have an intense desire to return to the womb—anybody's."

In 1964 Allen was invited to write and costar in his first film, *What's New, Pussycat?* (1965), a broad, episodic sex farce. He then wrote the light-comedy play *Don't Drink the Water*, which was staged in 1966 and released as a film in 1969. In the movie *Casino Royale* (1967) he played Jimmy Bond, a spoof of the he-man spy James Bond.

Allen soon discovered that his future lay in films. By 1968 he had essentially abandoned stand-up comedy,

The Hilarious Groucho.
"Groucho Marx was the best comedian this country ever produced," Woody Allen says. More effectively than any other comedian, Groucho "combined a totally original physical conception that was hilarious with a matchless verbal delivery."

though he did return to the stage occasionally in the early 1970s.

He both wrote and starred in *Play It Again, Sam*, staged in 1969 and released as a film in 1972. The story centers on a neurotic film critic trying to recover from the defection of his wife. He drifts back and forth between the worlds of reality and fantasy, in the latter of which he often confers with the ghost of the macho Humphrey Bogart.

Allen helped to prepare the scripts for, and then directed and starred in, the movies *Take the Money and Run* (1969), *Bananas* (1971), and *Everything You Always Wanted to Know about Sex* (*but Were Afraid to Ask)* (1972). The first is a mock documentary of a young man who aspires to become public enemy number one but flops. *Bananas* parodies Latin American revolutions, while *Everything You Always Wanted to Know about Sex* spoofs the popular sex manual of that name.

Allen coscripted, directed, and starred in *Sleeper* (1973). Set two hundred years in the future, the film satirizes sophisticated modern life.

Love and Death (1975), set in czarist Russia during the Napoleonic wars, is a mock epic in which the protagonist (Allen) is a self-professed "militant coward." Allen also wrote and directed the film, which spoofs nineteenth-century Russian novels.

The evils of blacklisting during the 1950s witch-hunting for Communists are the principal subject of *The Front* (1976), in which Allen had a major role.

With *Annie Hall* (1977) he returned to his triple role as coscriptwriter, director, and star. While telling the tender, introspective story of the breakup of a love affair, the film provides subtle insight into modern relationships.

After writing and directing, but not appearing in, the dramatic movie *Interiors* (1978), Allen made *Manhattan* (1979), a romanticized paean to his beloved New York City. Besides cowriting and directing the film, he starred as Isaac Davis, a successful comedy writer who quits his TV job to write a novel. Though imbued with much humor, the story is also a serious study of "selling out," both personally and artistically.

Allen then wrote, directed, and starred, as a comedy-film director, in *Stardust Memories* (1980). In it, he directs acid humor at both himself and overly serious movie fans.

After writing the play *The Floating Light Bulb* (1981), he made the film *A Midsummer Night's Sex Comedy* (1982), which he wrote, directed, and starred

Getting Physical

Not at all the helpless weakling he usually pretends to be, Allen was good at many sports in his youth, including baseball and boxing. Today he still participates in tennis and basketball.

Influences on Allen

Allen regards himself as a blend of Bob Hope and Mort Sahl—of traditional humor and the counterculture.

Writers who have influenced him include George S. Kaufman, Robert Benchley, and S.J. Perelman.

Woody Allen and Mia Farrow in a scene from *Hannah and Her Sisters.*

in. It is a light, sunny movie set near the turn of the twentieth century.

In *Zelig* (1983) Allen spliced himself into newsreel clips from the 1920s and 1930s. Besides playing the role of the human chameleon in the picture, he wrote and directed this "mockumentary."

Allen then wrote, directed, and starred in *Broadway Danny Rose* (1984). It is the story of a small-time talent agent who falls in love with the girlfriend of a second-rate nightclub singer, the agent's own client.

Allen wrote and directed, but did not appear in, *The Purple Rose of Cairo* (1985), a fantasy about a housewife and her movie hero, who walks off the screen and into her gray life.

In *Hannah and Her Sisters* (1986), which Allen wrote, directed, and starred in, he dealt with some of his familiar topics: adultery, upscale New York City life, and the modern existential crisis—cast in a humorous mold. But he also incorporated new elements: the celebrating of family life and the finding of love.

Radio Days (1987), which Allen wrote, directed, and narrated (but did not appear in), is a nostalgic

Wearing Disguises

Though philosophically a lover of humanity, Woody Allen is shy with individuals. To avoid being recognized in the streets, he tries to blend in with other pedestrians by wearing a hooded parka in the winter and other disguises during the rest of the year.

Woody Allen (far right) on location.

story about the effect of radio on people's lives during the medium's golden era, the 1930s and 1940s.

Allen then wrote and directed the dramatic films *September* (1987), an homage to the Swedish filmmaker Ingmar Bergman, and *Another Woman* (1988).

His "Oedipus Wrecks," which he wrote, directed, and starred in, is one of three short films strung together as *New York Stories* (1989); Allen's story centers on a young man whose mother tries to sabotage his love life. ☆

MOREY AMSTERDAM
The Human Joke Machine

Morey Amsterdam is one of the great one-liner specialists. He wrote the famous Will Rogers quip "Our congressmen are the finest body of men money can buy."

In his own stage acts, Amsterdam asks his audience for topics and then fires back a stream of jokes on those

The typical Morey Amsterdam expression.

Morey's Cello

When Morey forsook a cello career and turned to comedy, his violinist father was disappointed. But Morey continued to practice on the cello, and when he gave a concert with the Los Angeles Philharmonic, it was his father's proudest moment.

Principal Hobby

Because one of his principal hobbies is the study of history, Amsterdam has created many history-related jokes. Examples:

In 1898, at the Chicago World's Fair, Little Egypt danced the first belly dance seen in America. That's how they started Navel Observatory Time.

Freud was the first psychiatrist to lie on the couch with a patient. That's how he invented socialized medicine.

subjects. If an audience does not respond, he will do it for them by turning his head and calling out, "Hey, why don't you tell some drunk jokes?" He punctuates his punch lines and spaces out the laughs by frequently doodling on his ever-present cello.

Amsterdam was born in Chicago, Illinois, on December 14, 1914 (sometimes listed as 1912). He was raised in San Francisco, where his father was concertmaster of the San Francisco Symphony Orchestra. Family guests included such musical celebrities as Enrico Caruso, Ignace Paderewski, and Lily Pons.

Morey took up the cello, but he switched to comedy in his teens. He wrote jokes for radio personalities Jack Benny, Robert Benchley, Bob Hope, and others. Soon the youth was successfully performing his own material on radio.

Amsterdam has written a number of novelty songs, notably his signature tune, "Yuk-a-puk." The title is a nonsense word that divides the lyrics into comic stanzas. For example: "I got an aunt named Minnie, weighs 264. When she sits on the chair, there's so much there, most of her sits on the floor. Yuk-a-puk, yuk-a-puk, yuk-a-puk, yuk-a-puk, yuk-a-puk."

In the 1940s, besides continuing as a radio star, Amsterdam became a pioneer on TV. In 1939 he headlined the first Los Angeles experimental TV program. Later he was a panelist on the TV game show *Stop Me If You've Heard This One*, the first series to be telecast with a live studio audience; it began as a local Los Angeles program in 1945 and went out over a network during 1948-49. He hosted his own network variety series, *The Morey Amsterdam Show*, from 1948 to 1950.

His "five happiest years in show business" were those he spent as the wisecracking Buddy Sorrell in the TV situation comedy *The Dick Van Dyke Show* (1961-1966). The character was much like the actor himself: a veteran comedy writer with a knack for sharp one-liners.

Later Amsterdam made TV guest appearances and performed at dinner theaters and nightclubs in Las Vegas, New York City, London, Hong Kong, and elsewhere. He also acted in several movies, including *Beach Party* (1963), *The Horse in the Gray Flannel Suit* (1968), *Sooner or Later* (TV, 1979), and *Side by Side* (TV, 1988).

In the early 1980s Amsterdam had triple-bypass heart surgery. Within months he was back in action, still earning his reputation as the Human Joke Machine.★

Laughing at Himself

Morey Amsterdam says he is so corny that when he dies he will not be buried—he will be shucked!

Amsterdam and Al Capone

Amsterdam likes to tell the story of his relationship with the gangster Al Capone. As a teenager in the late 1920s. Amsterdam performed at Colosimo's, a notorious Chicago speakeasy and mobster hangout. "Maybe they thought I had a machine gun in my cello case," he says, "but the racket guys loved me. Al Capone called me 'Kid.' He'd pick me up and drive me out to his home in Cicero. He'd cook spaghetti for me, and I'd play Italian songs for him."

Contented Comic

"I'm the most contented comedian I know," Amsterdam boasts. "I have no neuroses. I'm calm as an anchor. I don't feud or fuss."

His calm is helped by the fact that he never drinks alcohol or smokes.

BEATRICE ARTHUR
Maude and Dorothy

Beatrice Arthur specializes in portraying comic characters of the commanding, acerbic type. She won national fame as the cause-conscious heroine of the TV sitcom *Maude* (1972-78). Since 1985 she has played the no-nonsense Dorothy in the comedy series *The Golden Girls.*

Arthur was born in New York City, New York, on May 13, 1926. Her original name was Bernice Frankel.

As a teenager she amused her friends with imitations of Mae West. Later, after a brief period as a medical-lab technician in a hospital, she decided to enter show business.

Arthur studied acting for two years under Erwin Piscator at the Dramatic Workshop of the New School for Social Research. Because of her height (5′9½″) and her deep, powerful voice, she was cast in the title role, a classic heroine, of the Dramatic Workshop's production of *Lysistrata* (1947), her first stage appearance.

Turning professional, Arthur joined the players at the Cherry Lane Theater in Greenwich Village. There she played many important roles, such as Inez in *No Exit* (1948), Kate in *The Taming of the Shrew* (1948), and Hesione in *Heartbreak House* (1949).

In 1951 Arthur became a member of the stock company at Atlantic City's Circle Theater, where she appeared in *The Voice of the Turtle* and other productions. In 1953 she worked as the resident comedienne at the Tamiment Theater in Pennsylvania. She sang and acted as Lucy Brown in the off-Broadway production of Kurt Weill's *The Threepenny Opera* (1954).

In *Shoestring Revue* (1955) Arthur delivered a comedy monologue and devastated audiences with her rendition of a torch song about cocktail prattle. In 1957 she appeared in her first Broadway comedy, *Nature's Way.* After portraying Yente, the matchmaker, in *Fiddler on the Roof* (1964), Arthur won her greatest Broadway acclaim with her performance in the musical comedy *Mame* (1966), as Vera Charles, Aunt Mame's savagely witty, cynical, and hilarious friend.

Hobbies and Habits
Beatrice Arthur is a gourmet cook, an avid gardener, a voracious reader, and a collector of antique furniture. She rarely watches TV, even *The Golden Girls.*

Prefers Musicals
Of her performance as Vera Charles in the musical comedy *Mame,* Arthur modestly declares, "I was brilliant on the stage." Musicals are "where I feel that I'm the greatest."

Lost Weight
Since leaving her Maude role in 1978, Arthur has lost about thirty pounds. She wears stylish, expensive clothing.

Favorite Foods
Arthur's usual lunch is salmon salad and white wine. She also likes Mexican food.

In the early 1970s the TV producer Norman Lear, a fan of Arthur's ever since *Shoestring Revue,* tried to induce her to appear on the new TV sitcom *All in the Family.* She was reluctant, partly because she did want to leave New York for Hollywood and partly because she was simply not attracted to TV.

Finally she agreed to do a guest part in *All in the Family.* Her performance, aired in late 1971, was electric. The series was dominated by the character Archie Bunker, a reactionary, bigoted loudmouth. Arthur created the new character Maude, cousin of Archie's wife, Edith. Maude, an outspoken liberal, proved to be more than a match for Archie and gave him his long-overdue comeuppance.

Arthur's performance was so well received that the following year she was given her own TV comedy series, *Maude,* which ran till 1978. The character Maude, an aggressive libertarian and women's libber, made the country laugh at her own human foibles as she tackled such controversial topics as abortion, race relations, and pornography.

Arthur has appeared in very few movies. They include the filmed version of *Mame (1974),* Mel Brooks's *History of the World, Part I* (1981), and the poignant comedy-drama *My First Love* (TV, 1988).

As Dorothy in *The Golden Girls* (1985-) Arthur

Shy Streak

Despite her stage and screen reputation for forcefulness, Beatrice Arthur has always been timid about appearing as herself on TV talk shows. "I've never felt that easy in myself," she admits, "cause I think, 'Who the hell wants to listen to *me*?' "

Arthur is "the shiest woman I've ever known," says Estelle Getty, who plays Arthur's mother on *The Golden Girls.*

Animal Rights

Unlike her character Maude, Beatrice Arthur is not a political activist. "Maude was not me," she emphasizes.

There is one major exception, however: Arthur does campaign for animal rights. "I think fur coats should have a label on them, saying how they became fur coats," she proclaims. "People don't know the indignity, the horror, that animals go through." She has even removed struggling flies from flypaper.

Beatrice Arthur with Martin Mull.

again portrays a forceful character given to caustic comments. Living with her octogenarian mother and two middle-aged women, Dorothy is the long-suffering anchor of the household, coping with the quirks of the others. When her mother decides to spend the night with an eighty-five-year-old man, Dorothy, in a role reversal, commands, "Ma, you're not spending the night at Rocco's. Listen, you live under our roof—you live by *our* rules!" ☆

Barr started out as a stand-up comic.

ROSEANNE BARR
"Domestic Goddess"

Roseanne Barr's comedy is based on her stage persona as an embattled housewife, or, as she bills herself, a "domestic goddess." Her principal technique is the lampooning of family life. She says her comedy is about "married couples that love each other and yet can't stand each other. . . . Deep down you are happy. But sometimes your partner is going to drive you crazy." "My husband," Barr complains in one of her typical nightclub routines, "comes home and says, 'Roseanne, don't you think we should talk about our sexual problems?' Like I'm going to turn off *Wheel of Fortune* for that!" Since the autumn of 1988 Barr has starred in the TV sitcom *Roseanne*, an extension of her club act, which in turn is an extension of her life.

Influences on Barr

Richard Pryor is one of Barr's idols because of what she calls his "political" orientation. Other influences include Jack Benny, Irma Bombeck, Lenny Bruce, Carol Burnett, Rodney Dangerfield, Phyllis Diller, Totie Fields, and Steve Martin. "But most of all," she says, "above anyone on earth, I adore Jackie Gleason. That's what I want my series to be—*The Honeymooners,* only I'm Ralph."

Personal Characteristics

Barr speaks with a high-pitched nasal whine and chews gum frantically.

She used to smoke, but in 1986 she reported that she was trying to give it up.

Coworkers on *Roseanne* say that she can be difficult and short-tempered when things do not go her way.

Unfaithful Man

"Because a man is unfaithful to you is no reason to leave him," Barr maintains. "You should stay with him and make sure the rest of his life is sheer hell."

She was born in Salt Lake City, Utah, in 1952. In that predominately Mormon city, Roseanne, her brother, and her two sisters faced anti-Semitism and were frequently beaten by other children. Her rough childhood made her tough-minded but insecure.

Roseanne became rebellious. She would, for example, repeatedly wander down the middle of busy highways, forcing cars to swerve around her. At the age of sixteen she was finally hit by a car and seriously hurt. She spent the next eight months in the Utah State Hospital, where the principal concern was for her mental health.

Shortly after her release from the hospital, she dropped out of high school and moved to Colorado. There she got married, had three children, became a traditional suburban housewife, and struggled for years to make ends meet financially.

Debts finally forced her to take a job as a cocktail waitress in Denver. To get the job, she had to lose 95 pounds, from 200 down to 105. ("I've since gained it all back," she admits today.) Her first public jokes were caustic replies that she made to the suggestive comments of male customers.

With comedy fever rising in her blood, she visited a Denver comedy club in 1981. Angered by the sexism of the male comics, she quickly wrote a five-minute rebuttal, which the manager allowed her to deliver. Her little act was a hit, and soon she was on the road as a touring comic in Missouri, Arizona, Oklahoma, and Texas.

In 1985 Barr hit Los Angeles, where an appearance at the Comedy Store won her some guest spots on *The Tonight Show.* She quickly found herself in huge demand at major venues, such as Caesar's Palace in Las Vegas. In the summer of 1986 she toured with Julio Iglesias, and in 1987 she starred in her own HBO special.

Her routines picture domestic life as a kind of war of wills. "My husband asked me if we have any cheese puffs," she says. "Like he can't go and lift that couch cushion up himself." And, "My husband wanted more space, so I locked him out of the house." The children, too, participate in the battles: "My kids have a game they play on family vacations. They like to count how many Dairy Queens we pass before I grab the wheel and force the car off the road." "I figure by the time my husband comes home at night, if those kids are still alive, I've done my job." This "domestic goddess" does not waste energy on cleaning: "The floor will stay messy until Sears brings out a riding vacuum cleaner."

In the hit TV comedy series *Roseanne* (1988-), Barr continues to develop her feminist message. She portrays a factory worker who constantly berates her

Man Hater?

Barr complains about the male domination of the comedy and business worlds. "Men have actually brainwashed women into thinking that in order to be successful you have to be exactly like the men," she asserts. "And what I'm trying to say more than anything is no, you don't. I mean they're going to evolve us out of the human race if we let them. As soon as they figure out cloning, forget it. They won't need us for anything."

Such comments have caused some observers to brand her a man hater. Nevertheless, "I never apologize for what I say," she boasts. "And that's what sets me apart from a lot of other women comics."

TV Addict

"I can't take Los Angeles life," Barr laments. "I'm just a real private kind of gal. I'd like to stay home, and have a beer, and stare at TV. . . . I watch Oprah and Phil . . . . And then I watch Geraldo, and then I eat dinner, and then I watch Morton Downey, Jr."

Barr with Rodney Dangerfield.

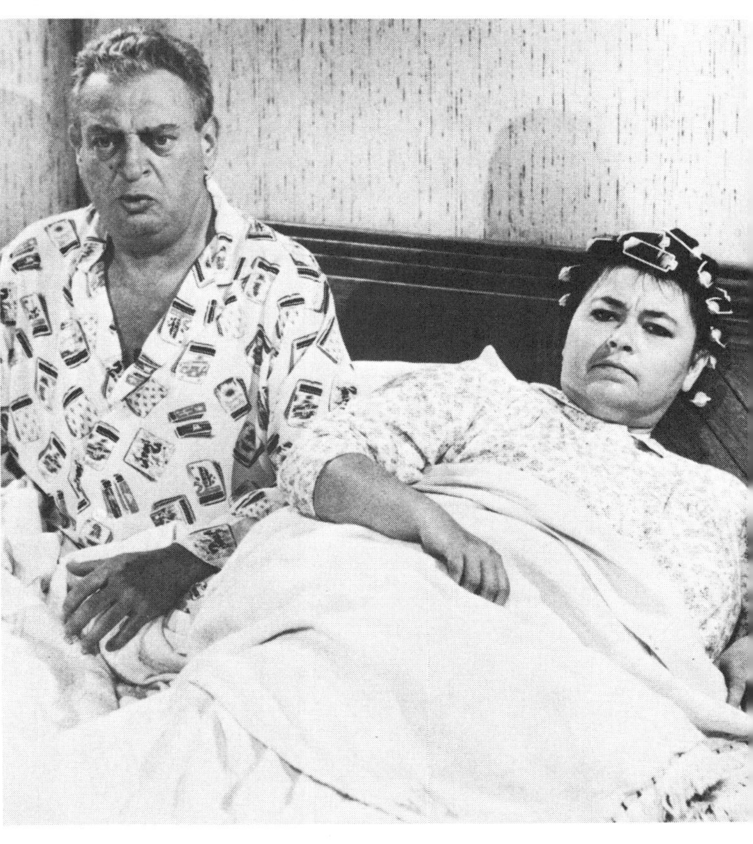

seldom-working husband and barks impatiently at her three children. Troubled by the father-dominance of most TV family shows, Barr wants *Roseanne* to be a realistic picture of the hardships and accomplishments of women. In one episode, Roseanne hears that a married couple she knows have divorced. "They shoulda stuck it out in the trenches," she responds sarcastically, "dodgin' that shrapnel with the rest of us that believe in true love."★

RICHARD BELZER
The Belz

Richard Belzer has been called vicious, vulgar, and self-destructive. Robert De Niro patterned his manic, half-crazed character in the film *The King of Comedy* (1983) after Belzer. "I realized I had a black side, like Lenny [Bruce]," Belzer admitted in 1981. "And I knew I had to overcome it."

Onstage he shifts rapidly from pure fun (Mick Jagger as a rooster) to fascinating insight (an insect making love to its mate before eating it) to questionable satire (Jack Benny asking Rochester to roll "a joint and turn on the stereo"). As an insult comic he is much harsher than Don Rickles. Belzer's tendency to resort to needless invective has hurt his career, as when he cursed at a female spectator and told her to get her feet off the stage. He has also physically attacked members of the audience.

Richard Belzer was born in Bridgeport, Connecticut, on August 4, 1944. Raised by a physically abusive mother and a weak father (who eventually committed suicide), he compensated for his unhappy homelife by clowning in school.

After one year at Dean Junior College in Franklin, Massachusetts, Belzer entered the army. But at his own prodding he was soon discharged for being mentally unfit. There followed several years of jumping from job to job. During that time he also took and sold illegal drugs.

In 1971 Belzer auditioned for, and won, a job on a video show called *The Groove Tube*. From there he moved into stand-up comedy at a New Jersey night-

Personal Habits
Before developing cancer, Belzer caroused self-destructively and had a combative attitude. Now he rests, exercises, meditates, and speaks softly.

Favorite Snacks
At breaks during work, Belzer snacks on cheese and crackers, which he washes down with mineral water.

Comedy as a Shield
Belzer sees life as a painful experience and comedy as a way of shielding himself from the cruelty of the world. "I carry a lot of sadness around with me that's just part of my whole history and life," he says.

Belzer (right) in *The Wrong Guys.*

club. In 1973 he made his first appearances at the Catch a Rising Star club in New York City, where he began to experiment with what became his confrontational style. By 1974 he was a regular there.

Later he had bit parts in several movies, including *Fame* (1980), *Night Shift* (1982), and *Scarface* (1983). Meanwhile, he continued to appear at the Catch a Rising Star in New York City and at the Comedy Store in Los Angeles.

In 1984 Belzer learned that he had cancer. Subsequently he went through an operation and many radiation treatments. That experience—along with maturation and some professional success—affected his stage manner. While continuing to hurl insults at the audience, he became less meanspirited, he stopped his physical attacks, and he began to aim some of his barbs at himself.

In the mid-1980s Belzer was particularly active on cable TV, appearing regularly on *Thicke of the Night* and hosting *Hot Properties.* In the movie *The Wrong Guys* (1988) he had a leading role as a sarcastic manufacturer of women's belts. Since then he has continued to be active both in clubs and on TV. ☆

Jewish Heritage Influence

In June 1986 Belzer, speaking at New York City's Jewish Museum, emphasized his pride in being Jewish and the importance of his ethnic roots in shaping his comic persona. "There is a definite connection between being funny and being Jewish," he stated. "The toughest room I ever played was my mother's kitchen."

Trademark

The dark-spirited comic constantly wears black sunglasses.

"Authentic" Entertainers

Mick Jagger, Robert De Niro, Bruce Springsteen, Richard Pryor, Marlon Brando—these are among Belzer's heroes, whom he calls "authentic." "The great ones—Pryor, Lenny [Bruce], Jackie Mason—all started out as something they weren't," Belzer says. "And they were all eventually accepted as great by being [themselves]."

Bout with Cancer

After his 1984 bout with cancer, Belzer explained the psychological effect it had on him: "You learn to cherish certain people more and stop wasting time."

JACK BENNY
Master of Timing

Jack Benny pioneered a new kind of humor in America. Ignoring the vaudeville tradition of pratfalls and pomposity, he introduced timing, subtlety, self-effacement, and rounded characterization.

He was particulary renowned for his comic timing. But it was not instinctive; he had to work to develop it. A well-trained violinist, he learned from his music studies the importance of rhythm, cadence, and especially silence. The classic example of this aspect of his artistry was on those occasions when, after being insulted, he would pause before coming out with a perfectly timed "Well!"

He was born in Chicago, Illinois, on February 14, 1894. His original name was Benjamin ("Benny") Kubelsky.

He was raised in Waukegan, Illinois, where he began to take violin lessons at the age of six. Later he studied at the Chicago School of Music. As a teenager he played in local dance bands and theater orchestras. He also played in the Waukegan Township High School Orchestra till he flunked out of school after his second term.

Benny never went back to school. Having little formal education profoundly affected him in later life. He became an avid reader, and he developed a sincere humility and simplicity that endeared him to his audiences.

After leaving high school he got a job playing the violin at a local vaudeville house. In 1912 he joined a pianist, and the musical duo began to perform classical and popular pieces on vaudeville stages. Originally billed as Benny Kubelsky, he soon took the name Ben K. Benny. In 1913 he changed pianists as well as the spelling of his stage name, to Ben K. Bennie.

In 1917 the act broke up and the violinist enlisted in the navy. There he began to play the violin in entertainments put on by and for the sailors. One night he was playing "The Rosary" when the audience started to boo him. He ad-libbed a navy joke: "I claim the Swiss navy is bigger than the Irish navy . . . but that the *Jewish* navy is bigger than both of them put together." It was the first time that he had ever talked onstage, and he brought

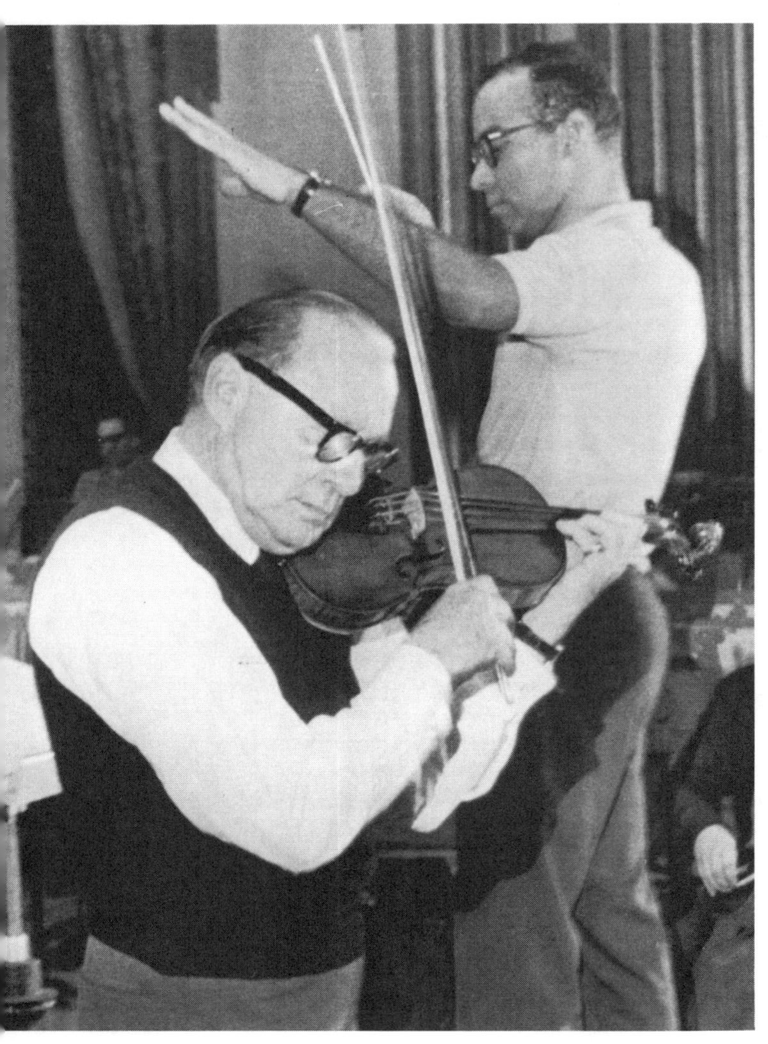

Cheapskate Image

Jack Benny's image as a cheapskate was only an act. In real life he spent money freely on himself and others. He owned one of the most extensive and expensive wardrobes in Hollywood, and he was an easy touch for individuals and groups who needed funds.

Hypochondria

Benny was forever worried about his health. Next to his bed he kept dozens of bottles filled with all sorts of medicines.

Violin Soloist

Jack appeared as a violin soloist with nearly every major symphony orchestra, including the New York Philharmonic, the Chicago Symphony, and the San Francisco Symphony. He especially liked performing under the baton of Zubin Mehta with the Los Angeles Philharmonic and the Israel Philharmonic. Benny played difficult violin concertos, a little slowly and slightly out of tune, but remarkably well for a nonspecialist.

Hobbies

Benny played golf, enjoyed card games at the Friars Club, and rooted for the Los Angeles Dodgers.

the house down. Later he acted a comedy part in a service revue. In 1918 he left the navy.

The following year he created a new vaudeville act as a single, billed once again as Ben K. Benny. He told jokes, performed comic bits on the violin, and even sang a little. In 1921 he billed himself for the first time as Jack (after the vaudeville comic Jack Osterman) Benny (after his own original first name).

Over the next several years he became a star vaudevillian. In 1927 he married Sadie Marks, who eventually took the stage name Mary Livingstone. She helped him in his vaudeville act and later on radio, in movies, and on TV.

In the late 1920s Benny began to appear in films, including *The Hollywood Revue* (1929), *Artists and Models* (1937), *Charley's Aunt* (1941), and *The Horn Blows at Midnight* (1945). His finest screen work was in *To Be or Not to Be* (1942), as a Shakespearean actor who dresses up as a Nazi and outwits the Gestapo.

However, Benny gained his greatest fame through radio. *The Jack Benny Program* was phenomenally successful for over twenty years (1932-55). The basis for his long-lived popularity was that ordinary people could identify with him. He portrayed a consistent, realistic character involved in simple but carefully planned comedic situations. Moreover, he allowed himself to be the target of most of the humor, especially through the themes of his being "the world's worst violin player" and "the stingiest man in show business." (In reality he was a fine violinist and a gentle, generous man.) In Jack Benny's radio character, audiences found a forgivably fallible average guy confidently making plans only to have them explode in his face.

Frustrated with the conduct of others, the character would blurt, "Now cut that out!" When confronted with a difficult situation, he would pause before drawing out a "Hmmm." When a thief bellowed, "Your money or your life!" the miserly character would pause before replying, "I'm thinking it over!"

In the 1940s Benny wrote, "The public today demands more of its humor than a laugh at any price. It resents too much insulting, too much cynicism. In short, the public likes good comedy, but it likes good taste even better." Consequently: "Nobody gets hurt on our program. It's all in the spirit of fun. We try to follow one simple rule: if it hurts, it isn't funny."

Benny easily transferred his show to TV, where the series ran from 1950 to 1965. The audience enjoyed being able to see him raise his hand to his chin when he said, "Hmmm," to see him flatten his mouth and roll his

Personal Habits

Though always neatly dressed in business suits before audiences, Benny in private life tossed clothes on carelessly (such as brown slacks with purple socks, a green shirt, and a blue sweater.)

He smoked cigars and tended to let the ashes fall where they may. His wife teasingly called him a "slob."

Benny nervously bit his fingernails. He also had the habit of rubbing his thumbnail back and forth across his second finger.

Hollywood wits joked about Benny's wearing a toupee, but in fact he never used a hairpiece. However, in his late twenties his hair began to turn prematurely gray (an inherited family characteristic), and for the rest of his life he dyed his hair.

Benny had a low boiling point. He would erupt in anger quickly, but he never held grudges long.

What bothered him most was poor punctuality. His mania for being on time was a carryover from his traveling days in vaudeville. In later life he always arrived early for planes, rehearsals, and so on.

The maestro.

eyes when he paused to think, and to see him exaggerate his character's egotism with an affectedly refined walk across the stage.

Benny's character was so well known that he could, and did, walk out on a Las Vegas stage, fold his arms, look silently at the audience for almost one minute, and make the house roar with laughter. His opening line was "What are you laughing at?"

After his TV series went off the air, he returned to the small screen for many specials. He also gave live performances at hotels, nightclubs, and elsewhere.

In private, he was kind, gentle, and low-key. He used his violin and his comedy to raise millions of dollars for charity, Israel bonds, and symphony orchestras.

Benny died at his home in Beverly Hills, California, on December 26, 1974. He was universally mourned as the most beloved comedian of his time.★

Benny with Mary Livingstone.

GERTRUDE BERG
Molly

Gertrude Berg won fame principally by playing a single character, the lovable Jewish housewife Molly Goldberg. On radio, Broadway, TV, and film, the matriarchal Molly delighted audiences with her homespun philosophy ("Better a crust of bread and enjoy it than a cake that gives you indigestion") and her malapropisms ("It's late, Jake, and time to expire").

Gertrude Berg was born in New York City, New York, on October 3, 1899. Her original name was Gertrude Edelstein.

In her youth she wrote and performed skits and monologues for her father's resort in the Catskills. There she met the engineering student Lewis Berg, whom she married in 1918.

In 1929 she wrote a radio script about a Jewish family living in a ghetto on the Lower East Side of Manhattan. Gertrude herself read the script for a radio executive, who decided not only to take the story but also to hire her for the leading part.

Her show, *The Rise of the Goldbergs* (later called simply *The Goldbergs*), broke a path for later radio

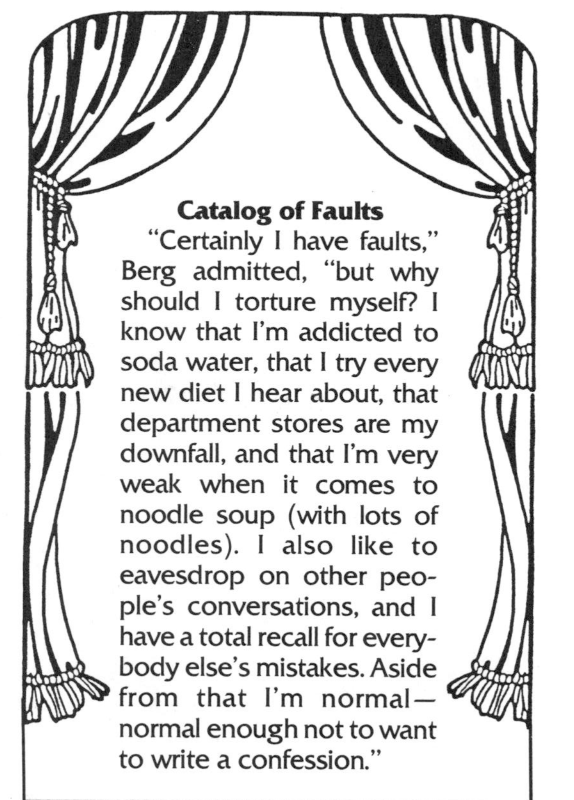

Catalog of Faults

"Certainly I have faults," Berg admitted, "but why should I torture myself? I know that I'm addicted to soda water, that I try every new diet I hear about, that department stores are my downfall, and that I'm very weak when it comes to noodle soup (with lots of noodles). I also like to eavesdrop on other people's conversations, and I have a total recall for everybody else's mistakes. Aside from that I'm normal—normal enough not to want to write a confession."

programs through its use of recurring characters in everyday settings. Molly, the mother, helped her family cope with the problems of urban life. The other principals were her husband, Jake; her son and daughter; and Uncle David. Others in the cast included Jewish friends and neighbors; but also represented were non-Jews, such as the Irish janitor.

Molly opened each show with a call to her neighbor, "Yoo-hoo, Mrs. Bloom," which became a national catchphrase. Another popular saying from the program was Molly's familiar reply to the knock on the door, "Enter, whoever."

The language on *The Goldbergs* sprang from Gertrude's own background. "We scarcely spoke Yiddish at home," she explained. "You'll notice there's no dialect [on the show], just intonation and word order." In the early episodes, however, the English was quite fractured, as in these passages spoken by Molly in "Jake, a Businessman" (1931): "Jake, it's Shabbes! You must go to voik, also today? . . . Oy, vat beezness! . . . Vhy don't you buy a bed and slip dere and finished! And dat's beezness? It's slavery—just like in *Oncle Tom's Cabinet!*" Later in the episode, when the Goldbergs had a telephone installed, Molly exclaimed, "Ken you emagine, you put your mout here und you

The Real and the Unreal

"I think that we all live in worlds that are part real, part unreal, sometimes wishing that the real might be touched with just a little of the unreal," Gertrude Berg once observed.

"My profession has been making believe. Almost every day I move from my real apartment to a stage apartment. I write words for characters who never were but aren't too different from people I've really known. I have enjoyed this double identity so much that I've never really asked myself 'Why?' "

Favorite Teacher

Lewis Berg, Gertrude's husband, introduced her to the world of the mind. "I was being directed from one idea to another," she said of his aid in her self-education, "instead of skipping here and there and finding things that interested me only because they were easy to understand. I learned how to learn, and that was something no teacher had ever been able to make me see."

When Lewis and Gertrude read H.G. Wells's *The World Set Free* they "finished feeling like idealists," she reported. After reading Romain Rolland's *Jean Christophe*, they "felt like romantics."

Lewis also guided Gertrude into a love of plays, operas, museums, and classical music.

Gertrude Berg as Molly Goldberg.

give a talk, 'Hulloh!' And right avay it henswers you beck! Soch a brains vat pipple got!"

The Goldbergs avoided excessive stereotyping and attained immense popularity among both Jews and non-Jews. Jews enjoyed the program because they were proud to identify themselves with the personalities, culture, and rituals depicted. Most Jews related to the strong family bonds, the struggle for financial stability, and the ideal of motherhood personified in Molly. The show was widely praised for fostering interracial understanding.

The Goldbergs aired on radio nearly continuously for over twenty years: 1929-34, 1937-45, and 1949-50. Gertrude Berg wrote and starred in all of the episodes. She also appeared as Molly in the Broadway play *Me and Molly* (1948), in the TV series *The Goldbergs* (1949-55), and in the movie *Molly* (1951).

In her later years she diversified her roles. She was highly praised for her performance as a middle-aged Jewish widow who finds romance with a Japanese man in the play *A Majority of One* (1959).

Gertrude Berg died in New York City on September 14, 1966.☆

MILTON BERLE
Uncle Miltie

Milton Berle, one of comedy's legendary masters, combines wild ad-libs, over fifty thousand memorized jokes, and physical humor. The resulting barrage has overwhelmed audiences for more than sixty years.

"Good evening, ladies and germs," begins a classic Berle monologue. "I mean ladies and gentlemen. But why should I call you ladies and gentlemen? You know what you are. I just want to [burp]—I don't remember eating that. I just got back into town from Florida. I flew in. My arms are very tired. [Pause with facial expression of surprise.] These are the jokes! What is this, an audience or an oil painting?"

Milton Berle was born in the Harlem section of New York City, New York, on July 12, 1908. His original name was Milton Berlinger.

At the age of five he won a local talent contest by doing a Charlie Chaplin routine, and his mother im-

Top Friar
Milton Berle has served as president of the Beverly Hills Friars Club.

Real TV
Live TV was "real" and "fun" for Berle. Tape, retakes, and canned laughter have "robbed TV of its spontaneity."

Favorite Food
Berle ate poorly till he married Ruth Cosgrove in 1953. Today turkey is his favorite food.

mediately set out to make the youngster a star in show business. She secured parts for him in many silent movies, beginning with an episode in the serial *The Perils of Pauline* (1914), in which he was tossed from a moving train. Later he appeared in *Tillie's Punctured Romance* (1914) with Chaplin himself, as well as *Rebecca of Sunnybrook Farm* (1917), *The Mark of Zorro* (1920), and other films. He also performed onstage in kid acts and in the Broadway musical *Florodora* (1920).

By the time he was in his midteens, he had already struck out on his own as a stand-up single comic in big-time vaudeville. His mother sat in the audience at every show, laughing wildly and warming up the rest of the crowd. One of his earliest ad-libs, to the sound of one voice laughing, was "Thanks, mom."

In 1931 he added nightclubs to his schedule. But the major break in his career came when he was asked to act as master of ceremonies at vaudeville's famous Palace Theater in New York City early in 1932. Later that year he hit Broadway as a star comedian in the *Earl Carrol Vanities* revue. He returned to Broadway in several more shows, including the *Ziegfeld Follies of 1943.*

Berle developed a brash style as a wisecracking streetcorner comic and put-down artist. His stage style truly reflected his offstage aggressiveness and self-confidence. He had no compunction about using material by others, feeling that he could tell the jokes better than anyone else. The columnist Walter Winchell dubbed Berle "the thief of badgags."

One of Berle's most famous comic bits, dressing in drag, evolved from a real-life incident. One of his girl friends lived at the Barbizon, a strictly women-only residence in New York City. He dressed up as a stylish Barbizon girl to get through the lobby and into the lady's room, where the drag was soon abandoned.

In the late 1930s Berle began to make movies. His early films included *New Faces of 1937 (1937), Rise and Shine* (1941), and *Always Leave Them Laughing* (1949).

In the 1940s he frequently performed on radio. But his essentially visual brand of humor did not fare well over that medium.

On television, however, Berle made his greatest impact in show business. He was among the first to perform on TV, with appearances in experimental broadcasts in 1929 and 1933. Then, from 1948 to 1953, he hosted the most popular variety series in TV history, *The Texaco Star Theater* (also known as *The Milton Berle Show*). His buffoonery helped to spur the purchase of TV sets by lower-income families all over the United States.

Some of the many faces of Milton Berle.

A Lot of Regrets

"I have a lot of regrets about things I did and said, for the way I pushed and shoved and bullied during those hysterical years," Berle has admitted about his heyday. "My only defense, which is no defense, is the pressure." If a youth becomes a star too early, it will be "a miracle if that kid doesn't grow up to be a man who believes he's Casanova, Einstein, and Jesus Christ all rolled into one."

Literary Achievements

Berle has turned to writing in his late years. His works include the books *Milton Berle: An Autobiography* (with Haskel Frankel, 1974) and *B.S. I Love You: Sixty Funny Years with the Famous and the Infamous* (1988).

Workaholic

As a child Milton Berle liked reading, but now, he admits, "I've lost the pleasure and the patience for it. I'm a rotten spectator at a play or a movie, because I can't turn off my performer's critical eyes. I play a little golf, but I don't really have the patience for it. All sports, to me, are something you do for relaxation when you're not working. But if I'm not working, how can I relax?"

He says he does not get many laughs out of his personal life. His favorite activity is "anything where I can use makeup, take a bow, and hear laughs and applause."

Poker Player

In the 1950s Berle used to play poker twice a week with friends, including Dean Martin, Tony Curtis, and Ernie Kovacs.

Gambling Addiction

Berle lost over $3 million gambling on horse races up to 1954, when he finally quit betting on the ponies.

More of the many faces of Milton Berle.

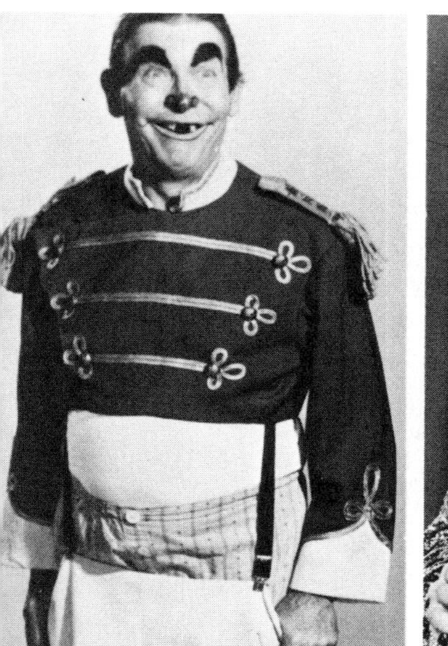

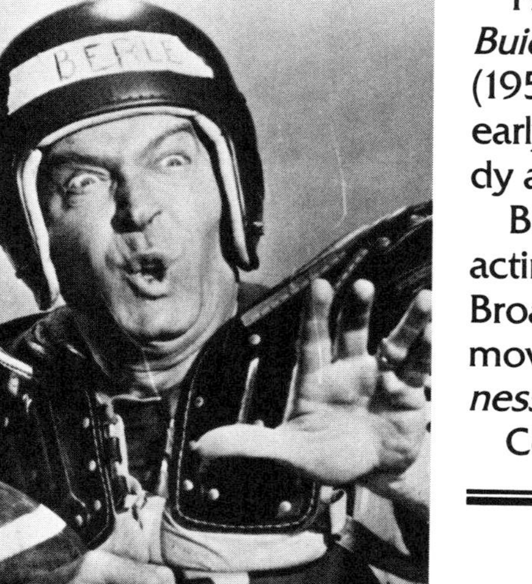

He became known affectionately as Uncle Miltie and respectfully as Mr. Television, TV's first superstar. Even though his shows were telecast live, Berle never used cue cards. When he muffed a line, he actually became funnier by extricating himself with ad-libs drawn from years of working in vaudeville and nightclubs.

He hosted several later TV variety shows, notably *The Buick-Berle Show* (1953-55) and *The Kraft Music Hall* (1958-59), but with decreasing popular success. In the early 1960s he was a frequent guest star on both comedy and drama series.

Berle revealed a surprising gift for straight dramatic acting. He gave outstanding performances in the Broadway play *The Goodbye People* (1968), in the movies *Seven in Darkness* (TV, 1969) and *Family Business* (TV, 1983), and in many other works.

Comedy, however, has always remained the core of

Berle's life. He has returned to TV for numerous specials, and he has continued to give live stage performances. In his seventies he organized a vaudeville tour with George Jessel.

In 1984 Berle was among the first seven people inducted into the Television Academy Hall of Fame. In June 1985 he had quadruple-bypass heart surgery. The operation was a success, and soon he was making public appearances again.

In 1988 he starred in a TV special, *Milton Berle: The Second Time Around.* He also had a role as one of three elderly men trying to start their own business in the movie *Side by Side* (TV, 1988).

Berle has willed to the Library of Congress his file of over five million jokes. He has cataloged the jokes and cross-indexed them by subject, by who did them first and where, and by comics who used the material later.

The catalog will be an important lasting comedy treasure, just as Berle himself has been for so many years an invaluable living comedy treasure. ★

Milton Berle.

SHELLEY BERMAN
First Modern Comic Neurotic

Shelley Berman, at his peak in the early 1960s, broke ground as the first big-time comic to personify the neuroses, frustrations, and absurdities of modern life. Himself a frustrated actor, he popularized the "comedy concert," consisting of one-act miniatures and comic lectures. In one sketch, for example, he played Franz Kafka thwarted by long-distance telephone operators who kept stealing his coins and making him repeat names and numbers. The poet Louis Untermeyer praised Berman's "way of turning ordinary happenings into universal experiences."

Sheldon Berman was born in Chicago, Illinois, on February 3, 1926 (sometimes listed as 1924). After serving in the navy during World War II, he struggled unsuccessfully for ten years to make it as an actor. Finally, while working with the Compass Players, an improvisational group based in Chicago, he made the transition to stand-up comedy.

The Critical Documentary

Berman says that his career was seriously hurt by the TV documentary "The Comedian Backstage" (*Du Pont Show of the Week*, 1963). The film recorded Berman giving a live stage performance. During his long seriocomic "Father and Son" routine, a phone could be heard ringing offstage. A few days earlier he had specifically requested that the phone be taken off the receiver during his act. After his performance, cameras followed backstage, where he railed at all of the stagehands. The film, however, shows him apparently yelling only at his young agent, Marty Klein. According to Berman, viewers saw him as "a child, an idiot, a fool." His reputation for being overbearingly demanding has dogged him ever since then.

Years later he reflected on the incident: "I thought the public would understand that I am a human being who loses his temper once in a while when things go wrong." But, instead, "people started looking at me in a negative way. It hurt a whole lot."

He centered his act on the telephone, a prop discovered while doing improvisations. "I couldn't find a partner to work one night," he has explained, "so I simply used the telephone—that's how the telephone began." In one telephone monologue, called "Morning after the Night Before," a man gradually learned of the drunken mayhem he had caused at a party the previous night.

The telephone led to another trademark, a bar stool. He felt that it was illogical to do a ten-minute phone-call routine standing up; but, he explained, "if I sat in a chair I couldn't be seen, so I borrowed a stool."

At first his topics were the miseries of everyday existence, such as coping with TV commercials, trying to hide spinach caught between his teeth on a date, and struggling to keep a paper napkin on his lap. One of his best-known routines was "Buttermilk," in which he lamented about the "ugly white map" left behind after buttermilk has been enjoyed.

Soon, however, he began to add darker, more hysterical material. In one routine, a man whose finger

Berman steps out with Janet Blair.

was bleeding profusely could not find a doctor; he deliriously called a gynecologist and then feebly explained his mistake by saying that his cut finger was on a "rather feminine" hand. Another routine covered the futile attempts of a man to get help for a woman hanging on to a ledge outside a building. Many commentators rated Berman second only to Lenny Bruce as a "sick comic."

Berman was also the darling of the intellectuals, whom he delighted with his forays into Kafkaesque dark comedy. In one routine, for example, a man called a hotel desk to complain that his room had no window, then no light switch, and finally no door.

Berman soon rose to the top spot among comics in the United States. He appeared on all of the major TV variety series and became the first comedian to perform at Carnegie Hall.

Tiring of his role as a "cerebral" comic, Berman broadened his act by creating a schlemiel character who could not get dates and who had only fair-weather friends. However, at about the same time, Berman's star began to fade, partly because of an unflattering 1963 TV documentary about him, and partly because of competition from newer comics, such as the easy-going Bill Cosby and Bob Newhart, and the sex-oriented Woody Allen. Such performers offered a strong contrast to Berman's tense, concentrated style, which he had developed to compensate for his extreme shyness and nervousness onstage.

Seeing the handwriting on the wall, Berman turned increasingly to acting, which, in fact, he had never abandoned. He had appeared in a stock production of *Damn Yankees* (1959), and, at the peak of his stand-up comedy success, had performed roles in the movie *The Best Man* (1964) and in episodes of such TV drama series as *Peter Gunn* and *Twilight Zone.* Beginning in the mid-1960s Berman tried to minimize his comic stints while performing in numerous stage productions of *The Odd Couple, Two by Two, The Rothschilds,* and *Fiddler on the Roof.*

In recent years Berman has largely returned to his true forte, the comedy concert. Today new audiences are rediscovering the unique humor that made Berman an important pioneer in modern comedy. ☆

Contemporary Comics

"They're wonderful," Berman says of Richard Pryor, George Carlin, and other contemporary comics. "They're nervy, they're truthful, and they're very, very honest. Sometimes their honesty is so bold it makes you wince. But then, Cervantes and Swift made people wince."

Impatience

In the mid-1980s Berman was still displaying combativeness and irritability to interviewers. "I wish to hell we could all be comfortable working together in this world," he said in 1984, "but I can't be comfortable."

On Saying Kaddish

The lowest point in Berman's life came in 1978 when his twelve-year- old son, Joshua, died of a brain tumor, and Berman could not gather ten men to form a minyan to say the Kaddish. Since then he has often volunteered to talk consolingly to parents facing the same kind of loss.

Weather-beaten

"Isn't it awful to be thirty-four and look ninety?" Berman has said about himself.

SANDRA BERNHARD
"One Big Raw Nerve"

Sandra Bernhard brings a sense of menace to comedy. "When I'm onstage, I don't want to please people," she says. "I'd rather evoke a strong emotion that have the audience worshipping [me]. If you're the kind of person everybody loves, you're doing something very wrong."

Bernhard does parodies of famous women, talks about her childhood and her fantasies, pokes fun at commercials and clothing fashions, and directs alternatingly erotic and violent comments at male members of the audience. She is simultaneously coarse and vulnerable. When I'm onstage I'm one big raw nerve, a shipwrecked human being. But if you tell strangers your innermost secrets, they don't hold it against you."

Sandra Bernhard was born in Flint, Michigan, in 1955. She grew up there and in Arizona. After graduating from high school, she spent eight months on an Israeli kibbutz.

Returning to the United States, Bernhard began to work as a Beverly Hills manicurist-pedicurist in 1974. Her experiences working on people's feet gave her plenty of material as a starting point for a stand-up comedy act. She began to appear onstage in the Los Angeles area, at first part-time and then, in 1978, full-time. The Comedy Store was a major venue for her.

Bernhard developed impressions of Bette Midler, Tina Turner, Jacqueline Kennedy, Marilyn Monroe, and others. She made confessions ("I love sleeping on a full-length mirror"). She ridiculed fashion trends (her idea of a good time is "kicking the shoulder pads off Norma Kamali dresses"). She would select a man in the audience, come on to him, and then suddenly become violently angry at him. Sexuality played a large role in her act; she would frequently fondle her own breast.

Tall (5'10") and lanky (barely one hundred pounds), with thick lips and a prominent nose, Bernhard says her appearance had a lot to do with her entering show business. "I was stared at from the time I was able to remember," she points out. "So I figured if people want to stare at me, let them stare at me on the screen."

She did, in fact, make people stare at her on the

Role Models

Bernhard admires "people who take chances." When she was a small child, she saw *Hello, Dolly!* with Carol Channing, who served as an early influence on Bernhard. Later influences and role models included Bette Midler, Mick Jagger, and Tina Turner.

Hostile and Aggressive

Many critics have described Bernhard as being "hostile" or "aggressive." But she says, "I'm very vulnerable, full of sincere emotion, which is something most comics are afraid of." However, she admits to being special: "I create a spark that nobody else does."

Bernhard with Robert DeNiro in *The King of Comedy.*

screen when she won the role of Masha, a rich, neurotic groupie obsessed with a TV talk-show host whom she helps to kidnap, in the film *The King of Comedy* (1983). Her performance in that movie gave her career a tremendous boost. She has made cross-country tours, worked in major clubs, headlined at important theaters, appeared regularly on TV's *Late Night with David Letterman*, and had roles in more movies, including *Sesame Street Presents: Follow That Bird (1985)*, as the grouchy waitress, and *Track 29* (1987), as Nurse Stein, who engages in sex games with Dr. Henry.

In her recent stage performances, notably her one-woman show *Without You I'm Nothing*, Bernhard has broadened her act to encompass not only stand-up comedy but also theater, cabaret, performance art, and rock music (she has ambitions as a singer). She has also deepened her art by addressing certain aspects of contemporary social life, such as self-obsession and the establishing of values by advertising and pop culture.

Bernhard develops these and other ideas in her writing, which include magazine articles, screenplays, and the autobiographical book *Confessions of a Pretty Lady* (1988). ★

Luggage Lunatic

Though she strongly dislikes designer clothes, Bernhard has a strange love for luggage. "Buying luggage is a passion with me," she confesses. "There's something very seductive about luggage."

Androgynous Characteristics

"Both men and women can relate to both the man and the woman in me," Bernhard says. "Everybody lets go of his/her preordained disposition."

Booze

She prefers club soda to booze.

JOEY BISHOP
Sad-faced Funnyman

Joey Bishop had a long, slow climb to stardom. He never dazzled audiences with brilliant wit, never shocked them with "sick" jokes, and never challenged them with social commentary. He neither capitalized on his Jewishness nor avoided references to it. In 1960 *Time* magazine described him as a "sad-faced funnyman whose effortless humor seems spontaneous but is the product of endless preparation."

He was born in New York City, New York, on February 3, 1918, but was raised in South Philadelphia. His original name was Joseph Abraham Gottlieb.

He never wanted to be anything but an entertainer. His father played the ocarina and taught Joey Yiddish songs. The boy learned to do imitations, to tap-dance, and to play the banjo and mandolin. The first thing he ever bought for himself was a false nose. In 1936 he won first prize in an amateur show for his imitations of Joe Penner, George Arliss, and Jimmy Durante. In the same year Joey dropped out of high school.

After a couple of years of doing odd jobs, he teamed up with two other boys to form a comedy act. They were booked into nightclubs in New Jersey and Pennsylvania. The boys were driven to their engagements by a black youth named Glenn Bishop, whose surname they adopted, calling themselves the Bishop Brothers. They toured the Eastern burlesque circuit, played vaudeville, and performed in nightclubs and at Catskills resorts.

When his partners were drafted into the army, Joey Bishop went on alone. His solo debut came at a club called El Dumpo in Cleveland. During those early days in noisy clubs, he developed his offhand approach and became a master of throwaway lines.

In 1942 Bishop himself was drafted into the army. He spent three years with Special Services.

In 1945, released from the army, he resumed his career as a comedian. Within a few years he was beginning to make a name for himself in New York City.

In 1952 Frank Sinatra saw Bishop perform and asked the young comedian to join the singer's act. Soon Bishop became a full-fledged member of Sinat-

The Smallest Baby

At birth Joey Bishop weighed only three pounds and was, he says, the smallest baby ever born in the Bronx's Fordham Hospital.

Sports Activities

"I enjoy swimming and riding," the comedian once said, "but basically I'm a lazy bum." However, he is an excellent golfer and used to play regularly with fellow comedians Buddy Hackett, Phil Foster, and Dick Shawn.

New Goal

Bishop says he has reached a stage in his life where he wants "to just have fun . . . . Too many actors forget to enjoy themselves."

Charitable Works

Joey Bishop has served as fund-raising chairman of the National Cystic Fibrosis Research Foundation, and he has raised millions of dollars for other causes, such as a Philadelphia center for addictive diseases. He received a citation from Pope John XXIII for his work in behalf of Boys Towns of Italy.

ra's clan, along with Dean Martin, Peter Lawford, Sammy Davis, Jr., and others.

Bishop extended his range of activities by taking movie roles. His early films included *The Naked and the Dead* (1958) ("I played both parts," he joked), *Ocean's Eleven* (1960), *Johnny Cool* (1963), and *Valley of the Dolls* (1967).

He also became a big attraction on television, guesting on shows hosted by Jack Paar, Perry Como, Ed Sullivan, and Dinah Shore. Those programs gave national exposure to his comic personality, which was described in the magazine *Esquire* (1961) as that of "an eager, naive, slightly awestruck yokel with whom the mass-communicated audience can sympathize."

Throughout the 1960s and 1970s he was one of TV's most familiar faces. From 1961 to 1965 he

Bishop in *Valley of the Dolls*.

Joey Bishop (left) with Jan Murray.

Boxing Fan

Bishop, a longtime boxing fan, regularly attends prize fights in southern California.

Stock Jokes

"I'd like to work one club—just one club—where they have a Jewish orchestra and Spanish people dancing."

"This is a nice family crowd—so many middle-aged men with their daughters."

"I put Dean Martin on my show one night, and wherever he went the next day people recognized him."

starred in the situation comedy *The Joey Bishop Show*, and from 1967 to 1969 he hosted a late-night network talk show of the same name. In the 1970s he frequently guest-hosted *The Tonight Show*.

In the 1980s Bishop continued to make TV guest appearances and to work in nightclubs. In 1981 he made his Broadway debut when he filled in for Mickey Rooney for one month as star of the musical *Sugar Babies*, a nostalgic re-creation of burlesque. When he stepped into the cast he spoke to the audience: "Ladies and gentlemen, on an opening night there's a tendency to be nervous. Please don't be." They roared with laughter. He also played an occasional dramatic role, as in the movie *The Delta Force* (1986).

Bishop has explained his philosophy of comedy: "Taste is the big thing—taste and honesty. Then acceptance of your style and material will come." "It's a lot more important to be known as a great human being and a so-so comic than to be known as a great comic and not be accepted by the audience as a human being." ☆

STAGE DOOR

Giving Something Back

"No matter how great the comedian," Bishop has said, "if he didn't do something for humanity, I disliked him to a certain level." Comedians he has admired for going "beyond just making money" include Danny Thomas, Bob Hope, and Jack Benny.

ELAYNE BOOSLER
Trailblazer

Elayne Boosler is generally regarded as the principal forerunner of the new breed of women comics who address topical issues from a woman's point of view without being self-demeaning or pandering to men. Her approach can be seen in this one-liner: "The contraceptive sponge is just a way of making sex seem more like doing the dishes."

Boosler was born in New York City, New York, in 1952. As a child she studied ballet at the Joffrey. But she gave it up because, as she later explained, "I don't have a dancer's body."

In 1973 she was an aspiring singer. At the Improv, a New York City comedy club, she started as a waitress and then became a hostess, introducing male comics and singing between acts. Eventually she began to incorporate comedy into her own performances.

She was encouraged by the comic Andy Kaufman,

with whom she was inseparable for the next several years. Boosler and Kaufman took any small entertainment jobs they could get. In 1977 they broke up, though they frequently met on friendly terms till Kaufman's death in 1984.

In the late 1970s and early 1980s Boosler gradually built a national reputation, at first through performances on college campuses and in small clubs in places like Mississippi and North Dakota, and later by opening for such stars as Helen Reddy and Johnny Mathis. It was Reddy who, as guest host of *The Tonight Show,* gave Boosler her first important TV exposure.

Boosler has also appeared on *Late Night with David Letterman, The Merv Griffin Show,* and TV specials. She is a regular in Las Vegas and Atlantic City.

Many of her jokes pertain to single womanhood. She speaks of dates who are so unintelligent that they keep bookmarks in their *People* magazines. And she says that people who dine alone should have their own restaurant, called Just One, where patrons are given empty frozen-food packages to read while they dine.

Some Boosler material is a slick updating of traditional jokes, including Jewish stories. For example: "My brother's gay. My parents don't mind as long as he marries a doctor."

However, much of Boosler's humor is completely mainstream and universal in appeal. "When you're eating tongue," she asks, "how do you know you're finished?" And while she generally avoids self-deprecation, she does use fat jokes because nearly everyone can relate to them: "I'm so compulsive about losing weight, I weigh myself after I cough"; "You know you're getting fat when you step on a dog's tail and he dies." Other topics include safe sex and urban living.

Physically very attractive, Boosler has frequently had to deal with verbal taunts from primitive males in her audiences. Much smarter than such men, she simply brushes them aside with good-natured retorts. When someone suggested that she "take it off," she explained, "I can't; I have a cold." When someone asked, "Why don't you do a poster?" she replied, "I'm holding out for a stamp."★

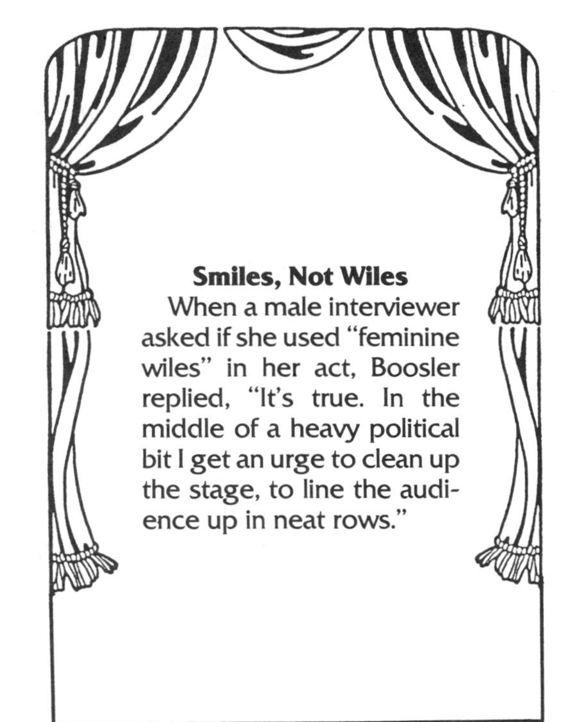

Smiles, Not Wiles

When a male interviewer asked if she used "feminine wiles" in her act, Boosler replied, "It's true. In the middle of a heavy political bit I get an urge to clean up the stage, to line the audience up in neat rows."

Favorite Humorists

As a child Elayne Boosler experienced the healing power of humor through Jackie Gleason's TV appearances. "He was so warm and expansive that he quelled the insecurity of my parents' being away."

Among members of her own generation, the greatest influences on her have been Robert Klein and Richard Pryor, "who changed the role of the stand-up comic into that of the town crier delivering the news about life and growing up."

Not a Woman's Comic

Boosler rejects pressure from extreme feminists who want her to use the stage to express their dogmas. "I'm a woman who's a comic," she says, "not a woman's comic."

VICTOR BORGE
Unmelancholy Dane

Victor Borge holds a unique place in the world of entertainment. Equally adept at stand-up monologues, sight gags, pure silliness (as in his "phonetic punctuation"), and musical humor, he has created an act of unparalleled hilarity and sophistication.

He was born in Copenhagen, Denmark, on January 3, 1909. His original name was Borge Rosenbaum.

From 1922 to 1934 he performed throughout Scandinavia as a concert pianist. At the same time, he occasionally appeared as a parlor comedian. His nervousness at music concerts became so intense that he finally decided to turn to comedy full-time.

Borge became one of Denmark's most popular entertainers. He worked as writer, director, actor, composer, and pianist on stage, screen, and radio.

Orchestral Performances
When playing the piano with an orchestral accompaniment, "I'm always terrified of making some mistakes," Borge admits. "With an orchestra you have to play up to standard, but I'm never tense in solo performance, because there I can always talk my way out of a mistake."

Borge and Boats
Victor Borge loves the sea. He lives near the ocean in Greenwich, Connecticut, and enjoys vacationing in Saint Croix, one of the Virgin Islands. "With me the three B's are Bach, Beethoven, and Boats."

A Private Farewell
Even though he was outside Denmark when the Nazis invaded his homeland, he sneaked back to Copenhagen for a final visit with his mother, who was dying of cancer at the age of ninety-four. "The hour she was buried, I alone played the organ in a church in Stockholm."

At home at the piano.

His public attacks on the Nazis put him near the top of their list of undesirables. "What's the difference between a Nazi and a dog?" he asked onstage. "The Nazi usually lifts his arm."

When the Nazis invaded Denmark in April 1940, Borge happened to be in Stockholm. Later that year he arrived in the United States.

Penniless, he went to work as a straight pianist. Meanwhile, he learned English largely by attending innumerable movies. Soon he was able to transfer his humor into the new language.

His first big break in America was landing a regular spot on the radio series *Kraft Music Hall*, hosted by Bing Crosby. Borge appeared weekly on the show for over fifty consecutive weeks during 1942-43. Later he hosted *The Victor Borge Show* (1945-47).

Since then he has performed in nightclubs, in theaters, and on TV. From 1953 to 1956 he starred in Broadway's longest-running one-man show, *Comedy in Music*.

Over the years, Borge has carefully built up hours and hours of surefire comedy bits from which he spontaneously builds a routine while onstage.

His accent, deadpan understatement, and stop-start speaking cadence beautifully set off his monologues. "Did you know that Mozart had no arms and no legs?" Borge asks. "I've seen statues of him on people's pianos." In Las Vegas, "My wife called down and asked for room service, and a half hour later they sent up a table and a dealer. Of course, my wife doesn't gamble, so she sent the table back. And then just before I left the apartment, I sent the dealer back. I don't gamble either."

Many of his jokes are based on peculiarities of the English language. For example: "My grandmother lived to be 102. She was born under Napoleon. Well, not 'under' Napoleon—you know what I mean."

Borge's sight gags include adjusting the piano stool in unexpected ways, slamming the piano lid on his fingers, and playing sheet music that has been placed upside down on his music desk (resulting in music that moves consistently in the wrong direction). All of these gags are based on memories of his own not-so-funny experiences as a nervous young concert pianist.

Borge's famous "phonetic punctuation" consists of assigning various sounds (pops, clicks, and so on—all made by the speaker's own mouth) to commas, dashes, periods, and other punctuation marks. Incorporated into a spoken sentence, these zany sounds produce some of Borge's most sidesplitting moments.

Michele Morgan and Victor Borge in *Higher and Higher*, an RKO Film.

Crediting His Faults

"Being the recipient of physical and mental facilities assigned to me before my birth, I am convinced that, as custodian, my efforts toward accomplishments consist mainly of a reasonable amount of discipline and devotion to elementary decency. Perhaps part of my good fortune may be credited to my faults, of which the greatest is modesty."

The Possible and the Necessary

Borge frequently ends his concerts with this classic quip: "I want to thank my parents for making this possible—and I want to thank my children for making this necessary."

Borge Beauties

"This concerto was written in four flats, because Rachmaninoff had to move four times while he wrote it."

"To be honest with you, I know only two numbers. One is 'Clair de Lune,' and the other isn't."

"I remember my grandfather. He was Danish after his mother, and Swedish after a friend of his father's."

"I have played all over the world—piano, of course."

O-o-uch!!!

Victor Borge riding the "A" train to Aqueduct Race Track with his daughter Rikke and the late jockey Michael Venezia.

His musical humor centers on his sly, unexpected shifting from one melody to another in midstream; the connection usually a tiny motive that is similar in both pieces, and the humor is often intensified when the shift is made from a serious classical piece to a light popular tune. Sometimes he deliberately plays a piece incorrectly, whether with wrong notes or with his own bizarre extensions of the composer's melody. Borge has also been known to pull out a pair of scissors and quite literally cut and paste together parts of different works.

Well into his seventies, Borge was still giving over two hundred comedy concerts a year. He has also conducted, and performed as soloist with, many major symphony orchestras.

Beloved the world over, Borge always shows sensitivity to the feelings of others. "A smile," he says, "is the shortest distance between people." ☆

DAVID BRENNER
Poor Boy from South Philly

David Brenner aims his humor at a mass mainstream audience. He refrains from shock, profanity, and social messages. "I have the premise that an entertainer's job is to entertain," he said. "If one person walks out of the audience upset, then I haven't really done my job."

His slick, professional, conservative style should assure Brenner of a long, prosperous career, which is his principal goal. "Comedy for me is just a means to an end," he has admitted, "a way of reaching my financial goals."

Those goals dominate his thoughts because of the extreme poverty of his childhood in South Philadelphia, where he was born on February 4, 1945 (according to published sources, though the actual year may be as much as a decade earlier). His father, Louis Brenner, had been a vaudeville comedian and song-and-dance man who quit the stage when he was young. Later he earned a bare living as a bookie, gambler, and insurance salesman. But he instilled a love for comedy in his son, who learned that "if you make fun of what hurts, it takes away some of the sting."

After earning a degree in mass communications at Temple University, David Brenner wrote and produced radio and TV documentaries in Philadelphia, Chicago, and New York City. But he felt that he could do more for the world by making people laugh.

In 1969 he decided to invest his savings ($9,000) in supporting himself for one year while he tried to make it as a comedian. During his trial year (later expanded to a

Memorial Mogen David

"I wear a tiny Mogen David (also called the Star of David and the Jewish Star) on a thin gold chain around my neck," Brenner says. "I wear it in memory of one of the more than one million Jewish children murdered by the Nazis in World War II." When asked if he knew any of the children killed, he responded, "I knew every one of them."

Brenner the Author

Brenner wrote his first autobiographical book as *Soft Pretzels with Mustard* (1983), named after a Philadelphia snack. A sequel was called *Nobody Ever Sees You Eat Tuna Fish* (1986). He also compiled a joke book entitled *Revenge Is the Best Exercise* (1983).

Likes a Showy Appearance

Though he flaunts jewelry less now than he once did, Brenner still tends to be daring and experimental in his clothing.

Life Is a Race

Brenner lives fast, always moving, doing, seeing, and experiencing. "I have always felt like I am in a footrace with Death," he explains. "I know that one day he is going to win, but until then, I am going to give him one helluva good race."

Boxing Fan

Brenner has been an avid boxing fan since the age of four. One of his favorite photos shows him standing with Muhammad Ali.

year and a half), he struggled in small nightclubs, bars, and other venues in New York City.

Brenner's savings were exhausted when he got his big break, a TV guest performance on *The Tonight Show* on January 8, 1971. Since then he has been one of America's most successful and visible comedians. Besides performing regularly in Las Vegas and Atlantic City, he has appeared on all of the major TV talk shows and has guest-hosted *The Tonight Show* many times.

In the early 1980s Brenner frequently performed in clubs with comedienne Joan Rivers. "Joan and I are as opposite as two performers can be," he said. "She's rapid-fire, while I'm a builder with a slow-paced delivery. She's bombastic and caustic, while I'm very gentle and don't attack anyone. . . . And Joan's humor can be dirty in a clean way, while I work squeaky clean."

In the fall of 1986 Brenner and Rivers competed against each other by hosting separate late-night TV variety shows. Neither series lasted long. His *Nightlife* ran into 1987.

Brenner carries a tape recorder constantly, and some of his material comes from true personal anecdotes. For example: "I sat down on a newspaper on the subway, and a guy asked me if I was reading it. I said yes, stood up, turned the page, and sat down again."

He revels in self-deprecatory humor, particularly about his prominent proboscis. "At first I thought it was going to be an extra arm. I kept waiting for the hands to appear." "I always admired people who use only one Kleenex."

One of his favorite topics is his rough neighborhood in Philadelphia. "I went into a bar once and said, 'What do you have on ice?' The bartender said, 'You wouldn't know him.' "

Brenner also questions the logic of common expressions and events. To the panhandler asking for "spare change," the comedian would say, "Oh, I'm glad I ran into you. I was about to throw all of these quarters into the street." Then there is the evangelist who cures people on television. "And he wears a toupee?" Brenner asks. "I don't get it! He can fix a guy's legs, but he can't put some hairs on his own head?"

Comedy has served Brenner's financial aims well. He owns a four-story townhouse on Manhattan's Upper East Side. He sometimes tells visitors to his luxurious home, "Four hundred years of Brenner poverty stops here." ★

David Brenner is his usually zany self on a TV talk show.

Favorite Stories

Among the many humorous stories that David Brenner enjoys are several that have influenced his thoughts and actions. Two of them follow.

The Fish Bowl: Two fish are swimming around in a fish bowl. One fish asks the other, "Is there a God?" The second fish answers, "Of course there's a God!" To which the first fish says, "What makes you so certain there's a God?" The second fish replies, "Someone changes the water."

Nothing: A rabbi was delivering a holiday sermon to his congregation. He ended it with a plea for funds for the synagogue.

"We are born nothing," he said. "We die nothing. If, in between, we can do something for our fellow man, we should do so. Each of us is nothing!"

A man in the front row stood. "Rabbi, my name is Finkelstein. I own the bank in town and I am nothing. I'll give $10,000!"

The man seated next to him stood. "Rabbi, my name is Goldstein. I own the haberdasher's and the drugstore in town. I, too, am nothing. I'll also give $10,000!"

From the back row in the balcony an old man wearing a worn, shabby suit stood up. "Rabbi, my name is Bernstein. I own the vegetable pushcart in town. I am nothing. I'll give $25!"

Finkelstein turned to Goldstein and whispered, "Look who's trying to be nothing!"

FANNY BRICE
Queen of Theater Comedy

Fanny Brice was America's premier comedienne associated with burlesque, vaudeville, and Broadway. She displayed a large, varied repertory, both as a singer and as an actress-clown.

Her vocal techniques included her satiric "concert-room vocalizing," her broadly humorous specialties (such as "I'm an Indian"), and her comic Yiddish-accented rendition of songs (such as "Sadie Salome, Go Home"). But she could also wring tears from her audiences by singing sad ballads, notably "My Man."

As an actress-clown, Brice was a pioneer in proving that women could create brilliant comedy without exploiting their sexuality and without relying on homemaking topics. She hilariously lampooned lady evangelists, fan dancers, tap dancers, and ballet dancers (she called them "belly dansehs"). Her specialty was mocking famous sirens of history, literature, and the screen. In her skits, she often adopted a Yiddish accent (actually she could not speak or understand Yiddish), thus enhancing the comic effect of the incongruity of hearing such seductive women as Eve, Madame de Pompadour, Camille, and Theda Bara speaking with the inflections of the Lower East Side of Manhattan. Other comical skits involved actual Jewish characters.

"I never did a Jewish routine that would offend my race," Brice insisted, "because I depended on my race for the laughs. In anything Jewish I ever did, I wasn't standing apart making fun. I *was* the race, and what happened to me onstage is what could happen to my people. They identified with me, which made it all right to get a laugh, because they were laughing at me as much as at themselves."

Brice was never cruel; she always performed with sensitivity and human understanding. "If you're a comic you have to be nice," she asserted. "The audience has to like you."

Brice further explained her approach to humor: "You must set up your audience for the laugh you are working for. So you go along and everything is fine, like any other act, and then—boom! You give it to them. Like there is a beautiful painting of a woman

and you paint a mustache on her." After "you get your first laugh—boom! You're going. You lose yourself; you become whatever it is they're laughing at."

Exhilarated by the joy of the moment, the madcap funny lady, with her mischievous eyes and wide, half-moon smile, would pull comic grimaces, cross her eyes, puff out her cheeks, slap her forehead, buckle her knees, and collapse her long, slender body.

Her play to the audience had begun early in life. She was born in New York City, New York, on October 29, 1891. Her original name was Fannie Borach. Her parents were saloon owners, and as a tiny tot she sang for their customers. She also got acting experience by going to Coney Island, feigning tears and pretending to be lost, and inducing passersby to give her carfare, which she proceeded to spend on hot dogs and amusement-park rides.

Determined to enter show business, Fannie quit school before she turned fourteen. She frequently won prize money as a singer at amateur contests. Soon she changed her name to Fannie (later Fanny) Brice, after John Brice, a friend of her mother's. The young entertainer made the change because she was tired of having her name punned by friends, as in "More-Ache" and "Bore-Act."

After several years of struggling, she began to attract attention with her singing and clowning on the burlesque circuit. The Broadway producer Florenz Ziegfeld spotted her and signed her for the 1910 edition of his *Follies* revue. Brice went on to appear in many of the annual *Ziegfeld Follies* productions throughout the 1910s and early 1920s.

In 1923 she headlined at the Palace Theater, New York City's prestigious vaudeville house. In 1925-26 she made a vaudeville tour.

Brice's later Broadway shows included the operetta *Fioretta* (1929) and the revues *Sweet and Low* (1930) and *Crazy Quilt* (1931). Her stage career reached its peak in the 1934 and 1936 editions of the *Ziegfeld Follies*.

Brice made six movies, including *My Man* (1928) and *Ziegfeld Follies* (1946). But she was never really comfortable in front of cameras: "Making pictures is like making love in public," she said. "You can't be at ease when somebody is watching."

She did, however, influence the films of others. Twentieth Century-Fox, without her permission, based the 1939 movie *Rose of Washington Square* on her life. She sued and won $30,000. Barbara Streisand

Skilled Craftswoman

Brice was a gifted dress designer (she designed the costumes for *Crazy Quilt*) and interior decorator (she decorated the homes of Eddie Cantor, Danny Kaye, Dinah Shore, and others).

Repressed by Fans

"Being a funny person does an awful lot of things to you," Brice confessed. "You feel that you must never get serious with people. They don't expect it, and they won't take it from you. You are not entitled to be serious. You are a clown. And maybe that is what made me dislike emotion. Once I cried in the movies, and I covered my face and bent my head. I admired the Chinese all my life because they would never show any feeling."

Fanny Brice in a Ziegfield production number.

sensitively portrayed Brice in the Broadway musical *Funny Girl* (1964) and in its movie adaptation in 1968, as well as in a film sequel, *Funny Lady* (1974).

Radio proved to be a good medium for Brice's talents. She became best known to millions of listeners for her creation of the impish little-girl character Baby Snooks. Brice had invented the character, modeled after the real-life child star Baby Peggy, as part of her vaudeville act in 1912. At a party in 1921 Brice revived the character to perform the burlesque song "Poor Pauline" as a six-year-old child might sing it. Baby Snooks then appeared on the stage in *Sweet and Low* in 1930, as well as in the 1934 and 1936 editions of the *Ziegfeld Follies*. Also in 1936 the precocious brat was introduced to radio listeners on *The Ziegfeld Follies on the Air*. She then made regular appearances on *Good News* from 1937 to 1940, when the program changed its name to *Maxwell House Coffee Time*, where she remained a fixture for the next several years. In 1944 the enfant terrible (who constantly badgered her father with question, "Why-y-y, daddy?") was given her own radio series, *The Baby Snooks Show*, which remained on the air for the rest of Brice's life.

Art Lover

Brice was an avid art collector and briefly took up oil painting. She was among the first to generate a serious interest in art in the Los Angeles area.

Food Favorites

Friends praised Brice's cooking, especially her spaetzle, spaghetti, and Hungarian goulash.

Hobbies

Brice enjoyed playing poker and collecting jewelry (especially if she could later brag about getting high quality at bargain prices). One summer she went on a hypnosis jag, insisting on hypnotizing everyone who came near her. She often succeeded.

As Baby Snooks became increasingly established as an individual entity, Brice almost completely abandoned her natural voice in public, preferring to speak in Snooks's mischievous-little-girl tones. In interviews, the entertainer often referred to "Schnooks" as if the child were a real person.

At the age of fifty-nine Brice suffered a massive cerebral hemorrhage at her home in Beverly Hills, California. She died five days later, on May 29, 1951.

☆

Albert Brooks in *Broadcast News.*

ALBERT BROOKS
Hollywood Brat Who Made Good

Albert Brooks, son of the famous radio comedian Harry Einstein (known as Parkyakarkus), grew up among professional comics and Hollywood personalities. Absorbing the comic spirit early in life, he became a professional stand-up comedian before the age of twenty-one. Later he gave hilarious performances in other people's movies.

But his real niche is making his own film comedies as writer-director-star. His pictures are cynical yet optimistic: they acknowledge the pain of existence yet also point out that much of the pain is needlessly self-inflicted. He sees the world as being full of absurdities created by the ridiculous side of human nature. Brooks has stated his creed: "Since I find reality funny, the better I can mirror it, the funnier the movie will be."

Albert Brooks was born in Los Angeles, California, on July 22, 1947. His father, the radio comedian Harry Einstein, tested the boy's sense of humor by naming the child Albert, knowing full well that the youngster would face years of teasing comparisons with the legendary scientist Albert Einstein.

The youth passed the test and soon became the class clown at school. After graduating in 1965 from Beverly Hills High School (where his schoolmates included Rob Reiner and Richard Dreyfuss), he studied for three years in the drama department at Pittsburgh's Carnegie Tech, intending to become a serious actor. Convinced by his friends that comedy was his true forte, Albert left college, changed his surname to Brooks, and turned to a full-time comedy career.

A Special Sense of Humor

Brooks's witty, intellectual approach to filmmaking has kept his audience size down. But "as people get used to me, they'll be more attuned to my sense of humor." he says.

A Private Person

Brooks tends to be secretive about his private life. "It's hard enough to have a successful relationship," he says. "I don't need the *National Enquirer.*"

Brooks with Goldie Hawn in *Private Benjamin.*

In 1968 he performed an inept-ventriloquist act on Steve Allen's TV show. Soon he did the same routine on shows hosted by Merv Griffin and Ed Sullivan. In 1969 Brooks was a regular on the TV musical-variety series *Dean Martin Presents the Golddiggers.* But he gave up the dummy act because he wanted to grow.

Turning to stand-up comedy, he scored big on *The Tonight Show* in 1972 and returned dozens of times. He also appeared frequently on other TV talk and variety shows, took his act on the road in clubs and theaters, and issued the albums *Comedy Minus One* and *A Star Is Born.*

His stand-up routines included one as a mime who described his every action with a French accent: "Now I am walking down ze stairs. Now I am petting ze dog." He was also a shadow artist whose broken hand reduced him to such impressions as "a bunny hiding behind a rock." Brooks was a riot as an elephant trainer who had to replace his ailing pachyderm with a frog; "Find the nut, boy," the trainer commanded as the "blindfolded" frog, covered by a blanket, hopped about the stage.

Life Is Funny

"Most people don't find life funny as it's happening," Albert Brooks asserts. "I think that's the job of the comedian—to point out that it *is.*" The reaction he treasures most is when a viewer thinks, "Oh, my God! That's me!"

Attuned to Human Nature

"Most of the films are not about human nature anymore," Brooks lamented in 1985. "Metal against man—that's the theme of movies in this decade." In his own films, he has sought to return human interest to the screen.

Human values are also his principal personal interest. His former girlfriend Linda Ronstadt, the singer, reported, "He turned me into a real human being." Informed of the remark, Brooks quipped, "It's true. When I first met her, she was a Volvo."

Again, however, Brooks felt bored and stifled doing the same routines over and over again. He decided to turn to films.

In the drama *Taxi Driver* (1976) he played a campaign manager. For the TV series *NBC's Saturday Night Live* he created several short comedy films, including an interview with a blind cabdriver and a parody of network promos for new series.

Brooks had a brief but effective role in the comedy *Private Benjamin* (1980), as Yale Goodman, a high-pressure businessman who dies while making love on the bathroom floor on his wedding night. In the drama *Twilight Zone, the Movie* (1983) he had a small role in the prologue. In *Unfaithfully Yours* (1984) he played a whining brother-in-law. In the comedy *Broadcast News* (1987) he was a brilliant TV reporter who longs to be an anchorman but, given the chance, flops.

Brooks worked with other writers on the scripts for, and then directed and starred in, *Real Life* (1979), *Modern Romance* (1981), and *Lost in America* (1985). In the first, he portrayed an obnoxious documentary filmmaker who, while filming a "typical American family," manipulates and distorts the events in their lives. The picture is a devastating illustration of how the mass media have dominated and nearly destroyed family life in America.

In *Modern Romance* Brooks played a neurotic film

News Addict

Brooks loves to watch cable-TV news because, he explains, "TV news allows you an occasional glimpse of lives that are not staged." A poor sleeper, he often gets up at three o'clock in the morning in California to get news from the East Coast.

Personal Habits

Brooks enjoys solitude. Sometimes he lies in bed all day. He does not smoke or drink, and he does not eat red meat. "I'm a bland freak," he admits. "I love bland foods."

On location.

editor who struggles to find happiness with his girlfriend. The movie insightfully explores many of the realistic difficulties in maintaining a love relationship in the modern world.

Lost in America shows two yuppies, a man (Brooks) and his wife, who become fed up with the fast life, buy a motor home, hit the road in a voyage of self-discovery, and then repent their decision. The movie is a satire on the values of contemporary American baby boomers, who want simplicity yet also want luxury, and who want freedom yet also want the security of belonging to a corporate structure.

Brooks's intelligence shines through all of his films. Hence, he has struggled to win acceptance at big studios and from mass audiences. But among Hollywood insiders and a small cult of comedy fans, Brooks is regarded as the funniest in the business. ★

MEL BROOKS
Wild Parodist

Mel Brooks's wild, manic humor springs from self-confessed anger and fear. When Mel was 2½ years old, his father died, leaving the boy with a permanent sense of loss and outrage. "I may be angry at God or at the world," the adult Brooks has admitted. "And I'm sure that a lot of my comedy is based on anger and hostility." He also pointed out another source of his caustic side: "It comes from feeling that, as a Jew and as a person, [I] don't fit into the mainstream of American society."

Fear, too, generates much of his humor. He maintains that comedy is like a rubber ball; if it is thrown "against the hard wall of ultimate reality, it will bounce back and be very lively." Of the ultimate reality of mortality, he has said, "If Shaw and Einstein couldn't beat death, what chance have I got? Practically none." So he created his character of the two-thousand-year-old man, who explained that "everything we do is based on fear." Singing began as a screaming for help. The handshake started as a hand search, to make sure that the other person did not "have a small stone or a marble he'd stick in your eye."

Cathartic anger and fear permeate Brooks's great

Divinely Destined

"The two-thousand-year-old man is a pastiche of everyone around me," Brooks admits. "When I became him, I could hear five thousand years of Jews pouring through me. Look at Jewish history. Unrelieved lamenting would be intolerable. So, for every ten Jews beating their breasts, God designated one to be crazy and amuse the breast-beaters. By the time I was five I knew I was that one."

Personal Habits

Mel Brooks smokes tobacco, drinks moderately, frequently uses four-letter words, and is always "on" except at home. Anxiety-ridden, he demonstrates excessive nervous energy by moving, talking, and eating rapidly; occasional lulls are followed by explosive bursts.

Favorite Moviemaker

From the age of five, Mel Brooks has admired Alfred Hitchcock more than any other film director. Brooks's *High Anxiety* is an homage to the older master.

film comedies. About *Blazing Saddles* (1974), for example, he has said, "I wrote berserk, heartfelt stuff about white corruption and racism and Bible-thumping bigotry" in the Old West. "To me the whole thing was like a big psychoanalytic session. I just got everything out of me—all my furor, my frenzy, my insanity, my love of life, and my hatred of death."

Mel Brooks was born in New York City, New York, on June 28, 1926. His original name was Melvyn Kaminsky.

Growing up in the tough Williamsburg section of Brooklyn, he had to be careful of the way he gave vent to the hostility he felt at the loss of his father. "I learned to clothe [my anger] in comedy to spare myself problems—like a punch in the face."

His mother also contributed to Mel's future. "My mother had this exuberant joy of living, and she infected me with that. She really was responsible for the growth of my imagination."

In his teens he spent summer vacations working as a drummer and toomler (creator of comic tumult) at Catskills resorts. His main gag had him walking out on a diving board with a suitcase in each hand and announcing, "Business is terrible—I can't go on." Then he would jump into the pool. During those early years he changed his name from Mel Kaminsky to Mel Brooks (after his mother's maiden name, Brookman) to avoid confusion with the jazz trumpeter Max Kaminsky.

After graduating from high school and briefly attending Brooklyn College of the City University of New York, Brooks entered the army. He was trained as a combat engineer whose specialty was to deactivate land mines. His first action was in the Battle of the Bulge in December 1944. No wonder his later show-business career came to be marked by risk-taking.

After leaving the army in 1946, he returned to the borscht circuit, where he met the comic Sid Caesar. When Caesar moved into television, he invited Brooks to join him. For the next decade Brooks helped to write comedy sketches for Caesar's TV variety series: *The Admiral Broadway Revue* (1949), *Your Show of Shows* (1950-54), and *Caesar's Hour* (1954-57). Brooks occasionally performed on the shows.

His career languished for a couple of years. Then, in 1960, he made the first of a series of comedy records with Carl Reiner, another veteran writer-performer for Caesar. Reiner played the straight man, and interviewer, while Brooks was a comically blunt two-thousand-year-old Jewish man with a Yiddish accent.

Brooks sings "High Anxiety."

Roots in Yiddish Comedy

Mel Brooks says his style has been influenced by many comedians, including Sid Caesar, Laurel and Hardy, Martin and Lewis, and the Ritz Brothers. But "the Marx Brothers had the most influence on me because they were a pastiche of strong physical comedy and very brave comedy." By "brave" he referred, for example, to the team's "making sharp political comments on war and peace."

"The roots of my humor are in very old-fashioned Yiddish comedy as well, which is based on some failure—making fun of the inept, which is cruel." Stuttering, falling on a banana peel, and so on, come down to this: "Oh, thank God it's not me." "It's cruel but effective," Brooks concludes.

The old man had seen everything but been impressed by nothing. "As long as the world is spinning we'll be dizzy and make mistakes," he said. On being old he observed, "We mock the thing we are to be. Yes, yes, we make fun of the old; then we become them." On a lighter note, he gave a new twist to a standard Jewish joke: "I have over forty-two thousand children—and not *one* comes to visit me." He explained how to know when someone is dead: "Simple. You put a finger in his nose. If he doesn't say, 'Hey, take your finger out of my nose,' he's dead." The old man had met all of the great historical figures: "Jesus Christ? Yes, thin, thin, nervous. Wore sandals. Came into the store a lot. Never bought anything." The series culminated in a three-disc album entitled *The Incomplete Works of Carl Reiner and Mel Brooks* (1973).

Brooks began his motion-picture career in 1963 when he wrote and narrated the cartoon short *The Critic.* The film is a three-minute satire of arty, abstract animated cartoons. The narrator is a simple old Jewish man sitting in the theater. "Dis is cute. Dis is nice," he says. Then, suddenly: "Vat da hell is it? It must be some symbolism. I think it's symbolic of junk."

In his full-length films Brooks has functioned in one or more capacities (producer, writer, director, actor) to stamp each work with his unique brand of humor. His principal technique is to parody established film genres, with such knowledge of, and obvious affection for, the originals that the spoofs can quite accurately be called homages.

Brooks's first feature-length film was *The Producers* (1967), which he wrote and directed. It parodies the putting-on-the-show musical films popular in the 1930s. A crooked producer and a timid accountant want to bilk investors by staging a terrible play, whose early closing will allow the two swindlers to pocket the leftover money. Their plans go awry when the show, *Springtime for Hitler,* becomes a camp hit. The film was Brooks's way of attacking bigotry and expressing his outrage at the Holocaust.

After playing a bit part in *Putney Swope* (1969), Brooks wrote and directed *The Twelve Chairs* (1970), a comedy about greed in early Communist Russia. A highlight of the film is Brooks's own small role as Tikon, an ex-serf who yearns for his former master's beatings.

With *Blazing Saddles* (1974), a parody of Hollywood westerns, Brooks reached his full stride as a filmmaking artist. The story centers on a black man

What Touches Brooks

"There are only a handful of things that have genuinely touched me in my life: when I first heard Bix Beiderbecke play his cornet; when I first walked by a painting by Soutine; when I first read Tolstoy; when I first saw my wife, Anne Bancroft, on the stage in *Miracle Worker;* and when Sid Caesar alternately made me laugh and cry while doing his version of *Pagliacci* on our TV show. It was the thrill of the discovery of a true genius."

Getting Physical

Brooks enjoys swimming in his home pool.

Tastes in Food

Junk foods are not allowed in the Brooks home. His wife, the actress Anne Bancroft, cooks only healthful meals. He has a special fondness for her tamale pie and for his mother-in-law's Italian cooking.

Intellectual Pursuits

Brooks is a voracious reader. As a child he read a satiric Russian novel that he later turned into his film *The Twelve Chairs.*

He has a particular interest in psychoanalysis.

Brooks in *The Twelve Chairs.*

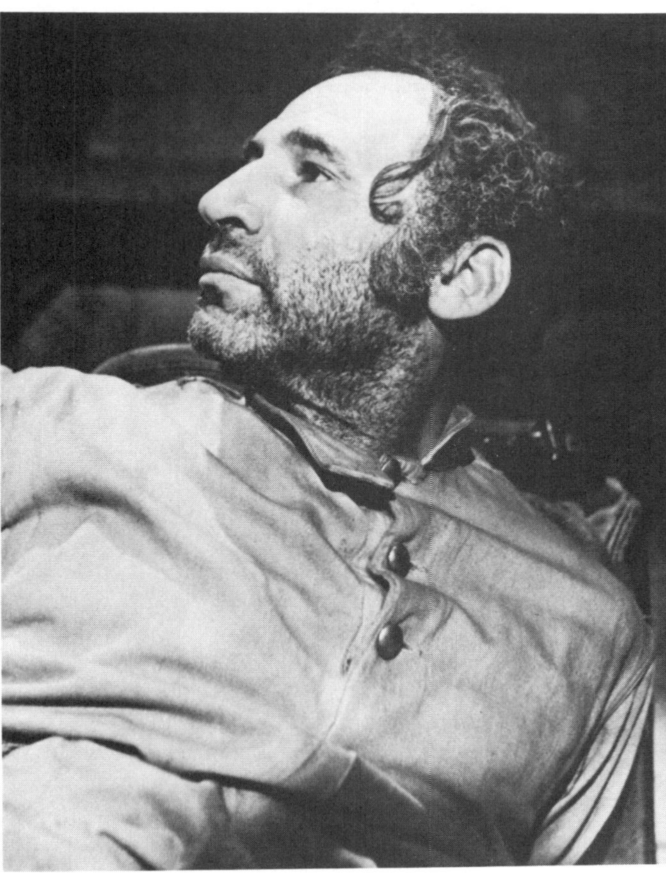

hired to defend a small town against a land-grabbing lawyer. Besides coscripting and directing the movie, Brooks played a villainous governor and a Yiddish-speaking Indian chief.

In *Young Frankenstein* (1974), a takeoff on 1930s horror movies, Brooks served as cowriter and director. He coscripted, directed, and starred in *Silent Movie* (1976), an affectionate spoof about a director trying to make a present-day silent picture.

High Anxiety (1977) parodies Alfred Hitchcock's thrillers. Brooks coscripted, produced, and directed the film. He also starred as Dr. Richard H. Thorndyke, a Nobel Prize-winning psychiatrist who suffers from a fear of heights.

Brooks wrote, produced, and directed *History of the World, Part I* (1981). He played several roles in the film, including Moses, Louis XVI, and Comicus, a stand-up philosopher who is out of work and settles for a job as a waiter (at the Last Supper he asks, "Are you all together, or is it separate checks?").

Brooks produced and starred in a remake of the classic 1942 comedy *To Be or Not to Be* (1984), in which a troupe of actors outwit the German Nazis during the latter's occupation of Warsaw in World War II. *Spaceballs* (1987), which he cowrote and directed, is a spoof of space epics; he also played a couple of roles, including President Scroob, a frantic megalomaniac. ☆

Mel Brooks reinterprets the history of the world.

A dramatization of the life of Lenny Bruce opened on Broadway in 1971.

LENNY BRUCE
"Sick" Comedian

"All my humor is based on destruction and despair," Lenny Bruce said. Understanding that everyone occasionally has sick or selfish thoughts, he stripped away what he regarded as the hypocrisy that usually covers up those thoughts and brought them into the open in his performances. He became the leading "sick" comedian of his time.

He was born in Mineola, New York, on October 13, 1926. His original name was Leonard Alfred Schneider.

When he was small his parents divorced, and he was passed back and forth between them. His conservative but caring father tended to spoil him, while his footloose mother sometimes took him to burlesque theaters but often left him on his own.

After serving in the navy during World War II, Bruce studied at a drama workshop. Soon he was working as a master of ceremonies in strip joints, telling frivolous jokes, and doing impressions of Maurice Chevalier and Frankie Laine. The clubs that he worked in were so small that he could experiment without fear of losing any ground in his career.

Bruce first began to attract serious attention in San Francisco in 1958. Much of his material was still tame, such as his movie satires and his genie joke. A genie is rubbed out of an old bottle by the owner of a candy store. The man says, "You can do anything? Then make a malted." The genie gestures and roars, "You're a malted!"

But Bruce's act increasingly included controversial jokes about vibrators, religion, homosexuality, and other subjects. "My mother-in-law broke up my marriage," he said. "My wife came home and found us in bed together." When introducing strippers, he would sometimes bare his backside, and occasionally he flipped the forbidden middle finger to members of the audience.

Lenny Bruce was perhaps the most courgeous and controversial comedian of his day.

Favorite Clothing

Lenny Bruce would buy Levi's in an army-navy store, bleach the pants with Clorox, and then take them to a tailor for redesigning into an extremely tight fit. He wore the pants with white boots.

Cleanliness Obsession

Bruce bathed or showered three times a day. To clean his insides, he regularly drank large quantities of mineral water.

Desire to Read

Bruce traveled with a mountain of reading matter, including novels, newspapers, magazines (especially the girlie variety), and books on drugs and show business. "Wouldn't it be great to just sit and read?" he mused. But the truth was that he lacked the patience and the concentration to read. When he tried, he complained of headaches. Therefore, he traveled with an intellectual companion, who kept Bruce informed through conversation.

Gaining a reputation as a "sick" comedian only made him become "sicker." He increased his use of four-letter words and added subjects like rape, toilets, and amputees. His attack on organized religion became more open.

Bruce was among the first entertainers to use "Jewish" material in front of audiences that were not exclusively Jewish. He often used Yiddish words. When police watched his act to catch him using profanity, he would switch to Yiddish vulgarities. More profound was his willingness to confront fundamental aspects of being Jewish in a gentile world. "Christians are lucky because your God, the Christian God, is all over: He's on rocks; He saves you; He's dying on bank buildings; He's been in three films; He's on crucifixes all over. It's a story you can follow. The Jewish God—where is the Jewish God? He's on a little box nailed to the doorjamb. In a mezuzah. I told my super, 'Don't paint God!'"

Bruce also showed a quiet sensitivity and human understanding. He spoke of the husband who begged his wife to "touch it, just once." And he felt the desperation of "people who come to a nightclub on New Year's Eve at 8:30. They sit there with a hat and a horn, waiting." Bruce understood the vulnerability of others because his performances laid wide open his inner self, leaving him completely vulnerable.

And it was not long before that susceptibility led to his downfall. In 1961 he was arrested twice: once for narcotics and once for obscenity. In 1962 he was again arrested twice, on the same charges.

The arrests had a profound effect on him. He spent large amounts of time studying law. And his performances suffered by his rambling on and on about his being harassed.

The end came quickly. In October 1965 he went bankrupt. And on August 3, 1966, he died of a drug overdose in Los Angeles, California.

"Satire," Bruce once observed, "is tragedy plus time." He himself did not have enough time to see the social liberalizations that he and others were calling for—or enough time to look back and see his own tragedy as a fleeting satiric reflection of the period in which he lived. But his rage against censorship, prejudice, and hypocrisy made him a cult figure among many after his death. ★

STAGE DOOR

Blue Room for a Blue Man

When touring, Lenny Bruce had a strange need to stay overnight in rooms painted blue. He was constantly wiring $50 to the next hotel to have his room painted the correct color.

Poor Dietary Habits

The comedian's staple foods were egg-salad sandwiches, ice cream, and boxes of Baby Ruth candy bars. Occasionally he indulged in huge meals, such as a nine-course Chinese dinner. He was always thirsty, and his favorite foods were soft, sweet, thick liquids, such as papaya drinks.

Bruce also went on health-food sprees, consuming grains, vitamins, and minerals. He thus lived the strange life of a man who constantly alternated between destroying himself with drugs and liquor, and building himself up again with health foods.

GEORGE BURNS
Show-Biz Methuselah

George Burns, now well into his nineties, has for years turned his advanced age into a comedy asset. "Thanks for the standing ovation," he says, "I'm at the point now where I get a standing ovation just for standing." "They're talking about making a movie of my life. I hope they do it quick—I'd like to see it."

He was born in a New York City, New York, on January 20, 1896. His original name was Nathan Birnbaum.

When Nathan was seven his father died. The boy immediately went to work at part-time odd jobs. He already had a love of show business, and he would sing as he sold crackers up and down the streets of Manhattan's Lower East Side.

A few years later he quit school and organized a singing quartet that performed wherever they found a crowd. Soon striking out on his own, he developed a variety of routines, including trick roller-skating, and in his early teens began to play the vaudeville stage. When he was fourteen, a case of stage fright led him to search for a prop that he could hang on to for security; he chose the cheapest thing he could think of—a cigar.

He changed his name to George (after the nickname for an admired older brother, Isadore) Burns (after the Burns Brothers coal company, from which he used to steal coal). But he frequently performed under a variety of other pseudonyms. He changed his name over and over again because, according to Burns himself, his early acts were so bad that he feared he would not be able to get jobs if managers knew who he really was.

He also went through a succession of partners, including a trained seal. One partner was Hannah Siegal, with whom Burns developed a Latin dance act and to whom he was briefly married.

He struggled in small-time vaudeville for a number of years. Later he admitted that his problem was that he could not deliver material as well as he could create it. That problem was solved in 1923 when he met Gracie Allen.

She was a young unemployed Irish-American Catholic trying to break into show business. Hearing that Burns was looking for a partner in his new comedy act, she asked for the job and got it. At first she play-

A young George Burns with his trademark cigar.

Happy Choice

After more than eighty-five years in show business, Burns loves it more than ever. "I'd rather be a failure at something I'm in love with than be successful at something I hate."

A Clean Act

Burns is proud that he has never used foul language or taken a cheap shot at someone to get a laugh. He has never been the subject of a scandal.

Cigars That Burn

"Expensive cigars are no good onstage," Burns explains. "They're so tightly packed—they go out. I smoke 35¢ domestic cigars. If I paid $4 for a cigar, I'd sleep with it."

Oh, George!

"Sometimes I get carried away with the part I played in *Oh, God!*" George Burns has admitted. "Yesterday when I was on an elevator, a woman got on and said, 'Nice day.' I said, 'Thank you.'"

Recreations

Burns used to love to play golf. But for many years now his main recreation has been bridge, which he plays every day.

ed the straight part, while Burns told the jokes. But audiences tended to laugh at her questions more than at his jokes. Burns and Allen switched roles and soon became a hit act.

In 1926 they married. Later that year they hit the big time by signing with the B.F. Keith chain of theaters.

Throughout the 1930s they also played supporting or cameo roles in a number of feature films. Among the movies in which they appeared were *International House* (1933), *Love in Bloom* (1935), and *College Swing* (1938).

Their radio series, *The George Burns and Gracie Allen Show* (1932-50), was one of the most popular in radio history. At first they drew from their episodic vaudeville routines. But in 1942 they changed the format to a situation comedy, with a sustained story line in each program.

In 1950 they entered the new medium of television. Their series, *The George Burns and Gracie Allen Show* (1950-58), was a domestic situation comedy in which they played under their own names, with him as a professional entertainer and her as his scatter-brained wife. The unflappable, dryly cynical Burns, the only character aware of the audience, would make comments and tell jokes to viewers between scenes.

In 1958 Allen retired. Burns revised the format of the series and tried to continue on TV with *The George Burns Show* (1958-59).

George plays God.

In 1960, at the age of sixty-four, he launched a whole new career for himself by developing a solo nightclub act, consisting of songs, reminiscences, and jokes. His trademarks were his cigar, his unfinished songs (actually performed as low murmuring), his self-deprecation, his raspy voice, and his sly wry delivery. After Allen's death in 1964, Burns added another element to his act: his preoccupation with being around very young women.

From 1964 to 1974 he continued his nightclub and concert work. But major solo success still eluded him.

That success finally arrived with his portrayal of the ex-vaudevillian Al Lewis in the movie comedy *The Sunshine Boys* (1975). His fame soared to even greater heights when he played the Deity in the films *Oh, God!* (1977); *Oh, God! Book II* (1980); and *Oh, God! You Devil* (1984).

Burns has continued to perform live as well. In 1983, for example, he worked at New York City's Palace Theater, where he had first appeared in 1924. he has also branched out into making recordings and writing many books, such as *Dear George: Advice and Answers from America's Leading Expert on Everything from A to B* (1985).

Burns still frequently appears on TV. He makes commercials, guests on talk shows, and performs on other programs. In 1983 he was honored in the TV special *George Burns Celebrates Eighty Years in Show Business.* His ninetieth birthday was celebrated in a TV special in January 1986. ☆

Exercise and Diet
Burns exercises for half an hour every day, and he walks as much as possible. He seldom eats red meat, preferring fish, chicken, and soup. Black coffee is his favorite beverage with meals. Occasionally he drinks a social martini.

George and Gracie
After Gracie died, "I was so upset for months and months," Burns recalls, "and finally I slept in Gracie's bed and I felt better. I go to Forest Lawn to visit her every month. I talk to Gracie. I tell her stories. I don't care what anyone says. I feel good talking to her."

When asked what his greatest asset is, he replies, "I was married to her for thirty-eight years."

Self-characterization
Burns calls himself "a neat old Jew."

RED BUTTONS
Little Guy with Troubles

Red Buttons has had a successful dual career, as a fine dramatic actor and as a leading comedian. "It is much harder to be funny than it is to be serious," he has said. His humor stems from his basic comedy persona as "a little guy and his troubles."

Buttons was born in New York City, New York, on February 5, 1919. His original name was Aaron Chwatt.

At the age of seven he began his show-business career by performing songs on street corners. On the Sab-

Red Buttons (right) with Marlon Brando in *Sayonara.*

bath he sang in a choir led by the great cantor Joseph Rosenblatt.

In his teens he sang and told jokes on the borscht circuit, in burlesque, and elsewhere. One job called for him to wear a bellboy uniform loaded with buttons, which, along with his red hair, led to his stage name.

In 1943 Buttons was drafted into the army and cast in the service play *Winged Victory* (1943), which was staged for Army Emergency Relief. After a long run in New York City, the show, with Buttons, was filmed (1944). He then toured in the production.

Following his discharge from the army in 1946, he appeared in a couple of Broadway shows and played the top nightclubs in the country. He was also invited to perform as a guest on TV shows, including Milton Berle's.

Buttons finally reached stardom when he was given his own TV series, *The Red Buttons Show,* in 1952. At first it was a musical-variety show, centering on little comic sketches in which he played several recurring characters, such as Buttons the Bellboy, the likable Kupke Kid, and Rocky Buttons (a punch-drunk prizefighter). His low-key humor went over well, and the show quickly became a major success. Button's familiar "Ho-ho" became a national catchphrase. However, during the 1953-54 season the program changed into a situation comedy and its ratings began to drop. The show left the air in 1955.

Admires Chaplin

While he likes much in the work of current cinema comedians, such as Woody Allen and Mel Brooks, Red Buttons still thinks that Charlie Chaplin was the best. "Ask me about Chaplin and I'll tell you I like *all* of what he did. He was funny, he was touching, he was pertinent to the times, and he had a great sense of social justice."

The next two years were difficult for Buttons. He worked very little, chiefly in nightclubs.

Then came a great turning point in his career. He was give the important role of Sergeant Joe Kelly in the movie *Sayonara* (1957). His sensitive tragicomic portrayal of Kelly won universal acclaim.

Since then Buttons has worked steadily as a character actor in films. His credits include *The Big Circus* (1959), *The Longest Day* (1962), *Stagecoach* (1966), *The Poseidon Adventure* (1972), *Pete's Dragon* (1977), and *Reunion at Fairborough* (TV, 1985).

He also bounced back as a comic. Since the 1960s he has been a major nightclub attraction in stand-up comedy.

His "little guy" jokes are still the most characteristic of his repertory. "With prices the way they are," he says, "I can't afford wheat germ anymore. Now I eat diseased wheat." "I took an economy flight. There wasn't any movie, but they flew low over drive-ins."

One of his best routines was created for a Dean Martin roast. Buttons fretted that the "greats of history never got dinners in their honor. "George Washington—who said to his father, 'If I never tell a lie, how can I get to be president?'—never got a dinner. Richard the Third—who said to Richard the Second, 'Your number is up'—never got a dinner. Michelangelo's girlfriend—who said to Angelo, 'Forget about paint; let's put a mirror on the ceiling'—never got a dinner. Captain Hook's brother— who said to Little Hook, 'For God's sake don't scratch it'—never got a dinner. And Uncle Ben—who was a credit to his rice'—never got a dinner."

"Down deep, basically," Buttons has said, "I love to clown." ★

Stress and Insecurity

The Golden Age of TV was not so golden for Red Buttons. "For fifteen years I used the same material in nightclubs, and I always got laughs," he recalled. "On TV I use a gag once and it's ready for the glue factory." His struggle to keep his ratings up led to insecurity and stress. One show was canceled when the comic fainted from overwork. In 1955 he said, "I never took a sleeping pill in my life until this year. This year I ate them by the bushel. It's a back-breaking, tension-packed grind." Later he said of his TV experience, "I was picked clean and left to die."

Red Can Be Fiery

In 1977 Buttons led a thousand members of a Beverly Hills synagogue to the French Tourist Office, where they poured five hundred bottles of French wine into the sewer to protest the release of Abu Daoud, a French terrorist involved in the 1972 Munich massacre of Israeli Olympic athletes.

SID CAESAR
Multicharacter Comedian

Sid Caesar remains best known as the star of the highly regarded early TV comedy-variety series *Your Show of Shows* (1950-54). His unmatched ability to ape many languages, sound effects, and human types put him into a class of his own.

Sid Caesar in *Fire Sale.*

Caesar with a playful Janet Blair.

He was born in Yonkers, New York, on September 8, 1922. His original full name was Isaac Sidney Caesar. Sid's father owned a luncheonette, where the boy learned to mimic the languages of Italian, Russian, Hungarian, Polish, French, Spanish, and other factory workers.

While attending junior high school, he began to earn money as a saxophonist. After graduating from Yonkers High School in 1939, he moved to New York City, where he studied to become a classical musician.

Simultaneously, however, another career was also opening for him. In the summers of 1939 and 1940, while working principally as a saxophonist, he helped to create and perform comic sketches on the borscht circuit. The following summer he worked as a comic in Monticello, while that autumn he returned to saxophone playing in New York City. In the summer of 1942 he performed as a comic at the Avon Lodge in the Catskills.

Late in 1942 Caesar entered the Coast Guard. There he helped to stage revues for the service personnel. Later he was part of the revue *Tars and Spars,* which was produced for general audiences in many American cities. One of his bits in the show was a conversation between Adolf Hitler and Donald Duck, with Caesar doing both voices. He also performed his soon-to-be-famous war-movie routine, a monologue in which he played several characters and created many sound effects, including those of aerial dog-fights. The tour culminated in Los Angeles, where the show was made into a movie that was released in early 1946.

Meanwhile, World War II had ended and Caesar had left the Coast Guard. He stayed in Los Angeles and appeared in another movie, *The Guilt of Janet Ames* (1947), in which he played a nightclub comic.

Then he returned to New York City and did some nightclub and theater work before spending a year with the Broadway revue *Make Mine Manhattan* (1948). After that, he entered the exciting new medium of television.

In 1949 he hosted the TV variety show *The Admiral Broadway Revue.* That was followed by *Your Show of Shows* (1950-54), *Caesar's Hour* (1954-57), and *Sid Caesar Invites You* (1958). Unlike many other early TV comedy-variety shows, which used stand-up comedy or slapstick vaudeville routines, Caesar's utilized some of the best comedy writers of the time (including Woody Allen, Mel Brooks, and Neil Simon) to create well-rounded sketches and a host of zany

In Tune With Music

Besides playing the saxophone, Caesar listens to classical music.

Avid Reader

Caesar reads a variety of subjects, including history and literature. He owns many books on Albert Einstein.

A Strict Diet

Since coming out of his dark period, Caesar has maintained a healthful diet. He eats two meals a day. The first comes at about 11:30 A.M. He begins with a whole grapefruit and a glass of orange juice, followed by a bowl of oatmeal sweetened with honey. Then comes canned fish (tuna, salmon, or kippers) with a slice of whole wheat bread. Dessert is Caesar's own concoction: a mush of dry cereal, low-fat yogurt, chopped walnuts, raisins, bananas, and other fresh or canned fruits. At night he has turkey or chicken with vegetables, followed by the dessert mush. In restaurants (he prefers Chinese and Japanese) he has poultry or seafood with vegetables; he then goes home for his dessert mush. Caesar also munches on the mush as a late-night snack.

characters played by Caesar himself. His most famous character was the Professor, who wore a squashed-in top hat, a tattered tailcoat, and an askew tie; the Professor pretended to know everything, but actually knew nothing. Caesar also did a monologue as a fly, including sound effects, and performed skits that parodied specific movies, TV shows, and operas. He revealed a genuine comic genius in his version of the opera *Pagliacci*, making the audience alternately laugh and cry.

Offstage, Caesar was shy and intellectual. But onstage, he hid behind a comedy persona that was brash and aggressive. When his TV series was canceled in 1958, he fell apart. In his autobiography, *Where Have I Been?* (with Bill Davidson, 1982), he confessed that between 1958 and 1978 his sense of insecurity and his difficulties in facing the pressure of success led to a dependence on alcohol and pills. Periods of despair alternated with periods of rage and violence.

"I worked," he wrote in his autobiography, "and I was there, but I really wasn't there." He was still effective in the Broadway musical *Little Me* (1962), playing seven roles. But, as he later admitted, he was working with "residual" capabilities.

Through the rest of the 1960s and most of the 1970s, he went through the motions in nightclubs, on TV, on the stage, and in films. In 1978 he finally hit

Caesar (left) with Bernadette Peters and Marty Feldman in *Silent Movie*.

Caesar with Myrna Loy.

Battling Depression

Beginning in his 1950s TV glory years and extending through his dark period (1958-78), when he was addicted to alcohol and pills, Caesar constantly battled depression. "I was so busy doing comedy, I had no time for humor," he later explained. "I couldn't laugh at myself for a long time.... But I found out that depression is 'I can't.' Laughter is 'I can.'"

Now he talks into a tape recorder every day, reminding himself to have fun with life.

Return to Exercise

In his twenties Caesar regularly worked out with weights at New York City's Gotham Health Club. When he was twenty-eight he stopped exercising and became enmeshed in his career and eventually in his use of alcohol and pills.

One of the signals of the end of his dark period was his joining, in November 1978, a Beverly Hills health club. There he began to lift weights, do pushups, and perform other exercises. He also began to swim in the pool at his Beverly Hills home.

rock bottom and began to turn himself around, largely through his own initiative. By the early 1980s he felt fully recovered in mind and body.

In 1981 Caesar toured in the stage production *A Touch of Burlesque* which was taped for release over cable TV in 1982. Since then he has appeared in several movies, including *Alice in Wonderland* (TV, 1985), in which he played the Gryphon, and *Side by Side* (TV, 1988), as one of three elderly men trying to start a clothing business for seniors. ☆

EDDIE CANTOR
Banjo Eyes

Eddie Cantor's performances as a comedian and comic singer were marked by energy and cheerfulness. In the 1919 *Ziegfeld Follies* he was billed as the "Apostle of Pep," and at the age of sixty he was described as looking like forty and acting like twenty. But his enormous popularity during his lifetime derived even more directly from his dignified yet boyish charm and his sincere human warmth.

He was born of Russian immigrants in New York City, New York, on January 31, 1892. His original name was Isidore Itzkowitz. He was orphaned at an early age and was raised in Manhattan's Lower East Side by his maternal grandmother, Esther Kantrowitz, a warm-hearted woman who greatly influenced the future entertainer's gentle, kindly character.

She was also responsible, inadvertently, for his eventual name and career. When she was enrolling the six-year-old in school, she mistakenly began to give the registrar her own name, Kantrowitz, but never finished it. The registrar wrote down "Isidore Kanter." Later the boy himself changed the spelling of his new surname to Cantor. Still later he changed the Isidore to Eddie because his girlfriend, Ida Tobias, liked the name Eddie.

Grandma Esther's ability as a mimic gave Cantor the idea of performing for others. He often sang and performed comic impersonations for his friends, sometimes combining the two skills, as when he pretended

Hobbies

In his spare time Cantor liked to read books and collect old records. He also wrote articles and books, including the autobiographical *Take My Life* (with Jane Kesner Ardmore, 1957).

to be Anna Held singing "I Just Can't Make My Eyes Behave."

At the age of thirteen he left school, determined to make a career for himself in show business. For several years he struggled in amateur-night contests, in a burlesque tour, and, as a singing waiter, in a Coney Island saloon.

In 1909 Cantor was hired as a comedian on a small vaudeville circuit. There he won praise for his ability to repeat the same act in various ethnic accents.

From 1910 to 1912 he performed as a blackface assistant to the comedy juggling team of Bedini and Arthur. When Cantor was allowed to sing "Ragtime Violin" as part of the act, he became so nervous that he skipped back and forth on the stage, clapping and gyrating his hands and rolling his eyes as he sang. Those gestures later became his trademarks.

From 1912 to 1914 Cantor toured with Gus Edwards's *Kid Kabaret* revue. There he met George Jessel, who became a lifelong friend.

In 1914 Cantor married Ida Tobias. Later he incorporated anecdotes about his wife and five daughters into his routines. He adopted "Ida, Sweet As Apple Cider" as his theme song.

The Cantors honeymooned in London. While there, he appeared in the revue *Not Likely,* in which he scored his first major success. Till then he had relied on imitations and dialects. In *Not Likely* he sang and performed comedy routines as himself.

Back in the United States later in 1914, Cantor renewed his vaudeville work as a blackface comedian and

Four Favorite Comics

To Cantor, the top pantomime comedian was W.C. Fields, especially as seen in his famous pool-table act, which spoofed the solemn manners of poolroom habitués.

Cantor's favorite comedienne was Fanny Brice, who had a tremendous power of concentration and an unmatched skill in hilariously burlesquing what others took seriously, such as ballet, literature, and movie stars.

Will Rogers was Cantor's choice for best monologist because of such homespun philosophy as this: "Don't worry if a man kicks you from behind—it only proves you're ahead of him."

The greatest of all comedians in Cantor's opinion was the black vaudevillian Bert Williams. "As a performer, he was close to genius," Cantor said. "Whatever sense of timing I have, I learned from him." Cantor also praised Williams for his economy of gesture.

Introduction to Literature

Eddie Cantor did not discover the joy of reading books till he was twenty-five years old. His teacher was his vaudeville friend W.C. Fields, who always traveled with a trunk full of books. Fields introduced Cantor to classics by Dickens, Hugo, Dumas, and others.

Personal Habits

After a 1952 heart attack, Cantor changed his lifestyle. Formerly, he would attend late parties or poker games every evening, eat a big meal at midnight, and go to bed after 3:00 A.M. From 1952 on, he went to bed early and arose early, ate several small meals during the day instead of one big late meal, exercised regularly, and adopted "a philosophy without fear."

Favorite Foods

Two of Cantor's favorite foods were meatballs and steak.

Fund-raiser

In 1920 Cantor began to give benefits for Surprise Lake Camp for underprivileged youngsters. He himself had attended the camp as a child.

In the late 1930s he helped to raise money for sending Nazi-victimized refugee children to Palestine.

He raised hundreds of millions of dollars for other causes, including hospitals, veterans, Catholic and Protestant projects, and the United Jewish Appeal.

Much of his work was done for the state of Israel, where he was affectionately referred to in Yiddish as the *schnorrer* ("beggar").

When President Franklin D. Roosevelt asked Cantor to organize a drive to raise money for fighting infantile paralysis, the entertainer suggested a plan in which each donor would be asked for only ten cents, calling it a "march of dimes." Roosevelt immediately adopted that slogan for the program. When Dr. Jonas Salk developed his polio vaccine in the 1950s, the money had come from the March of Dimes.

Eddie Cantor in *Ali Baba Goes to Town.*

singer. Breaking blackface tradition, however, he performed without dialect and without comedy clothes.

Cantor made his Broadway debut in the *Ziegfeld Follies of 1917*, followed by the 1918 and 1919 editions of the show. He then appeared in the revues *The Midnight Rounders* (1920) and *Make It Snappy* (1922). In a famous skit in the latter show, he played Max, a mousy tailor whose customer demanded a coat with a belt in the back; the "belt" he received was not the type he expected. The musical comedy *Kid Boots* (1923) was one of Cantor's most popular shows. In the *Ziegfeld Follies of 1927* he broke precedent by being the only star in the whole revue. That show was followed by the musical comedy *Whoopee* (1928). His last stage work was in *Banjo Eyes* (1941), the title coming from his nickname, which referred to his wide, expressive eyes.

In his stage appearances, Cantor performed some of his routines with, and some without, blackface. As was true of many other white entertainers of his time, such as Al Jolson and Sophie Tucker, Cantor's use of blackface was intended not as a racial slur but simply as a theatrical convention that helped performers overcome inhibitions. After gaining experience and confidence, they could come out from behind the "mask" and perform without the black makeup.

The development of sound movies in the late 1920s hurt the live theater. Cantor quickly jumped into the new medium, where his impish behavior and frantic pace fared well. Among his films were *Glorifying the American Girl* (1929), *Roman Scandals* (1933), *Ali Baba Goes to Town* (1937), and *If You Knew Susie* (1948). He also appeared briefly in, and sang for the music track of, the biopic *The Eddie Cantor Story* (1953), in which he was portrayed by Keefe Brasselle.

However, it was through radio that Cantor reached the peak of his popularity. He had his own radio variety show, under various titles, almost continuously from 1931 to 1949. Beginning in 1932, he pioneered the use of live-audience response on radio, where studio visitors had previously been admonished to remain silent.

In the 1950s he turned to television. From 1950 to 1954 he hosted *The Eddie Cantor Show,* a variety series. One of the highlights of the show was his regular skit character Maxie the taxidriver. In 1955 he hosted and occasionally starred in *The Eddie Cantor Comedy Theater,* a series of variety programs and comedy plays.

After a 1952 heart attack, Cantor reduced his activities. In 1962 his life changed even more drastically with the death of his beloved Ida. His own death, in Los Angeles, California, came on October 10, 1964.

George Jessel called Cantor "the most resourceful comic figure that there ever was in America."★

Cantor in *The Kid From Spain*, the 1932 Busby Berkeley musical.

JACK CARTER
Joke Salesman

Jack Carter's greatest comedic asset is his frantic nervous energy. The success of his furiously paced routines depends less on the material than on his delivery. He virtually "sells" the jokes to the audience through his aggressive mimicry, employing at least a dozen different facial and physical contortions, such as "the fadeaway," "the slow burn," "the turnaround," and "the walking freeze."

He was born in New York City, New York, on June 24, 1923. His original surname was Chakrin.

While attending New Utrecht High School in Brooklyn, he played Cyrano de Bergerac in a school production. Other early stage work included an appearance in a minstrel show.

Carter then entered the army, where he performed in service entertainments. Released, he began to build

Jack Carter in *The Horizontal Lieutenant.*

his professional comedy career, notably on radio's *Call Me Mister.* At that time his act consisted mainly of impressions of Fred Allen, Nat King Cole, Sidney Greenstreet, and other show-biz celebrities. Soon, however, he added songs and gags.

In the late 1940s Carter scored big as a guest on Milton Berle's TV series *The Texaco Star Theater.* Subsequently he hosted his own show *Cavalcade of Stars* (1949-50) and appeared regularly on *All-Star Revue* (1951-53).

Thereafter he frequently guested on TV, notably on *The Ed Sullivan Show.* In the 1970s he appeared on some TV game programs. That exposure made him a headliner in major nightclubs.

Carter has also carved a niche for himself as a reliable character actor. He had roles in the movies *The Horizontal Lieutenant* (1962) and *History of the World, Part I* (1981); and he acted in many TV series and stage plays, such as a New Jersey production of *Guys and Dolls* (1984), in which he portrayed Nathan Detroit.

In the 1950s Carter told this topical joke: "Truman said to MacArthur, 'OK, Mac, you're through. Pack up your pipe and get lost!' MacArthur replied, 'You can't do this, Harry. You'll ruin my Korea!' "

Real Estate Tycoon

Feeling a shift in the comedy marketplace away from himself, Carter now spends much of his time working in real estate, where, in fact, he makes more money than he does in show business.

Fear of Rejection

Jack Carter, like so many comedians, is an inveterate worrier with a deep sense of insecurity. "A comedian doing a solo routine is selling himself," he says. And if the audience does not laugh, the performer feels a sense of personal rejection. "That hurts, and that's why clowns must be the saddest people on earth."

On Getting Older

"It's getting tougher now," Carter admits. "When I was younger, I had a lot more gumption. As you get older, you get more timid because you are trying to hold your position."

A typical pose.

In the turbulent 1960s, the brash comedian told abrasive jokes. For example, a man sees a fat lady carrying a duck. "The guy says, 'What are you doing with that pig?' The fat lady snorts, 'That's not a pig; it's a duck.' The guy says, 'I'm not talking to you; I'm talking to the duck.' "

Today a typical Carter joke would run like this: "Canada ran out of silicone, and the girls up there are using hamburger helper."

Carter is a favorite in Atlantic City. ☆

California Vegetables
Since 1970 Carter has lived in California, where, he says, "the produce stores are like Cartier's. The tomatoes are real gems."

MYRON COHEN
Master Storyteller

Myron Cohen, master of the extended humorous anecdote, regarded himself not as a comic but as a storyteller. He would introduce the plot, savor the facial mannerisms and accents (Jewish and others) of the characters, and work his way to the punch line.

A private detective to his client: "I have the proof. Your wife is definitely cheating on you. What do I do now?" The client to the detective: "Follow my wife and that bum! Keep on their trail night and day, even if you have to track them around the world. And then I want a complete report on what he sees in her!"

Cohen was born in Grodno, Russian-ruled Poland (now Grodno, the Soviet Union), in 1902. Brought to the United States when he was a child, he later worked for many years as a textile salesman in New York City.

He told jokes to amuse his customers. Some quips were sly definitions: "A shoulder strap is a little piece of ribbon designed to keep an attraction from becoming a sensation." Others were one-liners based on puns: "I know a salesman who has one hundred suits—and they're all pending." However, as Cohen later admitted, "They liked my jokes, but they didn't always buy my material."

In the late 1940s he finally quit the garment industry and entered show business professionally. He became an overnight success. Though he had no foreign accent in his ordinary speech, he usually told his jokes in dialect, generally Yiddish but sometimes Irish or Italian.

Cohen developed a nice-guy image that truly reflected his own personality. He spoke with genuine humility, and his jokes were good, clean fun, such as this

A Special Friend
Cohen was close with comedian Henny Youngman for forty years. They often performed onstage together, and they even exchanged jokes.

About Audiences
"Audiences are the same everywhere," Cohen asserted, "whether you're in Vegas, South Africa, or Rockland. They all want to hear about something that happens to human beings."

Self-characterization
Myron Cohen was, according to the comedian himself, "a nice, pleasant little guy with nothing to prove." It is not hard, he said, to be a nice guy if you "like people" and "like what you're doing."

gem: "Here's one about the small-business man who after six months of valiantly trying to make ends meet decided to call it quits. He posted the following sign in his window: Opened by Mistake."

In 1952 Cohen hit the big time by appearing at New York City's Copacabana nightclub. For the next thirty-three years he remained one of America's leading entertainers. When other dialect comedians went out of favor, Cohen maintained his popularity because of his low-key manner, his inoffensive material, and his unique delivery.

In his later years he began to broaden his act to include modern topics, such as infidelity and race relations. But the jokes were always gentle and good-natured.

A black man in a Jewish district was bewildered at the sight of Orthodox Jews. "What the hell are they?" he asked a friend. "Hasidim," the friend answered. The first man retorted, "I see dem, too, but what the hell are they?"

An angry black man accused a Jew of bigotry: "I asked for directions, and he called me a black bastard!" The Jew, in his thick accent, defended himself: "No! You asked where the drugstore vas, and I said, 'You're a block passed it.'"

In 1976 Cohen had a heart attack. From 1976 to 1984 he worked with a pacemaker in his chest. In 1984 he had another heart attack, and he retired soon afterward.

Cohen died in Nyack, New York, on March 10, 1986.

★

Two Cohen Favorites

A typical Cohen joke was about two women in the Bronx hanging clothes out to dry. One woman asks the other, "Have you seen what's going on in Poland?" The other replies, "I live in the back—I don't see anything."

One of his personal favorites was the one about a skinny little guy who walks into a lumber camp, looking for a job. To impress a skeptical foreman, the shrimp fells a towering oak in ninety seconds. "Where'd you learn that?" asks the lumberjack. The little guy says, "In the Sahara Forest." "You mean the Sahara Desert." "Sure—now."

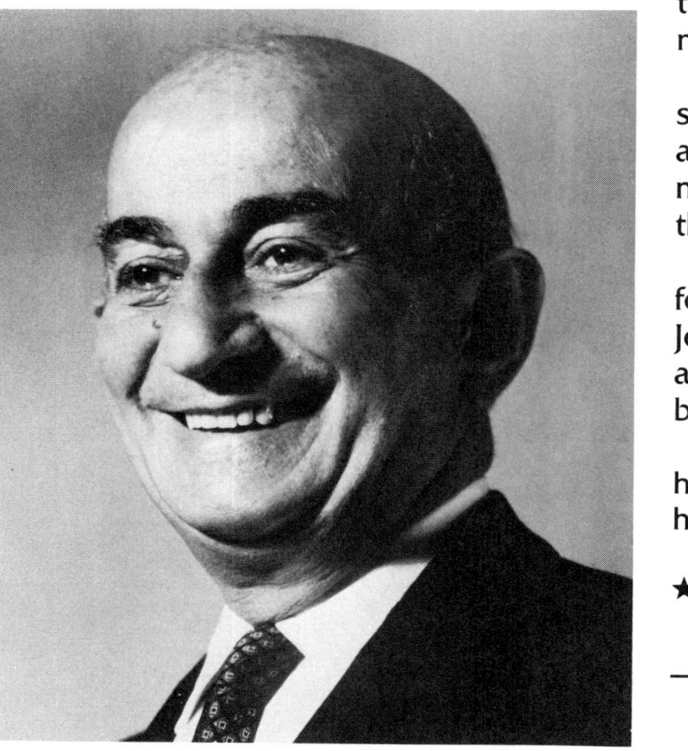

Myron Cohen.

IRWIN COREY
The Professor

Irwin Corey, in his stage persona as the befuddled, double-talking Professor, delivers wild "lectures" that turn into social and political satire. Wearing an overlarge frock coat, a bedraggled string tie, tennis shoes, and a mop of flying hair, he blends prepared gags with ad-libs.

Corey was born in New York City, New York, on January 29, 1912. Early in his career he showed an interest in straight acting. He appeared on the New York City stage in *The Emperor's New Clothes*

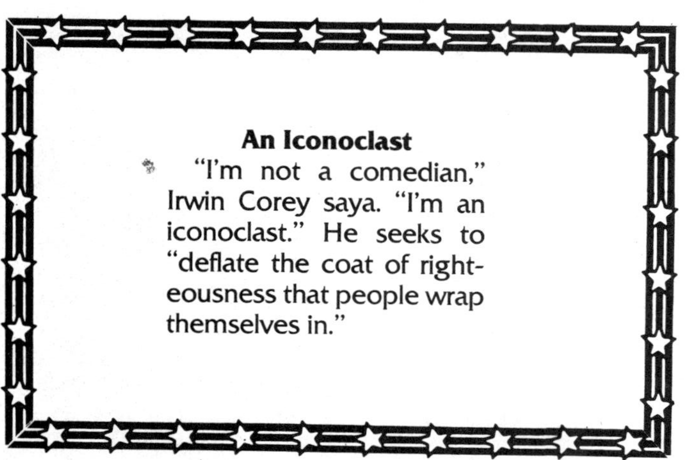

An Iconoclast

"I'm not a comedian," Irwin Corey saya. "I'm an iconoclast." He seeks to "deflate the coat of righteousness that people wrap themselves in."

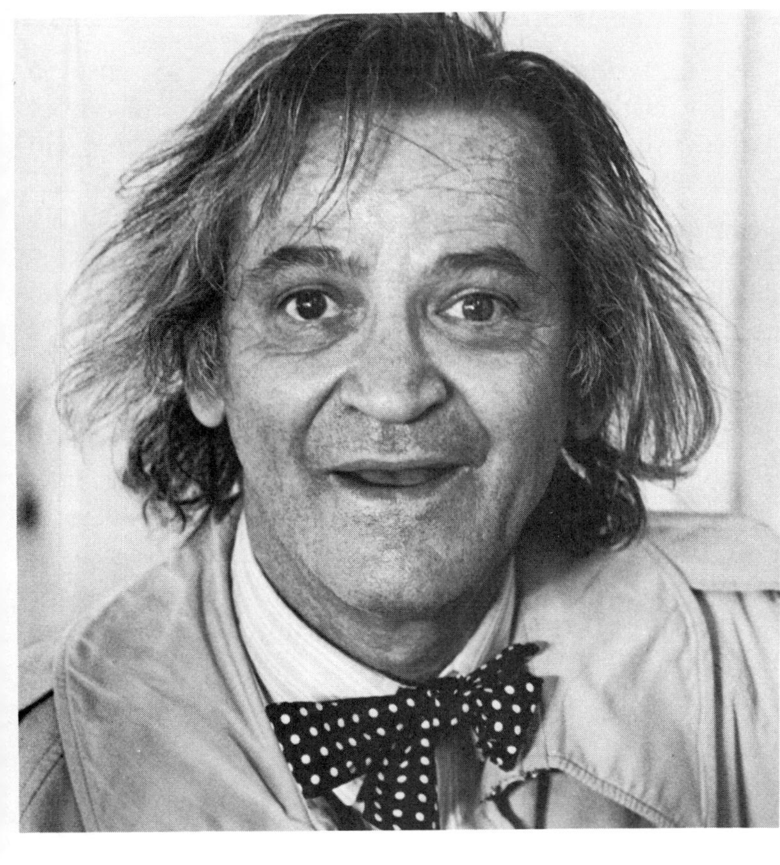

Corey Zingers

When he saw a sexy lady, Corey improvised this line: "Behind every beautiful woman there is a beautiful behind." On politics, he says, "You can't have a third party when the other two are the same."

Crazy Like a Fox

In 1943 Corey got out of the army by pretending to be crazy.

Former Boxer

In 1933 Corey won the Phoenix, Arizona, Golden Gloves boxing championship in the featherweight division.

Blasts "Scum"

When Corey was blacklisted from TV, his outbursts became even angrier. "I don't give a damn if I *am* self-destructive," he said. "I just don't want to be associated with scum," among whom he included politicians, show-business cliques, and comedians who play it safe or sell out.

(1941), *Mrs. McThing* (1952), and other plays.

But it was as a stand-up comedian that he began to make his mark. In the 1940s he appeared in major New York City nightclubs, and he worked on radio with the comedian Edgar Bergen.

In 1956 Corey described his Professor: "He just grew over the years. Sometimes I'm not sure what the Professor is going to say or do until I go on the floor and the character takes over. I'm not sure why, but everybody seems to love the poor-soul absentminded Professor. Just by looking at him you know he's lost in the clouds and doesn't know it. He wouldn't hurt a fly and he loves people. Even children laugh at him."

"Sir Isaac Newton and the law of gravity," begins one of the Professor's lectures. "There he was, walking through his apple orchard, and he saw an apple falling down from a tree, which amazed him because until that time—until the law of gravity was passed—all apples fell up."

An example of the Professor's gibberish: "New York, where the political view blightens the eye. More people per capita than any other city of the same size with the same per capita."

The Professor often uses audience participation to liven up his lectures. When that and his own ad-libbing falter, he calls on a stockpile of his standard lines. For example: "Life is memory. So if you don't do

Professor Irwin Corey.

Corey with Marlo Thomas in *Thieves*.

anything when you're thirteen, when you're fifty-one you got nothing to remember." If he spots an empty seat he might say, "It's impossible to capture the mind of the heterogeneous mass when they ain't even here!"

Corey was a popular guest on late-night TV talk shows till, in the 1960s, he began to utter controversial lines over the air. "Is there life after birth?" he asked in one routine. "Yes! Nixon is a great example of afterbirth!" Soon Corey was blacklisted by the major television networks.

"Comedy is a very interesting weapon in the hands of those who are fighting the injustices of society," Corey asserts. "Because people will remember a laugh more than they will a direct quote, however profound it is."

In recent years Corey has worked in nightclubs and has found acceptance on cable TV. He has also appeared in a number of movies including *Thieves* (1977) and *Crackers* (1984). ☆

NORM CROSBY
Mr. Malaprop

Norm Crosby has built his comedy career principally by using the device of malapropism, the misuse of one word for another that sounds similar to it. *Puberty,* for example, is confused with *poverty* in this line: "President Johnson declared war on puberty." To lend greater credence to his malapropisms, Crosby created a stage persona who seems perpetually bewildered.

The comedian was born in Boston, Massachusetts, on September 15, 1927. he attended the Massachusetts School of Art and planned to become a commercial artist. But he left school to enter World War II military service, during which he suffered a permanent partial hearing loss. Today he still wears a hearing aid, and he often jokes onstage about his inability to hear indistinct speech.

After the war, Crosby worked for a while in a Boston shoe store. Then he began to get comedy jobs throughout New England in nightclubs, at charity shows, and at stag dinners for fraternal organizations.

However, Crosby was still using standard material,

Embarrassing Allergies

Allergic to horses, Crosby nevertheless had to ride behind the Clydesdales in the 1983 Hollywood Christmas Parade. During the entire parade he was sniffing a nasal spray.

He is also allergic to dogs. His wife's parents keep canines, and when she visits her folks for holiday dinners, he has to stay home.

Some Crosby Gems

Mr. Malaprop speaks of "human beans," "trousers that need an altercation," a sports idol who is "an insulation to young players," and the human body's being "subject to so many melodies."

Sweet and Sour

Crosby is never without his favorite snack—licorice. However, in recent years he has had to curb his salt intake. He has particularly missed corned-beef sandwiches.

Charitable Activity

By staging an annual celebrity golf tournament, Norm Crosby has raised huge sums of money for the City of Hope National Medical Center and Research Institute (Duarte, California), where free treatment is given to those suffering from major ailments. He has also served as honorary chairman of the Better Hearing Institute of Washington, D.C.

A Prized Honor

When Crosby was given a spot on the famous Hollywood Walk of Fame, the star was placed, at his request, between the sidewalk stars of his idols Jack Benny and Red Skelton.

and he was desperate to freshen up his act for his New York City debut. He noticed that a friend of his constantly induced laughter through an unintentional use of malapropisms.

Crosby incorporated the technique into his act and made a hit in his first New York City appearance. Soon his career skyrocketed. He has perfected his style through years of polishing in nightclubs, at Catskills resorts, in concert halls and theaters, and on TV.

His routines take the form of lectures based on "hysterical truths." He explains the wisdom of great figures like "Sigmund Frood, who went into a lavatory and friggered out all for himself, on the sperm of the moment, that there was equalness between people." Crosby loves to receive a "standing ovulation."

He uses straight jokes as well. "Teenagers don't know what love is," he says. "They go for a drive, the boy runs out of gas, they smooch a little, and the girl says she loves him. That isn't love. Love is when you're married twenty-five years, smooching in your living room, and he runs out of gas and she still says she loves him—that's love!"

Crosby toured with Robert Goulet for three years and with Tom Jones for four years. Throughout the 1970s the comedian shared the bill in Las Vegas with many top-name singers, such as Tony Bennett and Liza Minnelli. From 1978 to 1983 he hosted the syndicated TV series *The Comedy Shop,* a showcase for stand-up comics. ★

Crosby gives the telephone a questioning look.

BILLY CRYSTAL
"Mahvelous" Mimic

Billy Crystal feels "at home in other bodies." Not a traditional joketeller, the gifted mimic creates comedy by humorously evoking alter egos of real and imaginary people. He has, for example mimicked Sammy Davis, Jr., singing "We Are the World" with Yiddish asides. Crystal has also done impressions of Muhammad Ali, Jewish relatives, and old jazz musicians. Among his fictional characters are Penny Lane, a transvestite; Rabbit, an octogenarian veteran of the old Negro Baseball League; and an unnamed elderly punch-drunk boxer who boasts that he broke his nose seventy-seven times in one fight. The comedian's most famous character is Fernando, inspired by, but only loosely based on, the late actor Fernando Lamas. Fernando's expression "You look maaaaaavelous" created a national catchphrase.

Billy (originally William) Crystal was born in the borough of Manhattan, New York City, New York, on March 14, 1948. (Some sources give the city as Long Beach, New York, and the year as 1947). He grew up in the Bronx (for two years) and in Long Beach, on Long Island, New York.

In his autobiography, *Absolutely Mahvelous* (1986), Crystal describes the influence of his early surroundings on his later career. His paternal grandfather was a Yiddish actor. His mother loved the theater and performed in shows at temple. One of his uncles, Milt Gabler, founded Commodore Records, which focused on jazz. Billy's father, who managed Gabler's shop on Fifty-second Street in Manhattan, often invited jazz musicians to the Crystal family home, where Billy met Billie Holiday, W.C. Handy, and other jazz greats. "We had swinging seders," he later recalled. Billy began to imitate the musicians' jive talk. He also performed for his family by mimicking the televised and recorded routines of professional comedians.

Crystal majored in theater at Nassau Community College and then studied TV and movie directing under Martin Scorsese at New York University. While at NYU, he worked as the house manager for the off-Broadway hit musical *You're a Good Man, Charlie Brown.*

A relaxed Billy.

Hollywood and New York
Though currently living in Pacific Palisades, California, Crystal hopes to move back to New York again. He likes to collect New York Yankees memorabilia, but he is also a Los Angeles Lakers fan.

Size Is Relative
Crystal, who stands 5′6″, likes to collect miniature furniture. "It gives me a great feeling of height," he says.

Crystal Cooks
One of Billy Crystal's favorite activities is cooking Japanese food.

In 1969 Crystal and two friends formed an improvisational troupe called successively We the People, Comedy Jam, and Three's Company. The trio played Greenwich Village clubs, small Eastern colleges, and trade shows for over four years.

Crystal then went solo. He struggled for the next couple of years (1975-77) with club dates and an occasional TV appearance.

After moving to Los Angeles, he was performing one night at the Comedy Store when he was spotted by the TV producer Norman Lear. Soon Crystal had a guest role in Lear's situation comedy *All in the Family*. Then the producer cast him as Jodie Dallas, the first openly homosexual character in the history of television, in the sitcom *Soap*, a spoof of soap operas.

During his four seasons with *Soap* (1977-81) Crystal also appeared in several movies. In the theatrical release *Rabbit Test* (1978) he played the world's first pregnant man. His other films included *Enola Gay* (TV, 1980). When not engaged in *Soap* or in movies, he returned to the live comedy circuit.

In 1982 he hosted his own short-lived TV series, *The Billy Crystal Comedy Hour*.

During the 1984-85 season he rejuvenated the slumping TV comedy show *NBC's Saturday Night Live* with his gallery of impersonations. Crystal cre-

Crystal about to present a Grammy Award.

In his younger days.

Creating Characters

"I like twisting my face and my voice and my mind into different characters," Crystal says. "But I do have a specialty. When I'm in trouble, under pressure, I fall back on being old and Jewish. I rattle phlegm . . . . I feel good."

Sports Activity

As a youth Crystal was a fine baseball player; he played shortstop for and captained his high-school team. Today he enjoys softball and tennis.

Learns From Others

Lily Tomlin and Richard Pryor, because of their ability to evoke tenderness and compassion through comedy, are among Crystal's favorite performers.

His stylistic model is Bill Crosby: "Like Crosby, I try to be honest out there. I just rap, just talk."

Crystal's heart, however, belongs to two giants of an earlier generation, as he explained while creating his 1982 TV series: "Since my two idols are Red Skelton and the late Ernie Kovacs, I try to combine elements of both of them."

Crystal (right) and Mickey Mantle on NBC's *Saturday Night Live*.

ated a borscht-belt comic, a phlegm-voiced Jewish weatherman ("The forecast for Thursday: don't be such a big shot; take a jacket"), and an elderly hippie with a Yiddish accent. He also did impressions of such show-business figures as Joe Garagiola and Yul Brynner. *NBC's Saturday Night Live* gave birth to the Fernando character, and in 1985 Crystal issued the album *Mahvelous*.

Since then he has performed on TV specials, hosted the Grammy awards (1987), appeared in the movies *Running Scared* (1986) and *Memories of Me* (1988), and toured the United States with his comedy act in nightclubs and on college campuses.

Stephen Holden of the *New York Times* wrote that Crystal has entered "the serious comedy territory occupied by Lily Tomlin, Woody Allen, and only a handful of others." Like those few others, Crystal can comedicly move an audience. He has described his own work: "Bittersweet. Nobody else will take a chance on doing anything with poignancy. I'm not that concerned with getting laughs. If I can move the audience, that's more important to me." ☆

BILL DANA
José Jimenez

Bill Dana remains best known for his portrayal of the comical Hispanic character José Jimenez, though the comedian dropped the role in 1970. Shy, humble, and inarticulate, José would break up audiences with his interview routines. As a frightened astronaut, he was asked what he planned to do during his long isolation in outer space. "I plan to cry a lot," José answered forlornly. Astronaut Wally Schirra later used the line for a gag.

Dana was born in Quincy, Massachusetts, on October 5, 1924. His original name was William Szathmary.

After attending Emerson College and serving as an infantryman in World War II, he entered show business with a last name borrowed from his mother, whose first name was Dena. In the early 1950s he was half of a nightclub comedy duo. But a back injury caused him to give up performing and to turn to writing.

He wrote for the young stand-up comic Don Adams before getting a TV staff job in 1956 on *The Steve Allen Show.* For two years he worked at that job. But his parlor entertainment impression of a Latin-American character delighted Steve Allen so much that the latter finally put Dana on the air.

José first appeared as a sidewalk Santa who spoke in mangled English; while ringing his bell, he shouted, "Jo, jo, jo." In subsequent programs the character held a variety of jobs. Here is part of a routine with Allen interviewing José as a submarine officer:

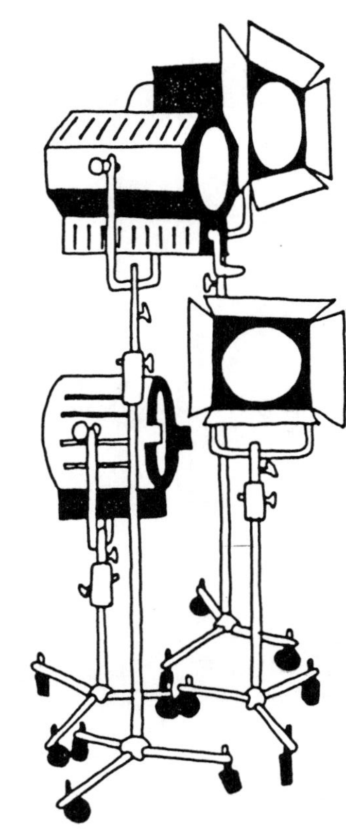

ALLEN: Congratulations on your tremendous feat.
JOSÉ: Thank you, but they're only size eight.
ALLEN: You stayed under water for eighty-four days. How come?
JOSÉ: They didn't want to come up before the submarine.
ALLEN: Under water all that time, did you begin to hate your friends?
JOSÉ: Just one time. During the third riot.
ALLEN: As an executive officer, you had a specific assignment—.
JOSÉ: No, I had the Atlantic assignment.
ALLEN: In those eighty-four days that you were submerged, did you have any mechanical trouble?
JOSÉ: Only with the ballast valve, the one that lets you go up.
ALLEN: How long did you have that problem?
JOSÉ: Eighty-three days.

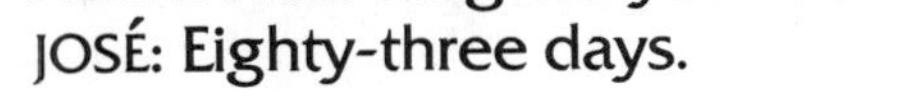

Triple Personality

At the height of his José Jimenez fame, the comedian Bill Dana explained his three personalities. "There's José Jimenez," he said, "actually the nice side of everybody. There's Bill Dana, who enjoys success to the hilt. And there's Bill Szathmary, who was tremendously insecure and had deep feelings of inferiority—but I think Bill Szathmary is just about gone now."

Bill Dana with Ann Margaret.

Adversity Breeds Humor

"Nothing breeds humor better than adversity," says Dana, who grew up during the Great Depression. "Maybe I even overcompensate today, but there's no better feeling than to look into my wallet and see real money."

Dana soon began to appear regularly as José in Danny Thomas's TV comedy series. From 1963 to 1965 *The Bill Dana Show* featured José as a bellhop at a New York hotel. The character also went over big on records and in nightclubs. His timid but dignified self-introduction, "My name—José Jimenez," created a national catchphrase.

In his nightclub act Dana also used straight monologues as well as non-Hispanic dialect stories. A Jewish mother, for example, was visited by her comedian son. The son shows her a color picture of a topless dancer in dark blue leotards. "When I work in nightclubs, Mama, this is the kind of girl I work with." The mother examines the picture and says, "That's the color I want the drapes."

Throughout the 1960s Dana received pressure from Latin-American groups who resented José because they thought that he was an insulting representation of their people. Dana finally came to agree that as a "Hungarian Jew" he had no right to portray José. On April 4, 1970, at a gathering of the Congress of Mexican-American Unity, he announced that "after tonight, José Jimenez is dead."

Later Dana successfully transferred many of José's jokes into Scotch, German, and Yiddish dialects. He recorded an album of Jewish humor, a parody of *Hee-*

Haw called *Hoo-Ha*. He has appeared in several movies, including *The Snoop Sisters* (TV, 1972) and *The Nude Bomb* (1980). And in 1982 he was a regular on the short-lived TV comedy series *No Soap, Radio.*

However, Dana has turned increasingly away from performing and toward TV writing and producing. He wrote the famous *All in the Family* episode in which Sammy Davis, Jr., gets the advantage on the bigoted Archie Bunker. ★

Intellectual Interests

Dana's home is filled with classical recordings, first-rate literature, pre-Columbian art, and his own paintings.

RODNEY DANGERFIELD
Comedian Who Gets "No Respect"

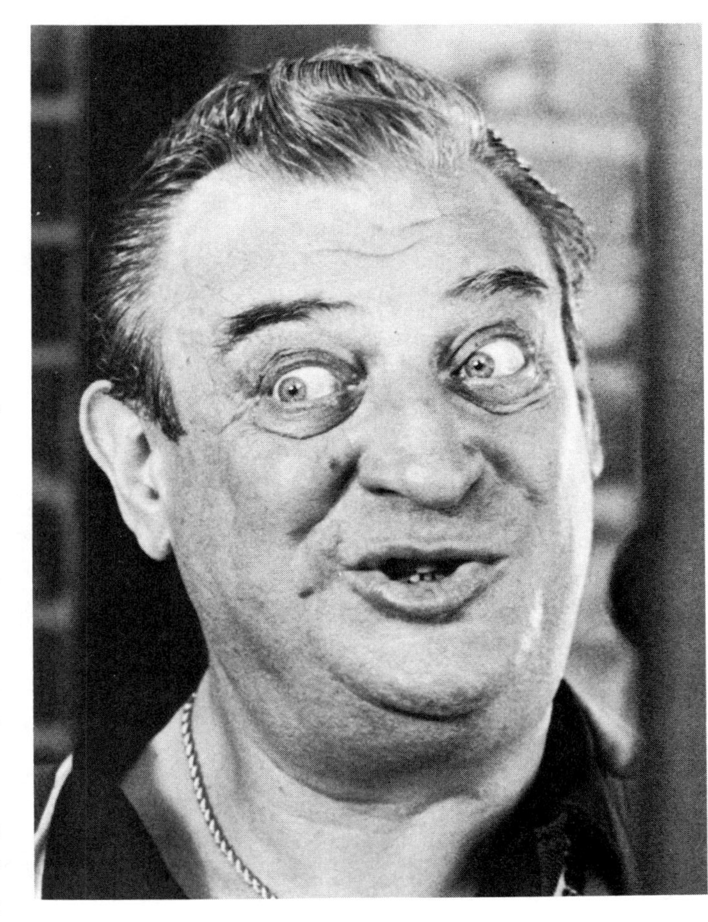

Rodney Dangerfield's success has been based on his creation of a unique comedic appearance and personality. His plaintive bugging eyes have been likened to fried eggs; and his brow-wiping, neck-craning, tie-adjusting, and shoulder-twitching suggest a thoroughly modern neurotic. The basis of his verbal humor is that, in his words, "I don't get no respect." "My mother never breast-fed me," he says; "she told me she liked me as a friend." Life has been going downhill ever since then: "My psychiatrist told me I was going crazy. I said, 'If you don't mind, I'd like a second opinion.' He said, 'OK. You're ugly, too.'"

Dangerfield was born in Babylon, New York, on November 22, 1921. His original name was Jacob Cohen.

He struggled through many difficulties as a child. His father, at one time a vaudeville pantomime comic under the stage name Phil Roy, ran out on the family when Jacob was a baby. Later his mother moved the family to the Kew Gardens section of the borough of Queens in New York City, a neighborhood that was actually beyond their means. The boy faced not only poverty but also the embarrassment of having a job that required him to deliver groceries to the homes of the well-to-do children with whom he went to school. His sense of inadequacy prevented him from dating

Appearances Can Be Deceiving

"People take a look at me and think I don't have any feelings," Dangerfield claims, "but I'm really a very sensitive person." What he wants is to have "peace of mind" and "to love and be loved in return."

Kids Like Dangerfield

Dangerfield is popular with youngsters, "I guess because I never grew up," he says. "My head is young."

Health Conscious

In the mid-1980s Dangerfield gave up smoking and started the Pritikin diet. His efforts have been diligent. "I don't know moderation," he confesses.

Dangerfield finally gets some respect.

the girls he liked. He also encountered anti-Semitism, even among his teachers.

At fifteen he began to write jokes as a way of escaping reality. "Comedy is a camouflage for depression," he would later admit. The first joke he ever wrote already showed him as a loser: "When I played hide-and-seek, they wouldn't even look for me."

At nineteen he began working in nightclubs at the Catskills resorts as a stand-up comedian under the name Jack Roy. For nine years he struggled. He already showed signs of being a good comedy writer, but as yet he lacked a distinct stage personality.

When he was twenty-eight he left show business to get married and raise a family. For the next dozen years he ran his own business, selling house paint and siding. During those years he continued to write jokes, and he sold some of them to Jackie Mason and Joan Rivers.

In his early forties Cohen/Roy decided to return to the stage, and he was booked into a Brooklyn nightclub that he had worked years before. To avoid embarrassment, he asked the club's owner, George McFadden, to bill him under a new name. McFadden chose the name Rodney Dangerfield, which the would-be comedian permanently adopted.

With his stage personality now clearly defined, as the loser who keeps trying, Dangerfield quickly found success. Soon he landed TV appearances on *The Ed Sullivan Show* and *The Tonight Show.* He also began to work in America's top nightclubs. In 1969 he opened his own place, Dangerfield's, in New York City.

His roles in several movies have solidified his position as a comedy star. In *Caddyshack* (1980) he was an endearing nouveau-riche boor. In *Easy Money* (1983) he portrayed a cheerful reprobate. And in *Back to School* (1986) he was a tycoon who returns to college.

TV has remained an important vehicle for him. He has often appeared on *The Tonight Show* and has guest-hosted *NBC's Saturday Night Live.*

Dangerfield is now probably best known to millions of Americans through his recent TV commercials for Miller Lite beer. He appears in the commercials with a number of former athletes, from whom he consistently gets no respect. ☆

Melancholy Comic

"I'm basically a down guy," Dangerfield admits. "I don't walk around smiling." Fame and success "came late in life. I'm too old to start doing cartwheels."

Loser's Laments

"My kid goes to a private school—he won't tell me where it is."

"I was a very ugly baby. When the doctor cut the cord he hung himself."

"The other day I called up to get the right time. The record hung up on me."

MARTY FELDMAN
Popeyed Comic

Marty Feldman was one of the few comedians who could make audiences roar with laughter just by looking at them. With large pop eyes as his central feature, he developed subtle facial expressions—such as a sly smile or a blank look of pure innocence—that added layers of meaning to his work and set him apart from the more obvious, aggressive kinds of comics. Yet he was also a master of zany slapstick, performing most of his own pratfalls and movie stunts.

Feldman was born in London, England, on July 8, 1934. His first ambition was to become a jazz trumpeter. In his late teens he led his own jazz band.

When his music career did not move forward, Feldman turned to acting and writing. He toured England's carnival circuit as an assistant to an Indian fakir, and he sold jokes.

Eventually he graduated to writing comedy sketches for British radio and TV. Among those for whom he wrote was David Frost, who later asked Feldman to be one of the writer-performers on the TV series *At Last the 1948 Show* (1967).

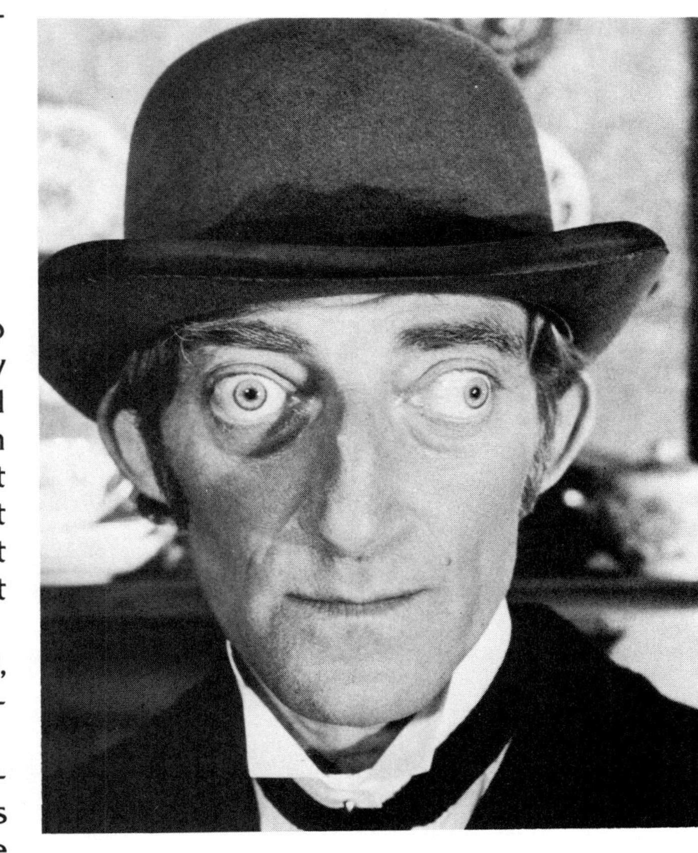

Feldman then had his own series, *Marty* (1968-69) and *Marty Amok* (1970), where he displayed great versatility in both verbal and visual humor. In one sketch he played a bookshop customer seeking an "expurgated" work on British birds. In another sketch he donned a judge's robe, burst into private homes, and announced, "I am your friendly neighborhood door-to-door judge." He created a hilarious effect when, as a bowler pacing off his approach, he marched halfway across the city. Feldman became one of the most popular entertainers in England, developing his own cult following.

In the 1969 film *The Red Sitting Room*, he had a small role as a male nurse. He then coscripted and starred in the comedy movie *Every Home Should Have One* (1970; American title, *Think Dirty*).

In 1970 he performed on the American TV musical variety series *The Golddiggers in London. The Marty Feldman Comedy Machine* (1971-72) was a comedy series taped in London and then shown on American TV.

Today Feldman is principally remembered for his brilliant comic portrayals in a handful of American films. In Mel Brooks's *Young Frankenstein* (1974) Feldman played Igor (which he pronounced "eye-gore"), the hunchbacked assistant to Dr. Frankenstein. In Gene

Wilder's *The Adventure of Sherlock Holmes' Smarter Brother* (1975) Feldman took the role of Orville Sacker, a retired London detective who assists Sigerson Holmes. *Silent Movie* (1976) was another Brooks film. In it Feldman portrayed Marty Eggs, who helps Mel Funn in an attempt to make a modern silent movie.

Feldman then set out to make his own films. He cowrote, directed, and starred in *The Last Remake of Beau Geste* (1977), a spoof of old foreign-legion adventure yarns. He also cowrote, directed, and starred in the biting satire *In God We Tru$t* (1980), subtitled *Gimme That Prime Time Religion*. In it Feldman played Brother Ambrose, a monk who, at his superior's request, leaves his cloister to perform an errand in the big city, where he becomes involved with religious hucksters.

On December 2, 1982, Feldman suddenly died of a massive heart attack in Mexico City, Mexico, where he had just finished his role in the film *Yellowbeard* (1983), a spoof of pirate pictures. He also appeared in the posthumously released movie *Slapstick of Another Kind* (1984). ★

A Confirmed Vegetarian

At the age of six, during World War II, Marty Feldman was evacuated from London to the countryside. There he had a pet rabbit named George. "One day he was my lunch," Feldman later recalled. After that episode he never ate meat again.

The adult Feldman liked pasta and fruit, and he ate cheese "the way other people eat meat."

"I won't eat anything that has intelligent life," Feldman maintained, "but I'll gladly eat a network executive or a politician."

Baseball Fanatic

After making *Young Frankenstein* (1974), Feldman moved to Los Angeles and soon became thoroughly Americanized, especially in his adoration of the game of baseball. "I love baseball," he exclaimed. "It's one of the best things about America. Vin Scully, the Dodgers announcer, is like some kind of god to me."

Nature Made Him a Clown

Feldman's bulging eyeballs, his trademark, were the result of a thyroid condition brought on by a childhood accident. He was short, with frizzy hair and a large askew nose. "Physically," he admitted, "I am basically equipped to be a clown."

TOTIE FIELDS
Rotund Comedienne

Totie Fields had the rare gift of being able to laugh at herself. Standing under five feet in height and weighing about 190 pounds, she ribbed herself for years about her own bulk. Near the end of her life, when she lost a leg, she joked about her artificial limb.

She was born in Hartford, Connecticut, on May 7, 1930. Her original name was Sophie Feldman. As a child she inadvertently created her own nickname by mispronouncing *Sophie* as *Totie*. Later she changed *Feldman* to the stage name *Fields*.

At the age of four she sang on a Hartford radio station. By the time she was fourteen she was singing on the borscht belt. Later she struggled for several years as a singer-comic in small nightclubs and strip joints. Her big break came in 1962 when she was asked to open for Chubby Checker in Pittsburgh. She finally hit the big time on her own when she was booked at the famous Copacabana nightclub in New York City. That

engagement led to an appearance on Ed Sullivan's popular TV variety series.

By then she had dropped singing for comedy, which she had gradually put into her act between songs. To prevent audience members from her heckling about her size, Fields started telling her own fat jokes. For example, after asserting that happiness was "getting a brown gravy stain on a brown dress," she reached the real punch line: "Why am I such a slob? Maybe it's 'cause the target's so big." She also told stories involving bizarre diets. Other topics included health foods and soap operas.

During the late 1960s and early 1970s Fields came to be widely regarded as being at or near the top spot among female comics in the United States. She appeared regularly at major nightclubs and on TV talk and variety programs (over one hundred times on Mike Douglas's show). Her following was particularly strong in Las Vegas, where she eventually settled.

In 1976 she began a courageous 2½-year struggle against a series of health problems. In April of that year she developed phlebitis, which necessitated the amputation of her left leg. Soon afterward she suffered two heart attacks. In 1977 cancer forced the removal of her right breast, and diabetes caused severe eye problems for her. She lost over seventy pounds the hard way—through illness.

Favorite Joke

Fields named this as her favorite joke: "Follow that cab!" "We have to. It's towing us."

Furs and Feathers

When she began to make big money, Totie Fields spent large sums on beautiful clothes, including bulky fur coats. "I break all the rules and wear everything: ruffles, ostrich feathers, fox coats. You look fat in fox anyway, so if you start fat, you only look a little fatter."

Generation-Gap Stories

Fields liked to draw on her family for humorous stories, especially ones pertaining to the ever-present problem of the generation gap. "My kid told me she was trying to find herself," began one such anecdote. "I said, 'Show daddy and me where you last saw yourself. We'll go there with a flashlight.' "

Self-criticism

"Totie Fields annoys me sometimes," Fields herself said in 1977. "I'm not that lady. I could never look at myself when I was fat. I'm a vain woman. I was disappointed in the way I looked."

Furthermore, "my voice is so offensive to me. It's not a nice *listening* voice. . . . I once made an album that was just great. You know, I've never listened to it. . . . Some of my shtick is annoying to me, too."

Nevertheless, Fields continued to work whenever she could, appearing onstage with a cane and a pivot chair. Her initial comeback, in April 1977, took place before a celebrity-packed house in Las Vegas. Many of her new gags were about her health problems, including her artificial leg. She performed throughout America, but her base was the Sahara Hotel in Las Vegas.

Totie Fields died of a heart attack in Las Vegas on August 2, 1978. ☆

BUD FLANAGAN
Leader of the Crazy Gang

Bud Flanagan holds a special place in the history of British comedy. As the partner of Chesney Allen and the leader of the Crazy Gang, Flanagan summed up the great music-hall comic tradition and left a permanent record of that art in his motion pictures. Broad and crude at one moment, he easily switched to wistful sentiment the next. Flanagan and Allen comically contrasted with each other: Allen was patient, dignified, and elegantly attired; Flanagan was playful, roguish, and dressed in a broken straw hat and oversize clothes. Flanagan delighted in periphrastic mistakes (such as "Fine Timber" for the name Goodwood), blurted out other verbal nonsense (as in "He's a eunuch; he's got no scruples"), and humorously hinted at vulgarity, often with a slyly placed "Oy!" His humor and personality were a blend of Jewish and British music-hall elements.

Flanagan, son of a cantor, was born in the Spitalfields section of London, England, on October 14, 1896. His original name was Chaim Reeven Weintrop, anglicized on his birth certificate as Robert Winthrop.

When he was ten he became a call boy at the Cambridge Music Hall. At twelve he made his theatrical debut by performing magic tricks in an amateur talent contest at the London Music Hall.

In 1910, inspired by the American vaudeville acts he had seen, he sailed for New York City. There he worked at odd jobs before touring the United States in a vaudeville act in 1911. In 1912 he acquired a partner, and they

A Royal Favorite

Flanagan was greatly admired by three reigns of British royalty. He appeared in more than fifteen variety command performances.

Tried Boxing

During his stay in the United States as a youth, Flanagan considered a boxing career, which lasted, he said, for one fight.

Working for Charity

Flanagan devoted much time to charity, both through the Grand Order of Water Rats and through his own Leukemia Fund, which he started as a memorial to his son, Buddy, who died at the age of twenty-nine in 1955.

Bud Flanagan (second from right) with the rest of the Crazy Gang in the film *Gasbags*.

appeared in New Zealand, Australia, and South Africa.

In 1915 he returned to England and joined the Royal Field Artillery. During World War I service in France he was gassed and temporarily blinded.

In 1919, after recovering and returning home, he formed a duo called Flanagan and Poy. He had adopted the stage name Flanagan as an act of revenge against an anti-Semitic sergeant-major of that name who had made the aspiring comedian's life miserable in the artillery. This act and another duo, called Flanagan and Poy, were both unsuccessful, and by 1922 he was driving a London taxi.

However, he soon returned to performing and teamed up with Chesney Allen, whom he had met in 1916. After an initial period of struggling, Flanagan and Allen became one of England's most successful music-hall comedy acts. They were outrageous, inventive, and endearing.

In 1929 they made their London debut. The following year they appeared in their first royal command performance at the London Palladium.

The team frequently joined seven other zanies to form a group called the Crazy Gang, with Bud Flanagan as its undisputed leader. Flanagan and Allen appeared with the Crazy Gang in *London Rhapsody* (1931), *The*

Flanagan's Character

Bud Flanagan was modest, decent, and honorable—qualities that shine in his autobiography, *My Crazy Life* (1961).

A Musical Hero

While working at the Cambridge Music Hall as a youngster, Flanagan heard Alec Hurley, who "sang tuneful Cockney songs in a quiet way." Flanagan modeled his own stage voice on Hurley's.

Little Dog Laughed (1939), and other shows. On their own, the duo worked in many more revues, including *Life Begins at Oxford Circus* (1935), *Many Happy Returns* (1937), *Black Vanities* (1941), and *Hi-De-Hi* (1943). They also made movies, such as *Underneath the Arches* (1937) and *Here Comes the Sun* (1945).

In 1945 ill health forced Allen to retire, and Flanagan went on alone. With the Crazy Gang he appeared in *Together Again* (1947), *These Foolish Kings* (1956), and several other extremely successful stage shows. Flanagan also worked with the Crazy Gang in the movie *Life Is a Circus* (1960) and performed on his own in the film *The Wild Affair* (1965). In his sixties he was still executing hilarious acrobatics.

He wrote many of his own songs. They included "Free," "Dreaming," and, the song with which he was most closely identified, "Underneath the Arches," which saluted the down-and-outs during the Great Depression.

Flanagan died in London on October 20, 1968. ★

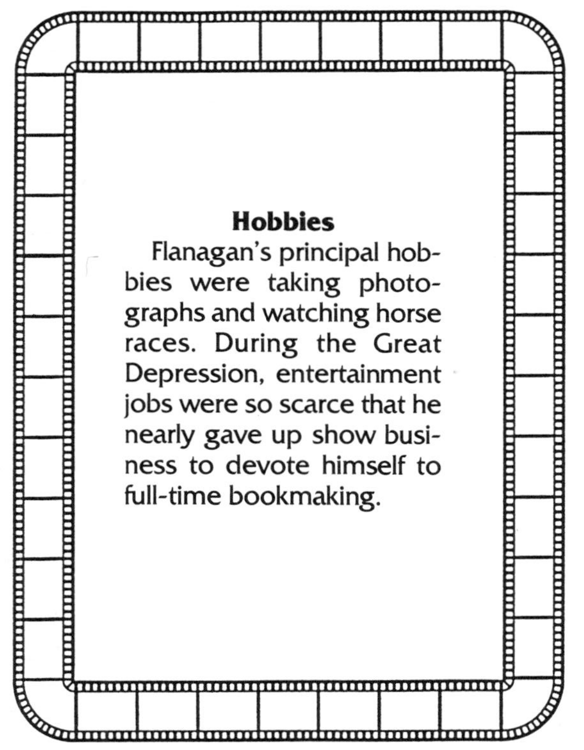

Hobbies

Flanagan's principal hobbies were taking photographs and watching horse races. During the Great Depression, entertainment jobs were so scarce that he nearly gave up show business to devote himself to full-time bookmaking.

PHIL FOSTER
Frank DeFazio

Phil Foster spent over forty years as a little-known, financially unstable stand-up comedian in nightclubs, in Catskills resorts, on radio, and on TV. But in 1976 he suddenly shot to stardom upon joining the cast of the TV sitcom *Laverne and Shirley* as the gruff but kindhearted Frank DeFazio. During the next seven seasons he finally attained security and became one of America's best-known comedians.

He was born in New York City, New York, on March 29, 1914. His original name was Fivel Feldman. His parents were Russian immigrants who had changed their surname to Feldman from Vishnodosky. Later the comic took the name Foster after the name of a Brooklyn street.

He began as a comedian and social director in the Catskills. Returning to New York City, he studied acting at the New Theater School and then joined a touring group that performed plays of Clifford Odets. While in Chicago with that ensemble, Foster went to a nightclub and loudly criticized a comedian working there. Challenged to take the stage himself, Foster did so, ad-libbed a comical Brooklyn Dodger fan, and won a job. There followed a succession of one-night stands as a comedian.

After World War II army service, he hit the road again and made some appearances on radio's *The Big Show* and *Monitor*. One of his most successful routines was a refinement of his early bit as a Brooklyn Dodger fan ranting from the stands.

In the 1950s he played the borscht belt and then hit the big time at Manhattan's Copacabana nightclub, at the Sands in Las Vegas, and at the Fontainebleau in Miami Beach. He also appeared on TV shows hosted by Sid Caesar, Jack Paar, and Ed Sullivan. His first movie role came in *Conquest of Space* (1955).

Foster later explained his early comedy: "I introduced a style that is very evident today. I just talked. I talked about my people, my family, my block. I was honest. Honesty is funny. Honesty is character. It always works."

In the 1960s and early 1970s Foster's career seemed to be stuck. He was highly respected by entertainment pros, but he could not get the big breaks leading to the big bucks. He appeared in a few movies, in-

A Favorite Story

Foster liked to tell a true story about a famous actress whom he and his wife knew when the actress was unknown. After she got a part on a TV series, she stopped seeing the Fosters. When the show was canceled and she became unemployed, she renewed her friendship with them as if nothing had happened. A couple of years later she won an Academy Award in a supporting role. Foster sent her a wire: "Congratulations—and goodbye again."

Learning Through Failure

Foster was grateful to have had his youthful apprenticeship in countless small, unimportant venues, where he could practice, experiment, and hone his skills. He felt that most young performers today do not have "a place to die," that is, a place to learn their craft through trial and error.

After *Laverne and Shirley* was canceled in 1983, he began to conduct classes in improvisation. "This is my contribution to reforestation," he explained. "This is a place where performers can fail. This is the place to die."

Phil Foster with Robert DeNiro (left) and Michael Moriarty in *Bang the Drum Slowly*.

cluding *Bang the Drum Slowly* (1973), and he continued to work in nightclubs and resorts.

Finally, in 1976, came the major breakthrough in his career when he won the role of Frank DeFazio, owner of a pizzeria, in the immensely popular TV sitcom *Laverne and Shirley*. The show ran till 1983 and gave Foster national renown.

During those years he made more movies, including *The Happy Hooker Goes to Washington* (1977) and *Gridlock* (TV, 1980). He also continued to make live appearances as often as possible, even at trade shows.

Foster died in Rancho Mirage, California, on July 8, 1985. ☆

Brooklyn Dodger Fan

Foster never missed a home game of the Brooklyn Dodgers from his childhood till the late 1950s, when the team moved to Los Angeles. He never forgave them for leaving New York. Even after he moved to Los Angeles himself, he had no interest in the team.

Sports Enthusiast

In his younger years Foster was active in handball, skiing, and hiking. Later he became a golf enthusiast: "All I live for is to play golf," he admitted.

Dream House

"What I'd really like to do if I made lots of money," Foster once said, "is buy a great big house and put an old comic in every room in it. A house full of comics—wouldn't that be something?"

DAVID FRYE
Satiric Impressionist

David Frye was by far America's top impressionist during the turbulent Nixon years 1968-74. Though a master mimic of a wide range of actors and other public figures, he made his greatest impact with his impersonations of politicians, especially Richard Nixon himself. Frye had an uncanny ability to duplicate not only the subject's voice and mannerisms but also his facial features, his other physical traits, and, most important, his fundamental effect on other people.

"Audiences need a way to vent their feelings and fears about these big political figures," Frye explained, "and they can do it with me. That's why it's so important to me to get not just a few characteristics but the whole presence of the man." To create each impression, he would spend many hours listening to tape recordings, studying photos, watching TV and videotapes, and rehearsing in front of a mirror. He tried to feel what it was like actually to *be* the subject. Then he would give his caricatured personalities monologues that created some of the fiercest and funniest political satire of the period.

Frye was born in New York City, New York, in 1934. His original name was David Shapiro.

He discovered his talent for mimicry while he was in his teens, performing impressions of total strangers shortly after meeting them. While attending the Univer-

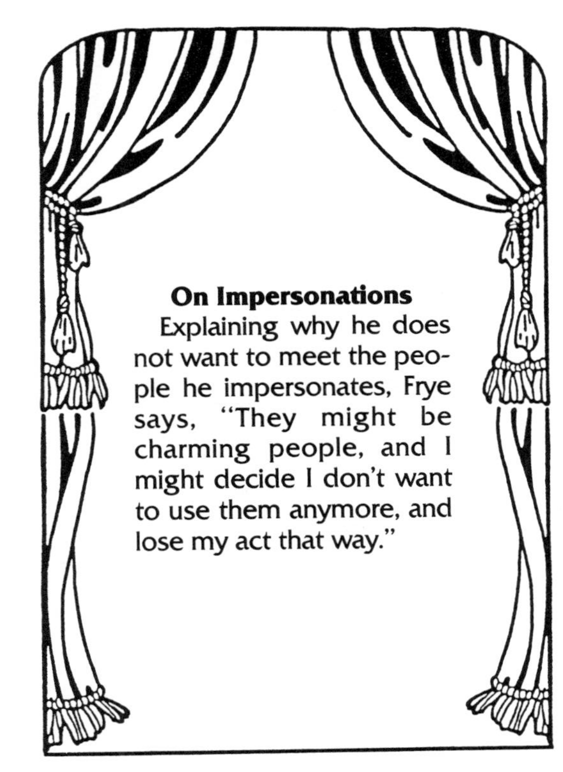

On Impersonations

Explaining why he does not want to meet the people he impersonates, Frye says, "They might be charming people, and I might decide I don't want to use them anymore, and lose my act that way."

sity of Miami, he did impressions of such show-business stars as James Cagney in campus productions and in Miami strip joints.

After four years of college and a stint in the army, Frye returned to New York City in 1959. He worked in his father's office-cleaning business during the days and performed in local talent shows in the evenings.

In 1962 an open audition led to two appearances on *The Tonight Show.* "I did JFK and they liked it," Frye recalled. "So they let me on again and I bombed."

The turning point in his career came when he added Robert F. Kennedy to his act in 1965. That impression went over so well that he began to add other politicians. His appearances on Merv Griffin's TV show in 1966 signaled the beginning of Frye's rise to star status.

His popularity skyrocketed during the 1968 presidential campaign. As a frequent guest on the Johnny Carson, Smothers Brothers, Ed Sullivan, and Dean Martin talk and variety shows, Frye broke up audiences with his mimicry of the candidates and other political figures. His effusive Hubert H. Humphrey blurted, "When I wake up in the morning, I say, 'Whoopee!' And I want to say I'm proud as Punch to be running for the presidency of the United States!" His bulldog-faced George Wallace growled, "I'm heah to say that I'm sick and tard of looters and rioters. Last week they burned down ma library in Alabama—both books, one I ain't even colored yet." His beaten President Johnson, peeringover a pair of spectacles and forcing an ear-to-ear smile, drawled, "My fellow Americans, I come here tonight—because I no longer have any place to go." Frye also gave devastating mimicries of a popeyed, self-important William F. Buckley, a gravel-voiced Nelson A. Rockefeller, and others.

But Frye's most effective impression was that of Richard M. Nixon. Beetling his brows, shrugging his slumping shoulders, puffing out his jowls, slightly opening a cruel mouth, and shifting his sinister eyes back and forth, the comedian's Nixon would say, "They call me Tricky Dickie. But I can't imagine why. I've got two good arms, two good legs, and two good faces—and I intend to take them to the public!".

When Nixon was elected to the presidency in November 1968, Frye could not have been happier. Nixon was a gold mine. In 1969 Frye released his first record, *I Am the President*, in which his Nixon said, "I am the president, and make no mistake about that!" The title became a national catchphrase and also the line by which many Americans would forever remember Nixon.

Difficulty Being Himself

Privately insecure, Frye, in the presence of others, seems uncomfortable as himself. He avoids eye contact and sidesteps questions about his personal life and his art, instead presenting nonstop mimicry of his stable of characters.

Humor in Nixon

In early 1974 Richard Nixon was in danger of losing his presidency. "Frankly I would prefer him to remain in office," Frye admitted. "There's no one as funny as he is. It's his gestures, his movements, his neurosis."

The comedian felt a special empathy with Nixon. "I'm a neurotic man," Frye confessed, "and neurosis comes easy to me."

STAGE DOOR

Between Art and Madness

Frye sometimes worries about the intensity with which he absorbs his impersonations. "The next step would be to become the person—and then I'd end up in the insane asylum."

When the Watergate scandal broke, Frye was given even more grist for his mill. Now his Nixon quipped, "My administration has taken crime out of the streets and put it in the White House, where I can keep an eye on it." When Nixon's lieutenants were forced to resign their posts, the parody Nixon said, "As the man in charge, I, of course, accept the full responsibility. But not the blame. Let me explain the difference. People who are to blame lose their jobs. People who are responsible do not."

When Nixon himself was finally forced to resign in 1974, Frye lost his favorite target. The comedian became erratic. Sometimes he had to take photos onstage as cue cards to remind him how to create his characters. There were even incomplete performances.

The Carter and Reagan years, with their relative domestic calm, have not lent themselves to Frye's kind of savage mimicry. Today his nightclub act consists principally of nonpolitical personalities, such as Howard Cosell, Billy Graham, and George C. Scott, though old times are rekindled with his still-brilliant William F. Buckley. ★

Unfilled Longing

Though best known as a political satirist, Frye actually has little political feeling. What he has long wished to do is to improvise characters, much in the manner of Jonathan Winters. But the full development of that technique has never quite materialized for Frye.

ESTELLE GETTY
Golden Mom

Estelle Getty has won fame in a succession of mother roles. Among them were Jewish moms in the off-off-Broadway play *Torch Song Trilogy* (1981) and the TV movie *Copacabana* (1985). But she is best known as Sophia Petrillo, the feisty, crotchety, comically blunt Sicilian mother in the hit TV sitcom *The Golden Girls* (1985-).

Estelle Getty was born in New York City, New York, in July 1923. Her original name was Estelle Scher.

As a youngster on the Lower East Side of Manhattan, she took lessons in dancing, elocution, and acting. She began her stage career as a member of Yiddish amateur neighborhood theater groups in Manhattan. At the age of eighteen she worked for a while as a stand-up comedienne in the Catskills, using a style that she later described as being a cross between Joan

Getty and Bea Arthur in *The Golden Girls.*

Rivers and Totie Fields. But audiences were not ready for female comics. "People did not like women doing that kind of humor," she later explained. "It was like public toe-sucking, they thought."

There followed many years during which she divided her time working as a secretary, raising two sons, and acting in the evenings. From her husband, a businessman named Arthur Gettleman, she derived the stage name Getty. She long labored in obscurity in Yiddish theaters, regional theaters, dinner theaters, summer stock, and experimental New York City stage productions.

Finally, at the age of fifty-eight, Getty won prominence with her role as the Jewish mother of a homosexual young man in *Torch Song Trilogy* (off-off-Broadway, 1981; Broadway, 1982). That success led to film and TV offers. She had a small part in the movie *Tootsie* (1982), portrayed the nagging Jewish mom in *Copacabana* (TV, 1985), played Cher's mother in *Mask* (1985), and excelled as the owner of a department store in *Mannequin* (1987).

But Getty has ensured her celebrity and endeared herself to millions principally through her role as the outspoken octogenarian Sophia Petrillo, who lives with her daughter and two other middle-aged women, on TV's *The Golden Girls* (1985-). Getty's brilliant

Estelle and Sophia

Like her *Golden Girls* character, Sophia, Estelle Getty acts and speaks with blunt honesty. "I've always done what I've wanted to do," Getty proclaims.

But unlike Sophia, who has white hair and stooped shoulders, wears plain clothes, and speaks and behaves gruffly, Getty has reddish brown hair and straight shoulders, wears chic clothes, speaks with elegant diction, and behaves with polite graciousness.

Late Bloomer

Though fame eluded her till she was in her sixties, Getty resents being called a "late bloomer." She says she's been blooming for fifty years.

Likes Anonymity

"People don't recognize me," says Getty, whose real-life appearance differs markedly from her TV role as Sophia on *The Golden Girls.* "I like that. I just go anywhere I want, with my shirt hanging out and no makeup. . . . There's something comforting about not always having to be on and always having to meet the public."

Getty in a scene from *Mannequin.*

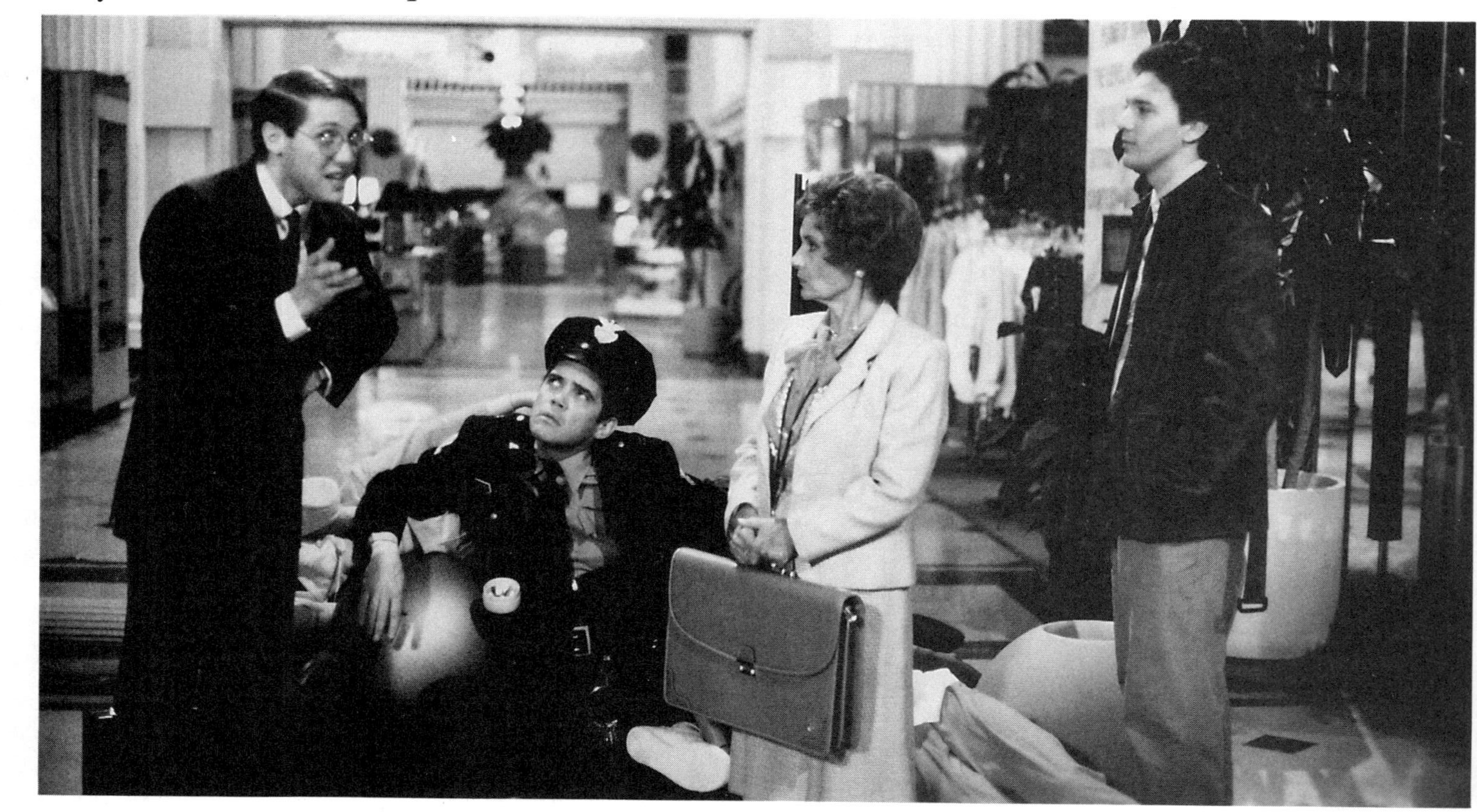

portrayal (for which she uses makeup to age herself twenty years) has effectively destroyed cliches about the inevitability of old-age mental and physical atrophy, as when she admits, "I haven't had sex for fifteen years, and it's beginning to get on my nerves."

Sophia's wisecracks are the highlights of every episode. Having recovered from a mild stroke that has had the effect of releasing her inhibitions, Sophia says precisely what she thinks. To her sweet but not-too-bright roommate Rose, Sophia blurts out, "I think there's a connection between your brain and wallpaper paste." When Rose puts a dish of food in front of her and says, "Where we come from, it's called shepherd's pie," Sophia responds, "Where I come from, it's called garbage." When another roommate, the libidinous Southern belle Blanche, boasts, "My whole life is an open book," Sophia cracks, "Your whole life is an open blouse." When a man-crazy young female visitor is leaving their home, Sophia's daughter, Dorothy, politely says, "We enjoyed having you"; to which Sophia adds, "And so did half of Miami." ☆

Funny Sophia

"I think there are people who use barbs as gratuitous put-downs," Getty observes. "I don't like rudeness, and I loathe cruelty. But I don't think that Sophia is really rude or cruel. I just think she's a funny lady."

Worries

A natural worrier, Getty has avoided one worry through her late success. "People who make it to the top when they're young have to worry about staying there," she explains. "The nicest thing about making it at this stage is that I don't have to worry about staying up here that long."

JACK GILFORD
Wistful Comic

Jack Gilford was one of the earliest stand-up comedians to abandon the traditional string-of-jokes act and to perform routines with variety, originality, and distinct themes. A gifted mimic, he gave comical impressions of Al Jolson, Rudy Valee, Laurel and Hardy, and others. He also invented abstract sketches, such as a takeoff on a surrealist movie. Gilford was the first to create a humorous sense for the line "the butler did it."

Today one of Gilford's most popular pantomimes is his impression of split-pea soup coming to a boil. He also gives impressions of animals, such as an owl and a chicken. His comical singing is a joy, as in his rendition of "California, Here I Come" in Yiddish.

In addition, Gilford has long been an outstanding comic actor on stage and screen. A meek, sad-eyed funnyman, he projects a uniquely wistful quality.

Jack Gilford was born in New York City, New York, on

Gilford in *Cabaret.*

Gilford on *Captain Kangeroo.*

Calm

Unlike most comics, who are nervous, insecure, and often strident offstage, Gilford radiates gentleness and serenity.

On Being Wanted

"If you can find something better than being wanted," Gilford says, "call me any time of day or night; call me collect and tell me what it is. Because whatever it is, it's very important."

Sense of Self

"I don't have a good objective sense about myself," Gilford confesses. "I feel I look much different than the character I'm playing, and I'm a little embarrassed when I see myself on screen and I recognize myself."

July 15, 1907. His original name was Jacob Gellman.

In 1934 he started his career as a comedian by appearing in an amateur show at the Bronx Opera House. Later than year he entered professional vaudeville, and in 1935 he began to tour in the *Milton Berle Revue.* Soon he added work on the borscht circuit and in nightclubs, especially New York City's Café Society Downtown and Café Society Uptown, where he performed off and on for many years.

In 1940 Gilford made his Broadway debut by appearing in the revue *Meet the People.* He was turned down for World War II service because he was in psychotherapy. But he toured the Pacific theater as an entertainer with the United Service Organizations (USO), returned to Broadway in *They Should Have Stood in Bed* (1942) and other shows, and appeared in his first films, including *Hey, Rookie* (1944).

After the war, he continued to work as a comedian in vaudeville, in nightclubs, and on the borscht circuit. In the late 1940s and early 1950s he began to perform on TV variety shows, including *The Texaco Star Theater,* hosted by Milton Berle. Gilford also resumed his movie work, in *Main Street to Broadway* (1953).

But his TV and movie appearances were interrupted in the early 1950s when he was blacklisted during the McCarthy-era witch-hunts for Communists. He then changed his career emphasis to stage roles.

In 1950 he portrayed Frosch, a nonsinging comic part, in Johann Strauss's operetta *Die Fledermaus* at the Metropolitan Opera. Gilford played the same role many times in the future. In *The World of Sholom Aleichem* (1953) he was the painfully shy Bontche Schweig, while in *The Diary of Anne Frank* (1955) he played the fussy, frightened Dr. Dussel. Gilford was the mute king Sextimus in *Once upon a Mattress* (1959), and in *A Funny Thing Happened on the Way to the Forum* (1962) he portrayed the timid slave Hysterium.

In the mid-1960s the blacklist lost its effectiveness, and Gilford began to get TV and movie assignments again. During the 1960s and 1970s he guested on many TV series, including *All in the Family,* and he was a regular on *The David Frost Revue* (1971) and *Apple Pie* (1978). He also appeared in many TV commercials, notably those for Cracker Jack. His films during that period included *Enter Laughing* (1967), *Catch-22* (1970), and *Save the Tiger* (1973).

However, he did not neglect the stage, where he acted in *The Sunshine Boys* (1973), *The Seven Year Itch* (1975), and other plays.

In the 1980s Gilford has continued to be active in a variety of outlets. Among his films were *Wholly Moses!* (1980), *Cocoon* (1985), and *Cocoon: The Return* (1988). On the stage, he played four roles in a revival of *The World of Sholom Aleichem* (1982), and he performed the one-man show *My Life in the Theater; or, How I Became an Overnight Success in Forty Years* (1987). In 1987 Gilford appeared at the Ballroom in New York City, his first nightclub performance since 1957 when he worked at the hungry i in San Francisco. In 1988 he guest-starred in two wonderful episodes of the TV sitcom *The Golden Girls,* as Max Weinstock, who marries the crotchety Sophia.★

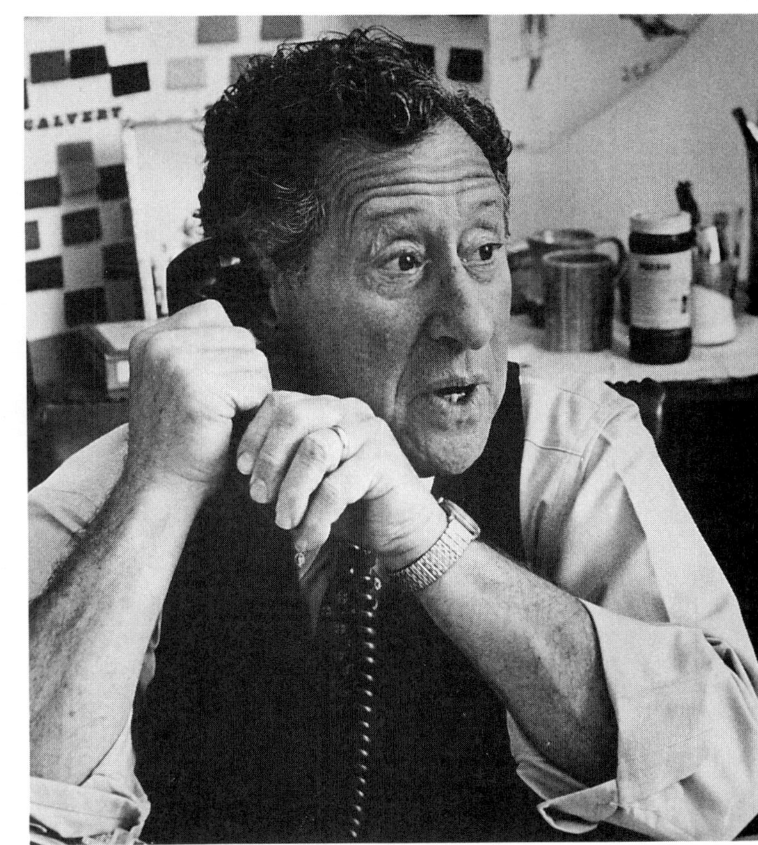

Gilford in *Save the Tiger.*

Bootlegging Mother
Gilford likes to tell true stories about his mother's booze-making activities during Prohibition. She was "the only lady on our street arrested for bootlegging."

Influence of Silent Movies
"Silent movies influenced me," Gilford states. "They were my acting school. I would try to do what I saw. I saw Laurel and Hardy when they were separate performers. I admired Charlie Chaplin and Buster Keaton."

Mementos
"My life is on these walls," Gilford says of the walls in his home. They are lined with paintings by his good friend Zero Mostel; photos of such costars as Buster Keaton, Jack Lemmon, and Carol Burnett; and other souvenirs.

Gilford and Mostel
Jack Gilford and Zero Mostel were close friends for nearly forty years before Mostel's death in 1977. They helped their wives write the book *170 Years of Show Business* (1978), the story of their four lives and careers. Gilford and Mostel liked to work together, as in the stage show *Once Over Lightly* (1955) and in the stage (1962) and film (1966) versions of *A Funny Thing Happened on the Way to the Forum.*

SHECKY GREENE
Vegas Comic

Shecky Greene is widely regarded as one of the must-see attractions in Las Vegas. His old-fashioned shtick, his range of facial gestures, his pantomimed sight gags, his ad-libbed comic song lyrics and patter, his interplay with audience members—all have endeared him to Vegas visitors for over thirty years.

He was born in Chicago, Illinois, on April 8, 1926. His original name was Sheldon Greenfield.

After spending three years in the navy he enrolled in 1949 at Wright Junior College in Chicago, intending to become a gym teacher. He got a summer job as a social director at a resort near Milwaukee, where he had to get up and tell jokes because the management could not afford to hire professionals. During the following year he studied at school and worked part-time as a comedian in nightclubs.

Leaving college, Greene was hired by a New Orleans nightclub for a two-week stint, but he ended up stay-

Proud Chicagoan
Greene is proud to belong to the tradition of Chicago comedians, such as Shelley Berman, George Gobel, and Jack E. Leonard. He says they have a special "Midwestern sound."

The Many Faces of Tevye
Yearning to be cast as the lead in a Broadway musical, Greene has compensated for that lack by incorporating musical-comedy routines into his act. He has, for example, presented exegeses of *Fiddler on the Roof,* each performance showing a different conception of the leading character, Tevye.

Greene Mellows
In the 1960s tales abounded of Shecky Greene's wild drinking, gambling, fighting, and destruction of casino property. But in 1976 he had throat surgery and temporarily lost his voice. That experience was followed by cancer surgery. His health problems plus the natural effects of aging have mellowed Greene. According to his press biography, "Shecky has a different attitude about himself and his career today. He is a new, much better Shecky, who is deeply loved and respected by his audience, peers, friends, and family."

Shecky Greene (second from right) in a scene from Mel Brooks' *History of the World, Part I.*

ing for three years. Later he worked at Martha Raye's nitery in Miami Beach. In 1953 he was the opening act for Ann Sothern at the Chez Paree in his hometown of Chicago.

Greene then hit Las Vegas, where he has been a permanent fixture ever since. However, he has had less success in other outlets, particularly TV, where his improvisations are discouraged and his ringsider repartee is impossible.

"If you've seen one nude girl, you've seen them all, begins one of his set bits. "Forgive me, ladies, but I don't believe there's anything sexy about a naked girl. My wife used to walk in front of me at night with a black lace negligee, and that was sex! Then I'd wait for her to go to sleep, and I would put on that black lace negligee—."

"I have a daughter who goes to SMU. She could've gone to UCLA here in California, but it's one more letter she'd have to remember. She's an A student. All she knows how to say is 'Ayyyyyy.' "

Greene is particularly successful with his sight gags, such as his impressions of famous personalities. He has mimicked Clark Gable, Frank Sinatra, Sophie Tucker, sex symbols, Richard Burton as Henry the Ninth, and Dean Martin spilling liquor on himself.

Greene has appeared in some movies, including *Tony Rome* (1967) and *Splash* (1984). Recently he has acted in TV situation comedies and adventure programs, such as *The Fall Guy*. ☆

Shecky Greene.

BUDDY HACKETT
Rubber Face

Buddy Hackett's humor tends to be based on an endearing combination of helplessness and craftiness. His comic delivery is aided by his awkwardly pudgy body and by his puckish elastic visage, which has been referred to as a "rubber face."

He is at his best on the stages of Las Vegas, where he has free reign with his raunchy anecdotes and his spontaneous interplay with audience members. Speaking out of the side of his mouth, in reverse English and with a heavy Brooklyn accent, he delights in shocking

A forlorn Buddy Hackett.

his audience with foul language and risqué remarks. He will, for example, shake hands with a ringsider in a low-cut blouse, stare at her breasts, shake hands again more vigorously, and then say, "Sometimes they jump out when you do that!"

Hackett was born in New York City, New York, on August 31, 1924. His original name was Leonard Hacker.

While growing up in Brooklyn, he spent some of his summer vacation time on the borscht circuit as a waiter, bellhop, and toomler (creator of comic tumult). After graduating from high school, he joined the army, where he spent three years in World War II service.

Returning to civilian life, he changed his name to Buddy Hackett and began to get small-time nightclub jobs as a comedian. Then, taking the advice of his friend Red Skelton, he brought to the stage his impersonation of a Chinese waiter. The routine was an instantaneous success and helped propel Hackett into engagements with major niteries and hotels throughout the country.

Soon he was offered acting jobs as well. He appeared in the movies *Walking My Baby Back Home* (1953) and *Fireman, Save My Child* (1954), the Broadway farce *Lunatics and Lovers* (1954), and the TV series *Stanley* (1956-57), in which he starred as the owner of a hotel-lobby newsstand.

The first role that really gave him a chance to show what he could do was that of Pluto, the lovelorn rustic, in the film *God's Little Acre* (1958). Hackett endowed the comic character with surprising depth and poignancy.

His later acting jobs included roles in the movies *The Music Man* (1962), *The Love Bug* (1969), and *Hey, Babe!* (1984). One of his most memorable performances was in the biopic *Bud and Lou* (TV, 1978), in which he portrayed the dual nature (entertainer and tyrant) of the famed comedian Lou Costello. Hackett has also appeared in TV dramas, such as 1980s episodes of *Quincy, M.E.* and *Murder, She Wrote*.

But stand-up comedy remains the center of his career. Nightclubs are his natural habitat, not TV, where his routines seem inhibited. In his act he alternates set jokes with ad-libs.

Here is a sample Hackett one-liner: "Think what a crowded elevator smells like to a midget." No subject frightens him. "If I wasn't a Jew I would be a Catholic," begins one routine. After poking fun at the Catholic practice of confession, he proceeds: "As soon as you become a Catholic you're very wealthy. The Vatican has paintings, statues, jewelry. I said to a cardinal, 'Your

Hackett's Heros

Asked to name the greatest influence on him, Hackett replied, "W.C. Fields, W.C. Fields, and W.C. Fields."

About George Burns, Hackett has said, "He's the nicest man I ever met. And the funniest."

On Off-color Language

Hackett uses earthier language onstage than off-stage. "My material has a purpose," he explained. "I use it to relieve psychological and physical pain." When people know that they are not alone in their pain, "they can laugh with relief."

Besides, "in my heart of hearts, I don't believe I'm doing anything off-color. I've been through poverty and war. I've seen it all. If those things can exist in this world, what's bad about a four-letter word?"

Love of Privacy

Privacy is important to Hackett. He tries to avoid the public. "You'll see me faster under an old car with Max, my mechanic, than in some fancy French restaurant." But if approached by fans, he will talk to them and sign his autograph.

He visits the Friars Club at odd times of the day. "By five o'clock it's too crowded and noisy. I hate the smell of cigarette smoke."

holiness, if you sold one of these paintings you could feed all the starving Catholics in Rome.' He said, 'Get outta here, you fat bastard!' Of course, he said it in Latin: 'Absconde, obeseri illegitimo!' "

In recent years Hackett has toured with his son, Sandy, who is a comic and a singer. ★

I'm a Cartoon

"I'm not a human being," Hackett says. "I'm a cartoon. And if I say something serious it comes out funny anyway."

GOLDIE HAWN
Kooky Comedienne

Goldie Hawn is widely regarded as the finest film comedienne since Carole Lombard. Combining slapstick with light romantic banter, and sexiness with innocence, Hawn typically portrays characters who are childlike but not stupid. Her success depends not on jokes but on comic timing, body language, and expressive openness.

Hawn was born of a Jewish mother and Protestant father in Washington, D.C., on November 21, 1945. She was raised in Maryland.

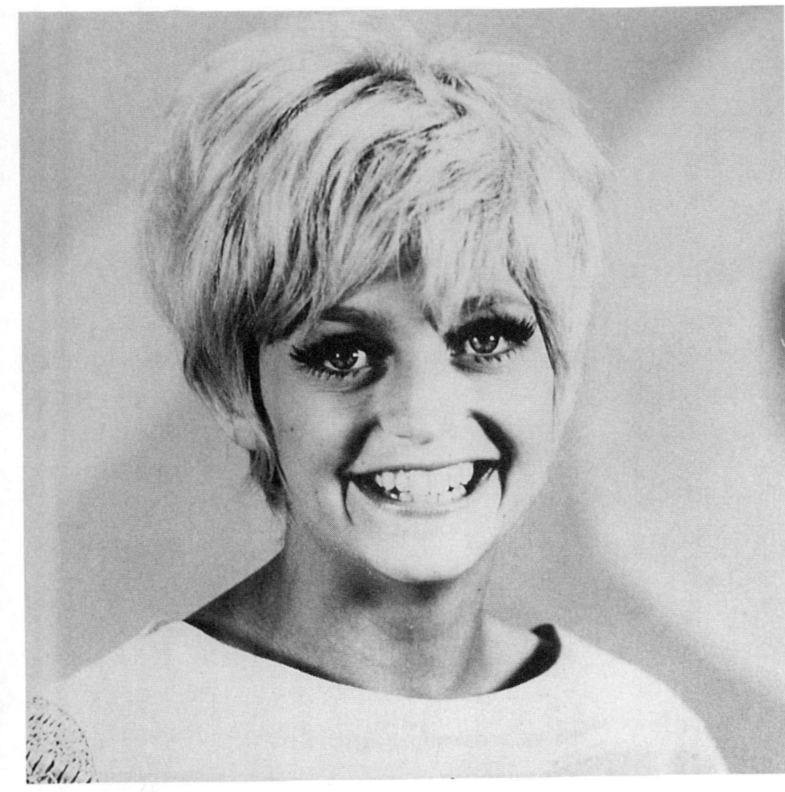

Goldie and Kurt Russell in *Overboard.*

Goldie's Special Appeal

"I have never thought I was funny," Hawn declares. People respond to her, she says, because of her "whole encompassing character. . . . It is the idea that I love people, that I love life, that I have a face and a body that are very expressive."

Old-fashioned

Describing herself as an "old-fashioned" and "very middle-class person," Hawn says that her goals have always included taking care of her own children in a nice house. She now spends as much time as possible at home, cooking and caring for her three children.

Goldie Hawn and Burt Reynolds in *Best Friends.*

At the age of three she began to study tap-dancing and ballet, and at eleven she added modern dance to her lessons. Her father, a musician in society dance bands, gave her voice lessons.

As a teenager she appeared in school and community dramatic productions. After graduating from high school, she studied drama for a year and a half at American University in Washington, D.C.

Hawn then went to work as a professional dancer. She danced in summer-stock musicals and performed as a go-go dancer in a Manhattan discotheque.

While dancing in the chorus on an Andy Griffith TV special in 1967, she was spotted by Art Simon, who became her agent. He helped her to get a small role as the wacky neighbor in the TV situation comedy *Good Morning, World* (1967-68).

Hawn then shot to stardom with her regular appearances on TV's *Laugh-In* (1968-70), a comedy series characterized by a kaleidoscope of one-liners. She wiggled and giggled as apparently another in the long line of show-business dumb blondes. But she endowed her offbeat persona with special qualities: an underlying awareness and a touching vulnerability.

In her first movie, *The One and Only, Genuine, Original Family Band* (1968), Hawn played a small part as a giggly girl. But in *Cactus Flower* (1969) she had a leading role and won great praise for her comic portrayal of the young mistress of a middle-aged dentist.

Her Characters Mirror Her Own Life

"There's a correlation between Judy Benjamin [in *Private Benjamin]* and my *Laugh-in* character," Hawn observes. Each struggled, as Hawn has in real life, to gain acceptance as "a person who has a brain." Hawn feels that her acting style and her gentle demeanor cause people to underestimate her. "I'm smarter than people give me credit for," she asserts.

Lives Simply

Dressing modestly, generally shunning Hollywood parties, and frowning on the drugs and promiscuity in the film industry, Hawn enjoys a quiet life, currently at a Colorado ranch house that she shares with actor Kurt Russell.

In *$* (1971) she portrayed a call girl and amateur bank robber. Her performance as the eccentric neighbor who falls in love a young blind man in *Butterflies Are Free* (1972) firmly established her as a leading comedienne. Among her other movies in the 1970s were *Shampoo* (1975) and *Foul Play* (1978).

In *Private Benjamin* (1980) she played the title role of a pampered young woman who has difficulty adjusting to life as a soldier. Hawn portrayed a lonely wife who finds work and romance in an aircraft plant during World War II in *Swing Shift* (1984). In *Protocol* (1984) she was a sweet, vulnerable, ditsy woman who foils an assassination attempt, becomes a protocol officer in the national government, and lectures federal officials on morality. In *Wildcats* (1986) she played a teacher who becomes the boys' football coach at a tough high school. And in *Overboard* (1987) Hawn was a spoiled heiress who develops amnesia. ☆

What Will the Child Become?

"I do have this quality that is very childlike," Hawn says. "But how long can it last? How long can you be cute?"

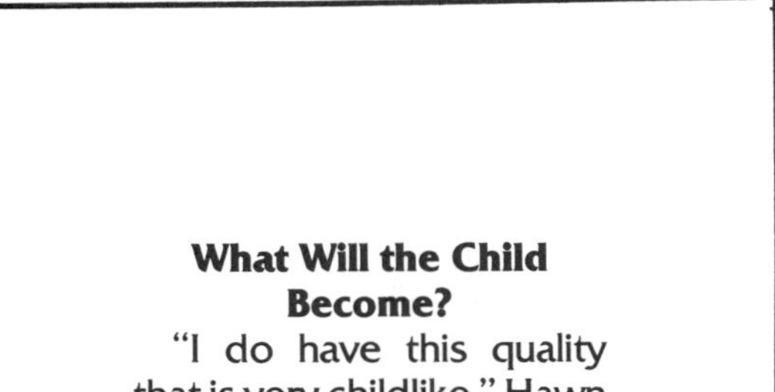

JUDY HOLLIDAY
Dumb-Blonde Genius

Judy Holliday had one of the most astonishing careers in show business. She performed in only a small number of plays and movies, most of them unremarkable except for the glow that she gave them. Yet she attained such a rapport with her audience and created such thoroughly endearing characterizations that her work (through films) continues to win the admiration of each new generation.

Holliday was generally typecast as a dumb blonde. In real life, however, she had a genius IQ of 172. Her characterizations, then, were thoroughly artistic creations, enriched by her mimic ability, vaudevillian talent, and expressive vulnerability. She gave her dumb-blonde persona a high-pitched, piercing, childlike voice, but she could suddenly drop to a deep pitch to deliver a humorous effect. And with just a tiny inflection in her voice, she could suddenly turn a scene from hilarity to poignancy.

June Holliday was born in New York City, New York, on June 21, 1921 (some sources give 1922). Her original

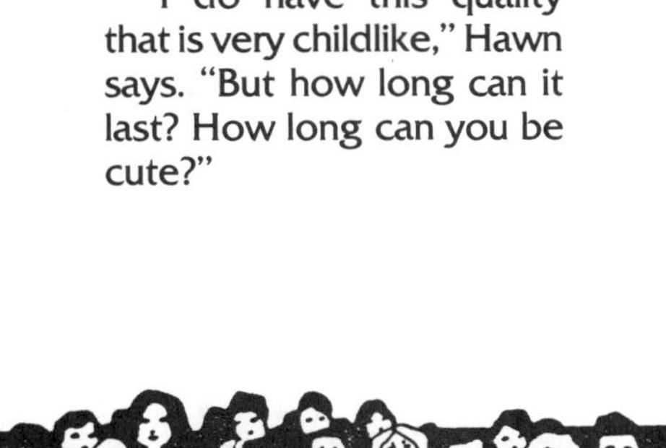

Judy in *Bells are Ringing.*

name was Judith Tuvim. From her father, a professional fund-raiser for Jewish and socialist causes, Judy derived her social consciousness. From her mother, a piano teacher, Judy acquired an interest in the arts.

In 1938 Judy graduated from high school. Shortly thereafter she worked briefly as a switchboard operator for Orson Welles's Mercury Theater. Then, with a few friends, including the future great lyricists Betty Comden and Adolph Green, Judy helped to form the Revuers, a topical cabaret act. They worked in nightclubs and had a thirty-two-week run on radio. Judy's gift for comedy showed itself immediately. During her tenure with the Revuers, she changed her name from Judy Tuvim to Judy Holliday (*tuvim* being a Hebrew word for "holiday").

In 1943 the Revuers were in Hollywood, California. While they were there, Holliday played bit parts in the movies *Winged Victory* (1944) and *Something for the Boys* (1944).

Returning to New York City, the Revuers disbanded. Holliday soon won a small role as a dingbat in the Broadway farce *Kiss Them for Me* (1945). She was the hit of the show.

Late in 1945 Jean Arthur was starring in the pre-Broadway performances of *Born Yesterday* when she

Favorite Performers

Judy Holliday liked the work of Judy Garland and Laurence Olivier. But her idol was Laurette Taylor, whom Holiday especially admired onstage as Amanda in *The Glass Menagerie.*

Recreations

Holliday read avidly, especially modern literature (she described herself as "one of those obnoxious children who read *War and Peace,* Schnitzler, and Molière"). She also enjoyed chess, poker, cooking, word puzzles (which she would work between scenes while filmmaking), collecting and refinishing antique furniture, and, in her late years, working in her garden.

Holliday in *Solid Gold Cadillac.*

became ill and had to withdraw. Holliday was called in as a replacement, and in just three days she learned and rehearsed the role of Billie Dawn, a corrupt tycoon's dumb-blonde mistress whose latent sensitivities are awakened, who learns to think for herself, and who finally scores a moral and financial victory in behalf of all "little" people over the wealthy megalomaniac junkman.

In early 1946 *Born Yesterday* hit Broadway and became a tremendous success. During the next few years Holliday played Billie Dawn well over a thousand times.

In 1949 she took a leave of absence from *Born Yesterday* to play a similar role in the film *Adam's Rib* (1949). She then returned to *Born Yesterday* for the filmed version, released in 1950.

In the early 1950s she frequently appeared on TV variety shows. But in 1952 Holliday, who supported many liberal social causes, was called before a Senate subcommitte investigating alleged Communist fronts. The subcommitte proved nothing against the comedienne, but it did succeed in casting a vague shadow over her. As a result, she was blacklisted from TV for a number of years.

However, her movie career blossomed. Basically continuing her dumb-blonde character, she made outstanding impressions in several films, including *It Should Happen to You* (1954), *Phffft* (1954), and *The Solid Gold Cadillac* (1956).

In 1956 she returned to the stage by making her musical debut, as Ella Peterson in *Bells Are Ringing*. Her old friends Comden and Green had tailored the role to take full advantage of Holliday's unique gifts. Judy also starred in the filmed version (1960).

In late 1960 she began to perform in the play that she felt would have the greatest impact on her artistic development: *Laurette*, based on the life of the actress Laurette Taylor. However, during the pre-Broadway tryouts, Holliday became ill. An examination revealed a lump in her left breast. When the lump turned out to be malignant, the breast had to be removed.

Her struggle to recover was as difficult psychologically as it was physically. In the ill-fated stage musical *Hot Spot* (1963) she made her last appearance as an actress.

Holliday died of cancer in New York City on June 7, 1965.★

A Quiet Person

Though criticized by some in her own profession (notably Humphrey Bogart) for not behaving like a glamorous movie queen offscreen, Holliday insisted that her personal life was her own concern. She avoided most Hollywood parties, and when she did attend she dressed plainly and tended to say little. She often appeared in public wearing blue jeans, workshirts, and no makeup.

Holliday preferred quiet dinners, casual socializing, and relaxed evenings at home.

Music Devotee

Holliday enjoyed classical music, show tunes, and, in her late years, jazz (largely because of her romance with jazz saxophonist Gerry Mulligan). She disliked folksongs.

Personal Habits

Holliday smoked cigarettes and worried about her looks. She knew that she had charm, wit, and intelligence; but she was concerned about her outer appearance. When she turned heads in public, she was always surprised.

Weight Problems

Throughout her life Holliday went on periodic eating binges and struggled with being overweight. On one memorable evening in the 1950s she consumed three complete dinners in one sitting at a restaurant and then went to a friend's house and ate a tuna salad.

When she grew too heavy, she would crash diet.

WILLIE HOWARD
Plaintive Broadway Comic

Willie Howard, in his vaudeville and Broadway revue sketches, played the perpetually confused little man. Anxiety-ridden and stoop-shouldered, he characteristically faced his problems with a comical, philosophical shrug. When sufficiently harassed, he could, through pure mischief, get the upper hand on his tormentors. But the core of Howard's stage personality was a plaintive quality.

Howard often spoke with a Yiddish accent in his routines. However, unlike Fanny Brice, who used the accent as a comical contrast to her non-Jewish characterizations, Howard used the accent to emphasize his ethnic identification. A master of dialect, he frequently combined his Yiddish accent with French, Spanish, Scottish, and other idioms.

Howard was also a fine singer and an outstanding mimic. His singing skills evidenced themselves in his celebrated opera takeoffs. His impressions focused on leading performers of the day, including the actors David Warfield and Charlie Chaplin, and the singer-entertainers Eddie Cantor, Maurice Chevalier, Al Jolson, Harry Lauder, and Jack Norworth.

Willie Howard was born of Russian parents in Neustadt, Silesia (now Prudnik, Poland) on April 13, 1886. His original name was William Levkowitz. He grew up in the Harlem section of New York City after his father, a cantor, moved the family to America.

After being expelled from school for disrupting classes when he was eleven years old, Willie began to pick up money by singing and clowning at amateur shows. At fourteen the boy soprano became a songplugger at a theater, where he would rise from his seat in the balcony and sing second choruses in support of some of vaudeville's great ladies, such as Louise Dresser and Anna Held. When his voice began to change, he turned to low comedy at a dime museum.

In 1903 he began a partnership with his brother Eugene. It was now that Willie assumed the name Howard, under which his older brother was already performing. Eugene soon became the straight man to Willie's comic genius. In their sketches the harried,

Willie Howard (feather duster in hand) anticipates a sneeze.

seemingly defenseless little Willie, as the waiter, bellhop, or other servant, would use gibes, impersonations, and slapstick to gain revenge for the boorishness and arrogance of the domineering upper-class character, played by Eugene. By 1912 the team—at first billed as Howard and Howard, later as Willie and Eugene Howard—had become one of vaudeville's most popular acts.

In 1912 they moved up to Broadway, debuting in the revue *The Passing Show of 1912.* Over the next twenty-eight years the Howards were one of the busiest acts on the Great White Way. They performed in four more editions of *The Passing Show,* six of George White's *Scandals*, and many other revues, including the *Ziegfeld Follies of 1934.* In addition, Willie starred in the book musicals *Sky High* (1925) and *Girl Crazy* (1930).

One of Willie Howard's most successful appearances was in *The Passing Show of 1921.* Among his sketches were a takeoff on the quartet from Verdi's opera *Rigoletto*, an impersonation of the Scottish entertainer Harry Lauder singing with a Yiddish accent, and a spoof of the stage musical *Mecca,* in which he adopted an Oriental singsong.

In 1940 Eugene left the act to become his brother's gag writer and business manager. Thereafter Willie performed in several more Broadway revues and in the book musical *Sally* (1948), but without his former level of popularity.

He died in New York City on January 12, 1949. ☆

Weird Inventions

Howard was fascinated by mechanical gadgets, and he amused his friends by concocting weird inventions. One contraption was a tiny violin held not under the chin but in the mouth; as the violin was bowed, the player produced a second melody by blowing into the instrument, where a harmonica was secreted. Another invention was a female mannequin that breathed; unfortunately, air from the motor shot the figure's nightgown to the ceiling. Howard's home resembled a toy shop.

Practical Jokes

One of Willie's favorite gags involved a backstage bulletin board, where he would tack up a note beginning "The company is invited to a party at—"; the rest of the note was indecipherable. He stood aside and enjoyed the readers' frustration.

Howard displayed a macabre sense of humor in one of his practical jokes. Whenever he stayed in a hotel, he would put a death mask (which he had purchased in a novelty shop) face up on a pillow, form his clothes into a body shape under the blankets, and then hide in a closet to watch the fun; when the chambermaid entered and saw the ghostly figure, she would invariably shriek and run from the room.

His Funniest Performances

Away from the stage Willie Howard tended to be morose. He had a constant craving to brighten that darkness by inducing laughter in others. Close friends said that some of his funniest performances were impromptu routines at home in front of small groups. He kept visitors in stitches with his impersonations and his wide-eyed, ingenuous fibs. His friend and producer George White said, "Anybody who don't like Willie, don't like children."

GEORGE JESSEL
Toastmaster General

George Jessel's fame in his late years rested on his melodramatic speeches at funerals, banquets, and fund-raising affairs for Israel and other causes. His ubiquitous presence at such events induced President Truman to dub Jessel the Toastmaster General of the United States. In his youth, however, Jessel was a versatile singer and actor.

He was born in the Harlem section of New York City, New York, on April 3, 1898. As a batboy for the New York Giants, he would entertain the ballplayers in the clubhouse after games—if they won. "If they lost, " he later reported, the manager, John McGraw, "would say, 'Get out of here, you little Jew! " And then I'd go to the visiting club."

Jessel was a child singer in vaudeville, where he performed as one of Gus Edwards's famous troupe of juveniles, including Eddie Cantor. Later Jessel developed a solo vaudeville comedy-and-singing act.

His "Hello, Mama" monologue became his most famous routine. Pretending to telephone his demanding mother, he swore that he knew nothing about the

Jessel and Horne

Jessel was escorting the young black entertainer Lena Horne into the fashionable 21 Club when the doorman stopped them. It was in the days when blacks were routinely excluded from such places. "Do you have a reservation?" asked the doorman. "Yes," Jessel replied. "Who made it?" "Abraham Lincoln, you son of a bitch!"

Helped Many Causes

Jessel devoted much time to aiding such causes as State of Israel Bonds and the City of Hope Medical Center. He also served as vice president of the Jewish Theatrical Guild. In 1952 he was voted Man of the Year by the Beverly Hills B'nai B'rith.

Bibliophile

Jessel loved to collect books. His favorite topic was religion, and he had one of the finest collections of books on the subject in the United States.

He also wrote many books, including *So Help Me* (1943), *You, Too, Can Make a Speech* (1956), and *The World I Live In* (1975).

Jessel with Ann Sheridan.

money missing from the cupboard, that he had not eaten a piece of the cake she had baked for charity, and that it could not be his cigar butt, because he did not smoke. "Say, mama, how did you like that bird I sent you for your birthday?" opens one of his best bits. "You cooked it! But, mama, that was a South American parrot! He spoke five languages—he should have said something?"

In 1925 Jessel left vaudeville to star in the original Broadway production of *The Jazz Singer.* His other Broadway credits included *Sweet and Low* (1930) and *High Kickers* (1941). He also acted in some movies, such as *Four Jills in a Jeep* (1944) and *The Busy Body* (1967), and produced many films and Broadway shows.

Jessel began his toastmaster career in 1925 when he served as an after-dinner speaker while campaigning for Jimmy Walker in the New York City mayoral race. As the years went by, he spent increasingly less time on other activities and increasingly more time on the dais.

His image was marred in the 1960s and 1970s by his maudlin songs and by his refusal to freshen up his act (many listeners did not understand his dated references to Eddie Cantor and his other contemporaries). But he particularly hurt himself through his humorless, vehement right-wing public posture. On a *Today Show* program in 1971 he wore a quasi-military outfit and

Jessel with daughter Jerrilyn in 1953.

Baseball Fan
Jessel liked watching professional baseball, and he often played in charity softball games.

referred to the *New York Times* as *"Pravda"* (a Soviet Union newspaper). After that, other TV talk shows refused to have him.

However, he continued to work as toastmaster. And he frequently appeared in nightclubs, where he sang, reminisced, and told risqué jokes. At the age of eighty he was still going strong.

Jessel died in Los Angeles on May 24, 1981. ★

MADELINE KAHN
"Clown with the Face of an Angel"

Madeline Kahn's career has run the gamut from serious opera to slapstick comedy. Beginning as a talented classical singer, she moved into musical comedy and from there into straight comic roles. Through motion pictures, in particular, Kahn has come to be regarded as one of the outstanding comediennes of her time.

She has a unique ability to endow her characters with dual qualities: physically sexy yet klutzy, vocally whining yet commanding, intellectually flighty yet conniving, and emotionally neurotic yet durable. Through all of these shifts and shades, the actress maintains a blank facial expression of neutrality and innocence. The film critic Rex Reed has dubbed Kahn "the clown with the face of an angel."

She was born in Boston, Massachusetts, on September 29, 1942. Her original name was Madeline Wolfson. When she was very young, her parents separated, and several years later her mother married a man named Kahn.

While being raised in New York City, Madeline took lessons in piano, dance, and voice. Her first significant public appearance came when she sang on *Children's Hour*, a New York City radio program.

In high school she appeared in plays. Then, at Hofstra University in Hempstead, on Long Island, New York, she majored in drama for two years before switching to music and then to speech. She performed as a classical singer in university productions and studied in an off-campus opera workshop. Kahn

Kahn relaxes in *Blazing Saddles.*

Therapy Helped Kahn

Years of private and group therapy helped Kahn overcome the shyness and insecurity that had inhibited her in her youth.

"I love to express myself," the mature Kahn has said. "I suppose it's a way of reaching out to other people. . . . It isn't easy, and sometimes it's scary."

Fundamental Influences

The most fundamental influences on Kahn are classical music and animated cartoons. "I know good from bad when it comes to cartoons," she asserts. "At three I talked fluently and learned the elephant's dance from *Fantasia.*"

graduated from Hofstra with a B.A. degree in 1964.

After a short stint as a schoolteacher, she performed as a singing waitress in Bellmore, Long Island, and then as a chorus girl in a City Center revival of *Kiss Me, Kate* (1965). For the next two years she sang opera and light opera with Green Mansions, an upstate New York repertory company.

Kahn's Broadway debut came in *New Faces of 1968* (1968), in which she made a strong impression with her singing of "Das Chicago Song," a parody of the Bertolt Brecht and Kurt Weill musicals. She went on to appear in satirical revues at New York City's Upstairs at the Downstairs club, sing the female lead in Leonard Bernstein's *Candide* (1968), and perform onstage in the musicals *Promenade* (1969) and *Two by Two* (1970). In the stage work *Boom Boom Room* (1973) she gave an impressive acting performance as a shallow, ambitious go-go dancer.

During the late 1960s and early 1970s Kahn often appeared on TV. She was a regular on the series *Comedy, Tonight* (1970) and guested on shows hosted by Johnny Carson, Merv Griffin, and others.

Kahn made her movie debut in *What's Up, Doc?* (1972), as a shrewish, frustrated fiancée. Her comic performance nearly stole the show from the film's star, Barbra Streisand. In *Paper Moon* (1973) Kahn was a Depression-era carnival dancer who teams up with a con man.

Madeline Kahn in *Clue.*

In Mel Brooks's western-movie spoof *Blazing Saddles* (1974) Kahn played the saloon singer Lili von Shtupp, a devastating burlesque of Marlene Dietrich's style in the famous German film *The Blue Angel* (1930) and in the American western *Destry Rides Again* (1939). Kahn gave one her most hilarious performances as her sexy Lili sneered, sulked, and pouted through *Blazing Saddles*.

In Brooks's horror-movie parody *Young Frankenstein* (1974) Kahn took the role of Dr. Frankenstein's primping, finicky fiancée. In Gene Wilder's *The Adventure of Sherlock Holmes' Smarter Brother* (1975), a takeoff on nineteenth-century detective stories, she played a music-hall dancer and sex tease who constantly changes her identity. In Brooks's *High Anxiety* (1977), a spoof of Alfred Hitchcock's thrillers, Kahn portrayed a glamorous but neurotic socialite.

Her later films included Brooks's *History of the World, Part I* (1981); *Yellowbeard* (1983); *Slapstick of Another Kind* (1984); *City Heat* (1984); *Clue* (1985); and *My Little Pony, the Movie* (1986).

In 1983 she starred in her own TV sitcom, *Oh, Madeline*. On May 11, 1988, at the Carnegie Hall salute to Irving Berlin on his hundredth birthday, Kahn gave a delightful vocal and visual rendition of the composer's comic song "You'd Be Surprised." During the 1988-89 theatrical season, she appeared on Broadway opposite Ed Asner in *Born Yesterday*. ☆

Exercises Daily
Physical exercises have long been an important part of Kahn's daily routine. Besides swimming half a mile and jogging one mile every day, she works out to the accompaniment of Jane Fonda's aerobics tape.

Love Life
Kahn believes that her love life has been hurt by her being a comedienne. "Men don't feel comfortable being romantic with a funny woman."

Prefers Quiet Life
Madeline Kahn avoids the show-business social whirl, preferring a quiet life in the privacy of her home. She has an unassuming personality and approaches her craft "seriously" but "not fanatically."

Kaplan as Mr. Kotter in *Welcome Back, Kotter*.

GABE KAPLAN
Kotter

Gabe Kaplan reached stardom as Gabe Kotter on the TV series *Welcome Back, Kotter* (1975-79). But he began his career as a stand-up nightclub comedian. In recent years he has won critical acclaim for his one-man stage show as Groucho Marx.

Gabriel Kaplan was born in New York City, New York, on March 31, 1945. After graduating from Brooklyn's Erasmus Hall High School, he took a job as a bellboy at a hotel in Lakewood, New Jersey. There he studied the performances of visiting comedians.

Soon he hit the road as a comedian himself, playing in small nightclubs and strip joints. His act at the Bitter End in 1968 was reviewed in *Variety*, but his formal, stiff style prevented him from making further progress.

Gradually, however, he relaxed and began to develop a closer rapport with audiences. A highlight of his act was his impression of a drunken Ed Sullivan insulting his guests. Kaplan also did routines about youths and high-school life, including this bit: "I heard your mother is like the Pennsylvania Railroad—she's been laid all over the country."

In 1972 he appeared on *The Tonight Show*. More TV work soon followed.

In 1974 a TV producer saw Kaplan's performance at a West Coast comedy club. The act included nostalgic bits about rowdy humor in a Brooklyn classroom. The routine was developed into the TV situation-comedy series *Welcome Back, Kotter*, with Kaplan as the high-school teacher Gabe Kotter.

Since the series left the air in 1979, Kaplan has acted in a few movies, notably *Fast Break* (1979). He has also appeared in Las Vegas and Atlantic City as a stand-up comedian.

But his most significant work in recent years has been his impersonation of Groucho Marx in the one-man show *Groucho*. During the course of the show, Kaplan's Groucho goes through a metamorphosis from the audacious young rascal of the movies to the mature host of *You Bet Your Life* to the wavering old man who appeared on *The Dick Cavett Show*. Kaplan's work was meticulous and moving. He opened with *Groucho* in 1983, and he has toured with it many times since then.★

Catching Up

Kotter gave Kaplan lifetime financial security. Today, he says, "I just work when I feel like it. . . . I started working so young, and I missed a lot in my twenties and thirties, when I was working all the time. . . . So now I'm doing a little catching up."

Kaplan enjoys traveling, especially in South America. He also plays golf, sails, and visits nightclubs to check out new talent. He's a good audience because he tends to laugh at almost anything.

Prefers Small Clubs

The money that he earned from *Welcome Back, Kotter* has given Kaplan the independence to be very selective in his work. He prefers appearing at small comedy clubs in out-of-the-way places because there, he says, "I'm really less self-conscious than in Atlantic City or Las Vegas, where, for some reason, people are more judgmental."

Comedy Idol

"His physical concept and effrontery were totally unique," Kaplan says of his comedy idol, Groucho Marx. Among the highlights of Kaplan's life were a couple of personal meetings with the aged Groucho.

Pro Poker Player

Enjoying poker so much that he became a professional card player, Kaplan won the World Series of Poker in 1980. He has hosted celebrity poker tournaments to aid the Cystic Fibrosis Foundation.

His First Love

Baseball was Kaplan's first love. He wanted to become a professional, but his real talent lay in show business.

Hate Mail

Kaplan has received hate mail for some of his material, such as his impression of Howard Cosell narrating the Crucifixion.

Spurns Celebrity Status

"After I got involved with *Kotter*, I realized I didn't have that hunger for recognition," Kaplan states. "I'm grateful for *Kotter*, but I know I'm not suited for show business.

MICKEY KATZ
Comic Musician

Mickey Katz in performance.

Mickey Katz earned fame for his unique combination of talents as clarinetist, saxophonist, vocalist, conductor, and comedian. In the mid-1940s he performed some of the comedy vocal "glugs" for Spike Jones's band. Later Katz created his own comedy recordings by inventing hilarious English-Yiddish parodies of well-known songs, such as "Haim afen Range" (from "Home on the Range") and "How Much Is That Pickle in the Window?" (from "How Much Is That Doggie in the Window?"). He capped his career with many years of touring in his own English-Yiddish fun-and-music stage show, which he called the *Borscht Capades.*

Meyer Myron ("Mickey") Katz was born in Cleveland, Ohio, on June 15, 1909. At the age of eleven he began to take clarinet lessons, at twelve he was entering amateur contests, and at fifteen he was a professional in local dance orchestras.

In 1927, at the age of seventeen, he began to tour with Phil Spitalny. In the early 1930s Katz played in Cleveland vaudeville orchestras under Maurice Spitalny, Phil's brother. During the summers in the late 1930s Katz led his own orchestra on boats out of Cleveland, while during the winters he had a jazz band that played one-night stands.

Most of World War II saw him leading an orchestra at a Cleveland theater-restaurant. In 1945 he formed a small comedy band, Mickey Katz and His Krazy Kittens, which played for a while in New York City before making a USO tour in Europe.

Available for Work

At the age of sixty-eight, Katz, in his autobiography (*Papa, Play for Me,* 1977), expressed his own view of himself:

> I still love to play my clarinet. I still love to make people laugh. I can still fit into my size thirty-seven tuxedo, and I'm still available for weddings, bar mitzvahs, and brisses.
>
> Yours, lox, stock, and bagel,
>
> Mickey Katz

Katz's Heroes

To Katz, Menasha Skulnick was the "clown prince of the Yiddish theater" and vaudeville's Harry Ritz, of the Ritz Brothers, was "one of the funniest men in the history of show business."

An Active Friar

From 1952 on, Katz was a member of the Friars Club. There, for many years, he was part of a regular bridge game with George Burns, George Raft, and Dave Siegel. Katz conducted the orchestra at many major Friars Club functions.

In 1946 he joined Spike Jones and His City Slickers. Katz played in the band, sometimes conducted it, and performed "glugs" and other comical throat sounds for the ensemble.

Katz's role as a comedian had actually begun when he was a teenager working with a Cleveland band on a local radio station. Besides playing in the band, he made up and performed English-Yiddish parodies of familiar bedtime stories, such as "Hanzel end Ganzel," "Little Red Rosenberg," and "Yoshke and the Beanstalk."

In 1947 he left Spike Jones and started making his own comedy recordings, in which he provided the lyrics and others prepared the musical arrangements. His first recording featured "Haim afen Range." The flip side was "Yiddish Square Dance," with Katz as an Arkansas hog caller calling a square dance in Yiddish. His second disc parodied the popular Latin number "Tico, Tico" as "Tickle, Tickle."

There followed a long series of side-splitting English-Yiddish comedy recordings. "Kiss of Fire" became "Kiss of Meyer":

When I look on you,
It burns by me a fire.
Come to Papa, bubele,
And have a kiss from Meyer.

"Davy Crockett" became "Duvid Crockett:"

Born in the wilds of Delancey Street,
Home of gefilte fish and kosher meat.
Handy wid a knife, O herzach tzi [listen to me],
He flicked him a chicken when he was only three.
Duvid, Duvid Crockett,
King of Delancey Street.

Among his other singles (and their sources) were "Dot's Morris" ("That's Amore") and "Shleppin' [Walkin'] My Baby Back Home." His "operas" included *Carmen Katz* and *The Barber of Shlemiel.* He also issued albums, including the all-instrumental *Mickey Katz Plays Music for Weddings, Bar Mitzvahs, and Brisses.*

In 1948 Katz formed a troupe to perform a stage revue in Los Angeles. He wanted to appeal to all generations, but he knew that older Jews would tend to expect Yiddish material, while fewer and fewer young Jews had a fluent knowledge of that language. Consequently he engaged young Catskills comedians to perform in English, vocalists to sing Yiddish folksongs, musicians to play "Jewish jazz," and himself to bridge

Clarinet Teacher

Joseph Narovec, a tall, aged Bohemian professor in Cleveland, taught Katz to play the clarinet, helped him get his first job with an orchestra, and, most important of all, encouraged the youth to believe in himself.

"Today I worship at Joseph Narovec's shrine," Katz said in his own old age. "He was the only clarinet teacher I ever had."

Father and Son

Katz was genuinely happy about the show-business success of his son Joel Grey. And many fans sent greetings from father to son and from son to father.

But Katz sometimes encountered people who insisted on comparing the two dissimilar performers (Grey the actor and Katz the musician). Once, after Katz had sung his opening number, a member of the audience rose and said, "Hey, Katz, I saw your boy Joel last night in *Cabaret*. He's better than you." Surprised, Katz replied, "How can you say that? You haven't seen me do anything yet." The woman said, "I've seen enough already."

the gap with his own English-Yiddish material. The resultant show was a tremendous success, and Katz toured with his *Borscht Capades* for many years.

One of the stars of the show in its early days was Katz's son Joel, at first billed as Joel Kaye. Later the boy went solo and became famous as Joel Grey. Father and son encouraged each other through the succeeding years.

Katz died in Los Angeles on April 30, 1985. ☆

Ham for Uncle Sam

According to his son Joel, Katz never had a strong stomach. When Joel was little, Katz would arrive home from work at four in the morning and awaken the boy so that they could share a bowl of raspberry Jello with sweet cream.

When Katz toured with the USO in 1945, he had to eat ham and beans. "It may be psychological, but I have never been able to digest ham or pork. But it was either eat ham or starve, so I ate ham for Uncle Sam. Plus becoming bloated from a steady diet of gassy beans, I sort of floated on and off the stage like a toy blimp."

He preferred traditional Jewish fare, such as corned beef.

ANDY KAUFMAN
Latka Gravas

Andy Kaufman was best known for his role as the meek, endearing Latka Gravas in the television sitcom *Taxi.* But elsewhere Kaufman was anything but meek. He delighted in the unexpected and the outrageous. The offbeat comedian wanted not only to generate laughter but also to provoke reactions of other kinds, including anger, confusion, and even boredom. His antics became so bizarre that in 1982 a national audience voted to keep Kaufman off the TV show *NBC's Saturday Night Live.*

Kaufman was born in New York City, New York, on January 17, 1949. He grew up in Great Neck, Long Island, and by the age of nine he was earning money by entertaining at children's parties. After graduating from high school, he studied radio and TV at Grahm Junior College in Boston.

Returning to New York City, he began to perform in coffeehouses and later in nightclubs and theaters. His act at that time (the early 1970s) included an impression of Elvis Presley, a Mighty Mouse routine, and a performance of a strange folksong from an island in the Caspian Sea. But his act centered on his characterization of the Foreign Man (a forerunner of Latka Gravas), who spoke with an odd accent and behaved in a manner completely lacking in self-confidence.

Later Kaufman developed a totally different character, Tony Clifton, an untalented but arrogant singer. During an engagement in San Francisco, Kaufman billed himself only as Tony Clifton (with no reference to the comedian's real name), and the singer's contemptuous

Kaufman as Armegeddon T. Thunderbird in *In God We Tru$t.*

Andy with Bernadette Peters in *Heartbeeps.*

behavior toward the audience resulted in his being pelted with bottles and cans during his performance. He finally had to wear a SWAT helmet and stand behind an industrial fishnet.

Eventually Kaufman, who regarded his work not as "comedy" but as "performance art," incorporated increasingly strange routines into his act. He induced audiences to imitate barnyard animals while he sang "Old MacDonald Had a Farm." He presented mock versions of the Radio City Music Hall Rockettes, the Mormon Tabernacle Choir, and Santa Claus. He delivered deliberately stale or unfunny lines. He read *The Great Gatsby* out loud, and when he asked the audience if they wanted him to stop and they said yes, he turned on a recording of himself reading *The Great Gatsby*.

One of his most provocative routines was his characterization of the Intergender World Wrestling Champion. He infuriated feminists by challenging women to wrestling matches and by crowing about his being undefeated in such bouts.

While angering many audience members, Kaufman nevertheless moved steadily upward in his career throughout the 1970s. His live stage performances were capped by his 1979 sold-out appearance at Carnegie Hall.

He also moved into television. From 1975 to 1982 he appeared many times on *NBC's Saturday Night Live*. On November 20, 1982, in an unusual live call-in ballot,

Friendly Person

Unlike many stars, who build a wall around themselves, Kaufman remained accessible to "ordinary" people. He often gave out his phone number to cabdrivers and others he met and liked.

Friends who needed money could rely on him to help.

The Wrestler

As a child, Andy Kaufman idolized the pro wrestler Nature Boy Buddy Rogers, whose role as the "bad guy" inspired the comedian's later performances as a confrontationist, particularly as the Intergender World Wrestling Champion.

In 1981 Kaufman made his "professional wrestling debut" at Cobo Hall Arena in Detroit. In April 1982 he suffered neck and back injuries from the pro wrestler Jerry Lawler, who had been angered by Kaufman's disparaging remarks about wrestlers and had challenged the comedian and would-be wrestler to a match.

Healthful Habits

Avoiding Hollywood's fast lane, Kaufman was a nonsmoker and nondrinker, believed in vegetarianism, ate health food, enjoyed yoga, exercised regularly, and practiced transcendental meditation twice a day. The type of lung cancer that he contracted was unrelated to smoking.

A Memorable Evening

At the end of his successful 1979 Carnegie Hall performance, Kaufman invited all 2,800 audience members to join him in a midnight snack. Buses hired by the comedian drove the crowd to Manhattan's New York School of Printing, where everyone enjoyed milk and cookies at Kaufman's expense.

viewers voted 195,544 to 169,186 to drop him from the show.

As Latka Gravas on *Taxi* (1978-83) Kaufman played a New York City taxicab mechanic of indeterminate overseas origin. His high-pitched accent and gentle manner were subject to sudden changes into a bewildering variety of multiple personalities, including a macho swinger. Latka became one of TV's most beloved characters. To rudeness and rejection, he would respond with a childlike, genuinely polite "Thank you veddy much."

Kaufman was a regular on *Van Dyke and Company* (1976). He also guested on talk and variety shows hosted by Johnny Carson, David Letterman, and many others.

In Marty Feldman's satiric motion picture *In God We Tru$t,* subtitled *Gimme That Prime Time Religion* (1980), Kaufman played Armageddon T. Thunderbird, a hypocritical TV evangelist. He was a lovesick robot in *Heartbeeps* (1981), while *My Breakfast with Blassie* (1983) showed him engrossed in conversation with the professional wrestler Freddie Blassie.

In 1983 Kaufman appeared on Broadway as the Referee in *Teaneck Tanzi: The Venus Flytrap,* a story about family members who solve domestic problems through wrestling matches. He also planted himself as an usher in the theater aisles, where he deliberately provoked heated arguments with audience members who did not recognize him.

In January 1984 Kaufman learned that he had lung cancer, but he continued to perform while undergoing treatments. On May 15, 1984, he was admitted to Cedars-Sinai Medical Center in Los Angeles, where he died the next day. ★

Offstage Introvert

The real Andy Kaufman was a decent, unassuming person, much like his Foreign Man and Latka Gravas characters. But his intense portrayals of such obnoxious characters as the singer Tony Clifton and the Intergender World Wrestling Champion eventually began to take over large chunks of his real life. Andy did not drink, smoke, or grossly curse; but as Tony—on or off stage—he drank, smoked, and cursed profusely. Andy was an introvert who had trouble talking with women, but as Tony he was an offensive extrovert. Andy never gambled, but Tony did. What began as a put-on nearly ended as a psychosis.

Kaufman (right) with Famous Amos in *Taxi*.

DANNY KAYE
Ambassador of Goodwill

Danny Kaye, for the last thirty or more years of his life, reigned as the world's undisputed prince of clowns. His work in behalf of the United Nations International Children's Emergency Fund (UNICEF) took him around the globe many times, and his

Ping-Pong Champ

In the 1960s Kaye developed a fanaticism for table tennis. He became the ping-pong champion of Beverly Hills.

Danny Kaye does an arabesque as Laurie Ichino watches.

humor—largely based on the universally understandable techniques of pantomime, mugging, and nonsense singing—won him the affection and admiration of people everywhere.

He was born in New York City, New York, on January 18, 1913. His original name was David Daniel Kaminski (sometimes spelled Kaminsky, Kominski, or Kominsky).

He grew up in the Brownsville section of the borough of Brooklyn, the toughest district in all of New York City. Danny survived by being the neighborhood clown. He always loved to make people laugh.

After dropping out of high school, he spent several years trying to build a career in show business, meanwhile supporting himself with odd jobs. During those years, he appeared as a summertime toomler (creator of comic tumult) on the borscht circuit.

In 1933 he was asked to join the dancing team of Dave Harvey and Kathleen Young, forming a group called the Three Terpsichoreans. On the opening

Musical Friends

Kaye was never happier than when he was in the company of musical giants, such as Arthur Rubinstein, Zubin Mehta, and Isaac Stern.

night, in Utica, New York, Kaye, an inexperienced dancer, accidentally fell during the performance. The audience began to laugh and applaud. Harvey whispered to him, "They love it. Don't get up." Kaye, in a false whisper that could be heard throughout the auditorium, replied, "I can't get up. I've split my pants!" Kaye's clowning became a regular part of the act, which played at vaudeville and burlesque theaters.

Late in 1933 the Three Terpsichoreans joined a revue troupe that worked its way westward across the United States and then sailed for the Orient in February 1934. By then Kaye was singing and monologizing in addition to dancing. To appeal to the non-English-speaking audiences of the Orient, Kaye learned to tell his stories in pantomime, to show emotions by making faces, and to entertain with scat singing (that is, the expressive vocalizing of meaningless syllables with an occasional recognizable word for emphasis).

After returning to the United States, Kaye could find only minor engagements for several more years. His career was stuck. He simply could not find the right material for his personality.

Then, in 1939, he teamed up with songwriter Sylvia Fine (whom he had briefly known when they were children) for *The Sunday Night Revue.* The show fold-

Cooking With a Passion

From the 1950s on, Kaye had a passion for cooking, particularly Chinese cuisine. He had an elaborate Chinese kitchen built into his home, and he purchased only the finest ingredients. Though usually eating little or nothing himself, he loved to prepare meals as presents for special people. Sometimes he would go to a friend's Chinese restaurant in San Francisco, give the chef the night off, and do the cooking himself. He also excelled at pastries and Italian food. Many experts regarded him as one of the best chefs in America.

Honorary Surgeon

The comedian watched so many operations—mostly at the Mayo Clinic—that the American College of Surgeons made him an honorary member. His intense medical interest also had practical benefits: once he gave artificial respiration to a fellow jet passenger who had apparently suffered a heart attack.

Danny Kaye as Hans Christian Andersen.

ed after only one performance, but it was the beginning for Danny and Sylvia.

That summer they worked together again, putting on *The Straw Hat Revue* at Camp Tamiment, a Jewish resort camp in the Pocono Mountains of Pennsylvania. In the autumn the show made it to Broadway, where Kaye finally began to develop a reputation and a following.

Soon his career as a major solo comedian was well under way. In 1940 he had a successful, now legendary, engagement at the elite New York City nightclub La Martinique.

The boost to his career can be traced directly to Sylvia Fine's sparkling melodies and absurd lyrics, perfectly tailored to showcase Kaye's personality and talent for dialect singing and for patter (humorous, rapid-fire) songs. There was, for instance, "Anatole of Paris," in which Kaye sang as a schizophrenic modiste with blue hair. In "Stanislavsky" he employed Russian dialect to poke fun at the Soviet artists of the Moscow Theater, where students were taught to "become" inanimate objects.

Sylvia, whom he married in 1940, was the most important force in his career. For the rest of his life, she not only wrote much of his material but also served as his personal coach and critic.

Kaye's performance at La Martinique led to a part in the major Broadway musical *Lady in the Dark* in early 1941. Later that year he appeared in another stage show, *Let's Face It.*

A sacroiliac problem kept him out of World War II military service. However, he aided the war effort by appearing at benefits and rallies to help sell war bonds and by performing at military camps and hospitals. He also appeared in United Service Organizations (USO) tours in Europe.

During the war, Kaye began to make movies, through which his talent became known worldwide. His first film was *Up in Arms* (1944). There followed a series of movies designed as vehicles for Kaye's unique comedic and musical versatility, including *The Secret Life of Walter Mitty* (1947), *The Inspector General* (1949), and *The Court Jester* (1956).

Kaye proved himself as a straight actor as well. In the film *Me and the Colonel* (1958) he played a Jewish refugee fleeing 1940 France in the company of an anti-Semitic Polish colonel. In *Skokie* (TV, 1981) he portrayed a Holocaust survivor confronting resurgent Nazism in contemporary America.

Kaye also performed on radio and TV variety prog-

Kaye conducting the Israel Philharmonic Orchestra.

Sports Lover

At Public School 149 and Thomas Jefferson High School, Danny spent most of his energy on sports, such as swimming and baseball. His athletic activities helped to develop the strength, coordination, and sense of timing that became so important in his vigorous stage and film routines. In later years he played golf and tennis.

In 1976 he became a founder and part owner of the Seattle Mariners major-league baseball team. In 1981 he sold most, and in 1983 the remainder, of his interest in the club.

UNICEF Spokesman

From 1953 on, Kaye was UNICEF's official ambassador-at-large to the world's children. He went into remote areas of Europe, Asia, Africa, and Latin America to visit children who were undernourished, diseased, or orphaned by war. Exuding an obviously genuine affection for them, he entertained the youngsters while teams of UNICEF workers administered medical and other aid.

Jet Pilot
Kaye was a licensed jet aircraft pilot.

For Relaxation
Smoking a pipe and playing golf were two of Kaye's favorite ways of relaxing.

Danny Kaye in *Skokie*.

rams. He hosted *The Danny Kaye Show* on radio (1945-46) and the very successful TV series of the same name (1963-67).

Also notable was his return, after a nearly thirty-year absence, to the Broadway stage in the musical *Two by Two* (1970), based on the biblical story of Noah. But he always preferred the freedom of concert appearances, where he could exercise his ability to improvise. Kaye, though he could not read music, frequently appeared on the podium with major orchestras, such as the Israel Philharmonic, conducting them with inspired hilarity.

In 1983 he had a heart bypass operation. He did not slow down much after his surgery. On January 1, 1984, he acted as the grand marshal of the Rose Parade. He also made UNICEF tours and appeared as a conductor. In September 1985, for example, he comically conducted the Los Angeles Philharmonic Orchestra at the Hollywood Bowl in a benefit concert for a musicians' fund.

However, complications stemming from his operation finally took their toll, and Kaye died in Los Angeles on March 3, 1987.

Because his humor was never unkind, was always solidly based in humility, was universal in appeal, and was channeled into helping the world's children, Kaye was internationally recognized as one of humanity's greatest treasures and as an independent ambassador of goodwill to people everywhere. ☆

Lazy Saturday
"My favorite way to spend Saturday is in and out of bed," King notes, "watching sports on TV and eating."

ALAN KING
Hostility Humorist

Alan King, with his chin aggressively thrust forward and his voice vigorously barking New Yorkese, gives vent to all of the daily frustrations faced by average middle-class Americans. His favorite targets are the professions and institutions that seem to dominate people's lives, such as medicine, politics, airlines, and telephone companies.

He was born in New York City, New York, on December 26, 1927. His original name was Irwin Alan Kniberg.

Expelled from high school because of truancy, he

became a drummer in a combo that played at weddings and bar mitzvahs. At the age of fifteen he began his comedy career in the Catskills and in New York City burlesque houses. Still in his teens he became a regular at Leon and Eddie's club in Manhattan. In the early 1950s he frequently toured.

King's big break came in 1956 when he appeared with Judy Garland at New York City's famed Palace Theater. He then toured with her.

In the late 1950s and early 1960s he was a frequent guest on the Ed Sullivan, Garry Moore, and Perry Como TV shows. Since then he has continued to work TV, as well as top nightclubs, casinos, and hotels.

King first made his reputation by focusing on life in suburbia. Of the overly dutiful housewife, he said, "How would you like to get up at 5 A.M. to go to the bathroom and, when you come back, the bed is made?"

He also has some sharp-edged nostalgia routines: "My mother was the worst cook in the world. Everything had to cook for four days. She never believed the butcher killed it! My mother made chicken soup with fat on the top. It used to congeal and you could skate on it!"

But his fame today rests on his role as the middle class's release valve for hostilities and feelings of helplessness built up against modern structures, institutions, and "experts." He has called the Long Island Expressway "the world's largest parking lot." When his house was burglarized, he could not collect insurance, because "the company told me I should have had fire *or* theft, not fire *and* theft." "Interior decorators are the greatest fraud ever perpetrated on the American public. We've had seven decorators in four years. No furniture, just decorators! My wife found two boys on

Charitable King

Alan King has donated his time and energy to many charities, and he has received over one hundred philanthropic awards. He founded the Alan King Diagnostic Medical Center in Jerusalem, endowed a scholarship for American students at the Hebrew University in Israel, and helped raise money for the Nassau (Long Island) Center for Emotionally Disturbed Children. King emphasizes that his philanthropy is "Talmudic" in motivation.

Jewish Syndrome

"When I was a kid I wanted to be somebody," King has said. "And then I found that amusing people is a helluva way to make a living. And now you might say it is the syndrome of the Jews: if you don't laugh, you die."

Favorite Sport

Not all of King's hostilities are released onstage by striking out at institutions. In his spare time he also enjoys striking tennis balls. "I can get out all my aggressions on the court," he says.

King also likes to attend tennis matches as a spectator and as a tournament director. He was the first celebrity to back a Grand Prix tournament.

King (left) with Billy Crystal and Jo Beth Williams in *Memories of Me*.

Madison Avenue. . . . If you watch them they'll take your eyeballs outta your head, put 'em on a piece of driftwood, hang 'em over the fireplace, and charge you for it!"

King has acted in comedies and dramas, both onstage and in movies. He appeared as Nathan Detroit in a New York City production of *Guys and Dolls* (1965). His other stage credits include *Applause* (1970). He was hilarious as the rabbi in the film *Bye Bye Braverman* (1968). Among his other movies were *Hit the Deck* (1955), *Lovesick* (1983), and *Memories of Me* (1988).★

Food Connoisseur

Alan King is a passionate eater, cook, and restaurant buff. "When I get up in the morning I have to decide what I'm going to have for dinner, or I can't get through the day," he claims. He was raised on his mother's kosher cooking, and he loved her brisket and boiled beef. Today his favorite meals are French, Italian, and Chinese dishes.

To keep his weight down, King usually skips breakfast and lunch. He generally gets up at the bizarre time of three o'clock in the morning to eat his one big meal of the day.

He has a chef at home, but King likes to cook for himself on weekends and for his friends whenever they visit. His specialties are sautés, shrimp, veal, roasted chicken, and "eggs all kinds of ways."

King often dines out, but only at a select group of fine restaurants, of which he is a connoisseur.

Food and Sex

According to King, good food is second in importance only to sex. "Except for salami and eggs. Now, that's better than sex, but only if the salami is thickly sliced and if you put catsup on the eggs and have a toasted bialy."

Dapper Comedian

King is one of the best-dressed men in show business. He keeps a large wardrobe of expensive vested suits for public events. At home he wears elegant bathrobes.

ROBERT KLEIN
Hybrid Comedian

Robert Klein blends a traditional stage appearance and a hip awareness, a traditional comedy discipline and a modern improvisational style, and a traditional repertory of outward-directed gags and a contemporary set of personal, hostility-releasing jokes. His standard gags attack annoying things: "Hawaiian Punch is 10 percent fruit juice. What's the other 90 percent? You're better off with paint thinner." His hostility is released in lines such as those that recall 1950s school civil-defense drills: "No talking," the teacher said. "Take these tags home. They're to be used in the event you're burned beyond recognition in a nuclear holocaust. And remember, no-o-o talking during a nuclear holocaust. I shall be taking names!"

Klein was born in New York City, New York, on February 8, 1942. After earning a B.A. degree at Alfred (New York) University, he spent a year at the Yale University School of Drama.

In the fall of 1963, while supporting himself by substitute teaching in the Mount Vernon, New York, school system, Klein made his first attempts at stand-up comedy. After doing well for a short time at Greenwich Village's Bitter End, he bombed.

Leaving solo comedy, Klein joined the improvisational group Second City in Chicago for the 1964-65 theatrical season, and in 1966 he made his New York City stage debut in a Second City revue. He then appeared on Broadway in the musical *The Apple Tree* (1966).

During the run of *The Apple Tree,* Klein decided to return to stand-up comedy. He honed his skills at the Improvisation, a Manhattan nightclub, before moving on to other niteries in Chicago, Los Angeles, and elsewhere. In 1968 he hit the big time by appearing on *The Tonight Show,* followed in 1969 by *The Ed Sullivan Show.*

Since then Klein has been a major figure in stand-up comedy. In recent years he has been particularly active on cable TV.

He has also continued his acting career. On the New York City stage he appeared in *They're Playing Our Song* (1979), and his film credits include *The*

Ego Satisfaction

"The people who handled me thought I was going to be another Jack Lemmon," Klein recalls. After several Broadway shows and some films, "it didn't pan out." But "somewhere along the line I discovered that for me ego satisfaction is a one-man show."

Off the Beaten Path

Preferring to spend as much time as possible at home with his family, Klein avoids travel and extra commitments. "I've turned down many TV series and commercials," he notes. "It's not exactly been an orthodox show-biz career. I'm off the beaten path, a well-kept secret. I'm not a household word. That's OK."

Choice of Material

"My perspective is that of an East Coast urbanite," Klein points out, "but [my material] is something that people can relate to."

A youthful Robert Klein.

Klein as a camp counselor in *Poison Ivy*.

Owl and the Pussycat (1970), *Stripes* (1981), and *Your Place or Mine* (TV, 1983).

In one of Klein's routines, he pokes fun at scientists who conducted research into the effects of marijuana by forcing monkeys to smoke their body weight of the weed every day for months. The scientists finally came up with the amazing discovery that the monkeys "showed abnormal brain waves."

Other targets of the comedian's wit are often selected from the news. "Why is it that flying saucers," he says, "without exception, land and expose themselves to total morons? Why don't they ever land in Carl Sagan's backyard?"

Klein also enjoys mimicry of easily identifiable types, such as phony panhandlers and TV hucksters. In recent years the middle-aged comic's topics have broadened to include fatherhood, aging, and mellowing. ☆

"I'm an Illusionist"

"I'm not a teacher, preacher, or prophet," Klein says. He sees his craft as "serious business." "When I'm on, the audiences have a wonderful time, and it looks like I'm having a wonderful time, too. And sometimes I am. But I'm working. I'm an illusionist, and my illusion is to make everything seem like one big good time."

Recreations

Klein is an avid book reader. He also has a passion for aviation; one of his favorite pastimes is using his shortwave radio to tune into dialogue between pilots and air controllers.

Leisurely Puffs

While Klein does not, like Alan King and George Burns, use a cigar as an onstage prop, he does enjoy smoking cigars in his leisure moments.

BERT LAHR
Cowardly Lion

Bert Lahr is best known for his comic, heartwarming portrayal of the Cowardly Lion in the 1939 film classic *The Wizard of Oz*. But he was far more than a one-role performer. The last great American comedian to be nurtured in classic burlesque before the genre degenerated into a peep show, Lahr eventually became one of the few performers to triumph not only in low comedy and high comedy but also in literary drama.

He was born in New York City, New York, on August 13, 1895. His original name was Irving Lahrheim (though his surname was misspelled on his birth certificate as "Laurheim"). His father was German-born, and his mother was of German descent. For the first six years of his life Irving Lahrheim spoke only German.

Lahr in MGM's *Meet the People*.

Lahr (right) as the Cowardly Lion in *The Wizard of Oz*.

As a youngster he enjoyed making his friends laugh by clowning around. He discovered the thrill of the stage when he performed in an eighth-grade class show, which was a kid act, that is, a spoof of classroom life, often couched in familiar but exaggerated dialects.

At the age of fourteen he dropped out of school. For six months he did odd jobs.

Then, in 1910, he began to find work in various professional kid acts. Irving Lahrheim became Bert Lahr.

In 1917 he entered burlesque, where he carved his individual identity as a "Dutch" (that is, German-dialect) comic out of the block of low-comedy stock humor. He experimented with funny gestures, faces, and noises; and he learned how to build humorous situations, which set him apart from the comedians who merely strung together bits of slapstick shtick and jokes unrelated to one another. More than any other comic, Lahr showed the pain of comedy, getting laughs by responding to verbal and physical abuse with exaggerated intensity in his gesticulating, grimacing, and bellowing. To express disbelief or amazement, he would utter a guttural "gnong, gnong, gnong," which became his vocal trademark. He was also fond of the sarcastic expression "Some fun, eh, kid?" Much of his humor was based on exaggerated dialect and on malapropisms, as in this passage from a song: "Ouououououououch—how dot voman could cook! . . . Her oyshters and fishes were simply—[in sensuous delight] malicious!"

By the early 1920s burlesque was in trouble because of competition from theater revues and silent films. In 1922 Lahr graduated from burlesque to vaudeville.

In vaudeville he performed a comedy sketch entitled *What's the Idea?* He played a drunken, ill-dressed, wild-spirited policeman. The line "What's the idea?" had an important part in the sketch. And when he took his bows, he yelled at the audience, "What's the idea? What's the ideeeeaa?" That expression became another of his hallmarks.

In 1927 Lahr made the step up to Broadway by appearing in the revue *Harry Delmar's Revels,* followed by the musical comedy *Hold Everything* (1928). Lahr's stock soon rose so high that the grand Broadway impresario Florenz Ziegfeld picked him to star in the last Ziegfeld extravaganza, *Hot-Cha!* (1932).

In *George White's Music Hall Varieties* (1932) Lahr ventured for the first time into satire, spoofing the elegance of the musical-comedy star Clifton Webb and the emotionalism of a concert baritone (singing "Trees" while surrounded by a pack of sniffing dogs). In *Life Begins at 8:40* (1934) Lahr satirized the British upper-

Beatrice Lillie and Nancy Walker

The witty, elegant British comedienne Beatrice Lillie won high praise from Lahr, who appeared with her in the revue *The Show Is On* (1936). "Working with Bea was one of my great experiences in the theater," he said. Both performers liked to base their humor on the deflating of pretentiousness.

He worked with the American comedienne Nancy Walker in the revue *The Girls against the Boys* (1959). In one skit they parodied the new music style of rock 'n' roll. As a comedienne, Walker was second only to Lillie in Lahr's esteem.

Unparalleled Insecurity

Nearly paranoid with the belief that some fellow performers were constantly trying to top him, Lahr insisted that when he was saying a funny line, nobody else onstage was allowed to move. Once he complained to the director that an actor had been moving; but the director, who had been watching the scene, denied that the actor had moved. "You're wrong," Lahr replied. "Tonight he was moving his facial muscles."

He was the epitome of the insecure comedian. When he was congratulated for his tremendous success in the hit Broadway musical comedy *Du Barry Was a Lady* (1939), he responded, "Yeah, but what do I do next year?"

Baseball Fan

A longtime baseball fan (his favorite team was the New York Giants), Lahr drew on his love of the game to add depth to his comical characterization of the ballplayer in "The Baseball Sketch," a segment in the revue *Two on the Aisle* (1951).

Fishing Enthusiast

Lahr was a longtime lake-fishing enthusiast. "Fishing makes me tired, hungry, and sleepy," he explained. "I throw off all my worries."

Lahr (center) in *Love and Hisses.*

class's speech affectations and sense of family honor. In *The Show Is On* (1936) he spoofed scat singing, screen royalty, British royalty, and outdoorsy he-men (in the comical "Song of the Woodsman").

Hollywood beckoned Lahr as early as 1929, when he appeared in the movie *Faint Heart.* A few years later he had parts in *Flying High* (1931) and *Happy Landing* (1934).

In the late 1930s he made several motion pictures, notably *The Wizard of Oz* (1939), in which he played the Cowardly Lion. The film's lyricist, E. Y. Harburg, had promoted Lahr for the part because "when the Cowardly Lion admits that he lacks courage, everybody's heart goes out to him. He must be somebody who embodies all this pathos and sweetness, yet puts on this comic bravura. Bert had that quality to such a wonderful degree."

Lahr, as the Cowardly Lion, incongruously and hilariously used New York City colloquial pronunciations (such as *noive* for *nerve*) even though the character was set in the imaginary land of Oz. Absolute gems of comic-song interpretation were Lahr's renditions of "If I Only Had the Nerve" and "If I Were King of the Forest." He gave both humor and humanity to his Cowardly Lion.

Throughout the 1940s and early 1950s Lahr alternated stage work and film appearances. On the boards,

A Natural at Comedy

His own matter-of-factness about his business contrasted with the romantic-heroic image that other people tended to create. "Everybody says I've got wonderful *timing,*" Lahr once stated. "Young actors have actually stood in the wings with a stopwatch, charting when a certain laugh would come. But you wanna know something? I don't know what the hell they're talking about."

Hobbies and Habits

Lahr had temporary enthusiasms for many activities, such as painting pictures, listening to stereo tapes, and watching small Japanese TV sets (which he would take to the dinner table).

One fancy, smoking cigars, caused a great deal of turmoil in his household. When his wife began to gag on the smoke, he would hold the cigar near the air conditioner, not realizing that the air current was not taking the smoke out of the house but putting it back into the room. If the room became too thick with smoke, he would finish his cigar in the bathroom.

he played in *Seven Lively Arts* (1944), *Burlesque* (1946), *Two on the Aisle* (1951), and other shows. His movies during that period included *Ship Ahoy* (1942), *Always Leave Them Laughing* (1949), and *Rose Marie* (1954).

In the 1950s Lahr began to appear on TV. He frequently performed his old revue routines on Ed Sullivan's variety show.

In 1956 Lahr played Estragon in Samuel Beckett's complex modernistic play *Waiting for Godot.* Lahr's approach was instinctive and theatrical, not intellectual. He saw the play as "two men trying to amuse themselves on earth by playing jokes and little games." His performance was universally praised.

Waiting for Godot opened a whole new chapter in Lahr's career. He began to appear in other great literary plays, including televised productions of Shaw's *Androcles and the Lion* (1956) and Molière's *The School for Wives* (1956). On the stage, he played Bottom in Shakespeare's *A Midsummer Night's Dream* (1960) and Pisthetairos in Aristophanes' *The Birds* (1966).

Lahr's last performance was in the film *The Night They Raided Minsky's* (1968), fittingly a story about burlesque. He died in New York City on December 4, 1967. ★

Lahr in *Ship Ahoy.*

JACK E. LEONARD
Insult Comedian

Jack E. Leonard was the first entertainer to build an entire career as an insult comedian. Though eclipsed in popularity in his later years by the younger Don Rickles, Leonard is still held by some critics to have been the more creative insult artist.

He was born in Chicago, Illinois, on April 24, 1911. His original name was Leonard Lebitsky.

He began his career as a standard stand-up nightclub comedian aiming his barbs at himself and at the outside world. But during one engagement, Leonard recalled, "I was on the bill ahead of Tony Martin, and all the ladies were too busy looking at each other's clothes to pay attention to me—until I told them 'When you cross the George Washington to go home, I hope the bridge falls.' "

The Price of Insults

"You can't work all the best places with an insult act," Leonard admitted. "They're afraid to book me because they don't know what I'm gonna come up with."

Indeed, he was once thoughtlessly booked at a Catskills hotel catering to Orthodox Jewish audiences. When he saw the yarmulkes, Leonard cracked, "Welcome, legionnaires." During his act, he snarled, "If Moses saw you he would have invented another commandment." After thirty minutes, he concluded, "Thank you, opponents," and walked off to a deafening silence.

Only an Act

"I only needle people I like," Leonard explained. "My friends know it's just for laughs."

He never used insults in anger. "When I'm really mad," he admitted, "I can't think of 'em."

Battle of the Bulge

In the mid-1950s Leonard reduced from about 250 pounds to about 200 pounds. "No pills, no injections—just pure willpower," he boasted. He often vacationed at the Harbor Island Spa in Long Branch, New York, where he worked at controlling his weight.

Youthful Activity

As a young man, Leonard worked as a lifeguard. He also entered Charleston dance contests.

From such occasional outbursts to get the audience's attention or to quiet hecklers, Leonard gradually developed a full-blown insult act. His naturally mumbling, sarcastic manner was well suited to such material. By the early 1940s his audacious act had established him as one of the nation's top nightclub attractions.

"An insult is only funny if it's really ridiculous," Leonard claimed, "and if it's aimed at some really big shot." Leonard loved to blast big shots. He told the visiting Duke of Windsor, "You've been in this country so long, you should have your second papers by now." The crooner Perry Como received this dig: "You have a very fine voice. Too bad it's in Bing Crosby's throat." A frequent guest on TV's *The Ed Sullivan Show,* Leonard did not hesitate to insult his stoic—and powerful—host: "Don't worry, Ed, someday you'll find yourself—and you'll be terribly disappointed. There's nothing wrong with you that reincarnation won't cure."

Ordinary audience members were also fair game. "You there, sir," Leonard would say. "I always wanted to know how long a man can live without brains. Would you mind telling us your age?"

Leonard also used straight jokes. "Remember the words of Norman Vincent Peale, who said, 'A family

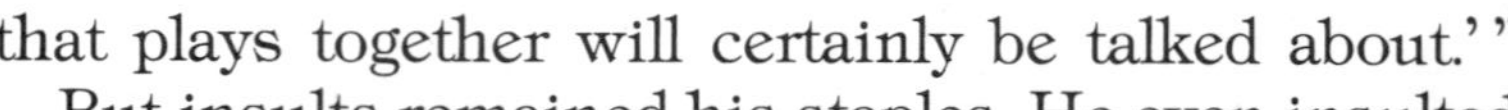

that plays together will certainly be talked about.'"

But insults remained his staples. He even insulted himself for being overweight: "You look like a nice bunch of people, and I'm a nice bunch of people, so maybe we'll have a good time." After he dieted and lost over a hundred pounds, he danced around the chubby Jackie Gleason and sang "Around the World in Eighty Days."

Leonard played a cameo role as a berserk entertainer in Jerry Lewis's film comedy *The Disorderly Orderly* (1964). He also starred in the movie *The Fat Spy* (1966).

In April 1973 Leonard had open-heart surgery. He died in New York City, New York, on May 10, 1973.☆

Fat Jack

Jack E. Leonard kidded himself about his obesity. Once he squeezed himself into a taxicab and told the driver, "Take me to a larger cab." Another time he joked, "You've heard of Sinatra the Voice and Durnate the Nose? I'm Leonard the Lump." He adopted the nickname Fat Jack.

SAM LEVENSON
Folk Humorist

Sam Levenson, a self-described "folk humorist," was a shrewd observer of the American domestic scene. Relying less on jokes than on personal recollections, he used his nightclub and TV monologues to stress the happy side of growing up poor in the old days.

Sam(uel) Levenson was born in New York City, New York, on December 28, 1911. He grew up in a large, poor immigrant family.

Levenson began his career as a high-school Spanish teacher. In the summers of 1940 and 1941, he served as master of ceremonies for an orchestra of teachers playing in the Catskills. That experience encouraged him to entertain after school and on weekends at luncheons, teas, and fund-raising events. In 1946 he took a five-year leave of absence from teaching.

In 1949 he earned a guest spot on Ed Sullivan's TV show. Soon more TV work followed, including a regular fifteen-minute informal lecture on each program of Jack Benny's new TV series in 1950. From 1951 to 1954 he was a panelist on TV's *This Is Show Business*.

Levenson hosted his own show, in various formats, in 1951, 1952, and 1959. Through the years, there were innumerable appearances on other TV game and talk shows, including *To Tell the Truth*. He also continued to work in nightclubs.

School teacher turned comedian.

His favorite topic was raising children. "You know what my mother's attitude was toward raising children? She used to say to my father, 'Go outside and see what Sammy's doing and tell him to stop!' "

Poverty had its lighter side to Levenson. "My mother used to buy one pound of meat and make three pounds of hamburgers. You know how? We had a slogan in our house. It said, 'Old rolls never die.' Everything went into a hamburger. After a while, my mother learned to make chopped meat completely without meat and I liked it that way." "In the old days, if you bought an order at the butcher's he threw in the liver for the cat. You remember? I will tell you the truth. We didn't always have a cat but we always had liver—you are looking at the family cat."

In 1958 Levenson reported that he had been offered a situation-comedy TV series. "I've turned it down," he said, "mainly because I refuse to play the part of an idiot father who is saved from danger by his kids. I prefer intelligent comedy that gives me an opportunity to say something about the American scene."

In later years Levenson tried to keep up with current events. Women's liberation, for example, brought this quip about the contemporary woman's plight: "You've got to look like a lady, act like a man, and work like a dog."

Levenson wrote several humorous books. Among them were *Everything but Money* (1966) and *In One Era and Out the Other* (1973).

He died in New York City on August 27, 1980. ★

Kosher Cooking

Levenson praised the food at New York City's Second Avenue Kosher Delicatessen and Restaurant, where "the very menu is a remembrance of things past, of a Jewish way of life all but destroyed by upward mobility." The chef was "privy to the highly inexact alchemy of traditional, instinctive Jewish cooking as handed down by word of mothers."

Levenson extolled the rye-bread sandwiches, the soups (chicken and matzo ball), and such main courses as chicken in the pot, boiled beef, Hungarian goulash, and gefilte fish with horseradish. He also relished the "Yiddish K rations": kasha (groats), kishske (stuffed cow's intestine), knaidel (dough balls), and kugel (noodle pudding).

Levenson Levity

"You know what one little grain of wheat said to another?" "What?" " 'Help! I've been reaped!' "

A pregnant bride and her groom were getting married. When the justice of the peace said, "Do you take this woman—," the groom interrupted, "I did."

Favorite Recreations

Sam Levenson's favorite recreations were books and music. His library covered such diverse topics as Freud and Chinese humor. His master's thesis was on the Spanish philosopher José Ortega y Gasset, and for his unfinished doctorate he was studying folklore. He began violin lessons at the age of eight and continued to play for the rest of his life.

JERRY LEWIS
Great Clown

Jerry Lewis is one of filmdom's most masterful exponents of physical comedy. He has also long provided laughter through his appearances as a stand-up comic.

As a film comedian, Lewis uses mugging and wild bodily movements for much of his humor. He is also adept at disguises and multiple characterizations. At the heart of his comedy is the ability to reduce the pain of shyness and failure through cathartic laughter.

The multitalented Jerry Lewis is a master of slapstick.

As a filmmaker (writer-director-star), Lewis tends to create episodic pictures. Individual episodes frequently rise to glorious moments of comic timing and visual inventiveness.

As a stand-up comedian, Lewis began with goofy physical routines. Later his stage presence became more sophisticated, though he by no means eschewed slapstick and mugging. Today his principal asset is sheer charisma.

Lewis was born in Newark, New Jersey, on March 16, 1926. His original name was Joseph Levitch. He came from a show-business family: his father, Daniel Levitch, worked in vaudeville under name the Danny Lewis, while his mother, Rachel Levitch (née Brodsky), was a pianist.

The boy was frequently left with relatives while his parents traveled the vaudeville circuit. Lonely, he gained attention by pulling faces and doing wild stunts.

When he was fifteen he was expelled from Irvington (New Jersey) High School for punching the principal, who had made an anti-Semitic remark. Young Levitch was transferred to a vocational high school, but on his sixteenth birthday he quit school forever and entered show business.

He billed himself as Jerry Lewis, taking his father's professional surname and adopting the first name Jerry because he wanted to avoid confusion with comedian Joe E. Lewis and boxer Joe Louis. Jerry developed a pantomime act in which he mugged and engaged in other physical comedy while popular songs and opera recordings were played.

For several years he played on the borscht circuit and in theaters and nightclubs in various major cities. But his career seemed to be stuck in low gear.

Then, in 1946 in New York City, he met the singer Dean Martin, with whom he soon formed a nightclub act. The crooning Dean Martin and the clowning Jerry Lewis played off each other beautifully. The act was a mix of prepared gags and ad-libs. While Martin tried to sing, Lewis would make faces, pop up with prop buck teeth, go into eccentric dances, and generally destroy the straight man, demolish the orchestra, and attack the audience (spilling food, putting cigars into drinks).

The team quickly became the hottest act in show business, and in 1948 they hit the big time with their appearance at the Copacabana nightclub in New York City. Also in 1948 they increased their following enormously when they got in on the ground floor of the new medium of television, appearing on the first show of Ed Sullivan's *Toast of the Town* and on Milton Berle's *The Texaco Star Theater.* From 1949 to 1952 they hosted their own radio series, and from 1950 to 1955 they had their own TV program (rotating with other hosts on *The Colgate Comedy Hour*).

But the duo's greatest fame came through films, beginning with *My Friend Irma* (1949). There followed a string of popular movies, including *At War with the Army* (1951), *Sailor Beware* (1952), *The Stooge* (1953), *Three Ring Circus* (1954), and, their final picture together, *Hollywood or Bust* (1956).

In 1956, after at least two years of increasing tension between Martin and Lewis, they split up. Martin tired of being the overlooked member of the team, and

Lewis (right) and Dean Martin are airborne.

Personal Habits

Jerry Lewis is a perfectionist, a chronic worrier, and a night person. Before his 1982 heart attack, he smoked cigarettes heavily and ate much junk food; after the attack, he quit smoking and began to eat more sensibly. He enjoys heat, and after his surgery he moved to Las Vegas.

Favorite Hobby

Lewis's favorite hobby is photography. Before his own heart surgery, he had taken graphic photos of open-heart operations performed by his friend Dr. Michael DeBakey.

Other pastimes include golfing, yachting, buying electronic gadgets, and collecting pictures of clowns.

he began to psychologically isolate himself from Lewis. The latter, emotionally drained by his efforts to renew the original chemistry between Martin and himself, initiated the formal and legal dissolution of their partnership. Their last performance together was at the Copacabana on July 25, 1956.

Lewis went on to star as a solo in many films, beginning with *The Delicate Delinquent* (1957). Playing the title role, he created one of his most memorable screen moments when, pretending to be a hoodlum, he feigned a knife attack on a female social worker, warning her that he was "slippin', baby."

In the title role of *The Bellboy* (1960) he did not speak till the final seconds. It was one of his finest performances, his brilliant slapstick skill equaling that of the masters of silent-film comedy.

The Nutty Professor (1963) was a departure for Lewis. He played the title role without his usual idiot-kid image. The story was a comedy version of *Dr. Jekyll and Mr. Hyde.* The lovable Jekyll-like professor contrasted with the hateful Hyde-like Buddy Love.

The Family Jewels (1965) provided Lewis with a vehicle for a tour-de-force performance. He played seven roles: Willard, the chauffeur; Uncle James, the ferryboat captain; Uncle Everett, the circus clown; Uncle Eddie, the airplane pilot; Uncle Julius, the fashion photographer; Uncle Skylock, the private investigator; and Uncle Bugs, the gangster. Julius was a spinoff of the nutty professor, while the gap-toothed, cheerful, and optimistic—but wholly incompetent—Eddie has to rank as one of Lewis's most inspired creations.

In his post-Martin films, Lewis has often served as producer, director, or writer as well as star. Examples include *The Bellboy* (producer, director, writer), *The Errand Boy* (1961; director, writer), and *The Family Jewels* (producer, director).

Among his other early solo films were *Rock-a-bye Baby* (1958), *The Geisha Boy* (1958), *Visit to a Small Planet* (1960), *The Ladies' Man* (misspelled without the apostrophe in the film, 1961), *The Disorderly Orderly* (1964), *The Big Mouth* (1967), and *Which Way to the Front?* (1970).

Lewis also worked on his own as a stand-up comedian on TV and elsewhere. He hosted his own TV variety series in 1963 and 1967-69.

In the early 1970s Lewis made *The Day the Clown Cried,* set in Germany during the Nazi era. He played the part of Helmut, once a great clown but now wasted by drinking that was brought on by his abhorrence of

The Beverly Hills Circuit
"I don't want the Beverly Hills circuit," Lewis declares. "I haven't got time for people who ask you how your grandchild is and don't listen to your answer."

Heart Attack Victim
Jerry Lewis says he experienced no vision of paradise during his heart attack and brief "death." Everything, he recalls, was "just black and bleak."

Lewis, the clown, in *Hardly Working.*

Jerry Lewis, the director.

the Nazi regime. Helmut is arrested by the Gestapo, interned in a concentration camp, and forced into clowning to help control Jewish children being marched into the ovens. The film remains unreleased, locked up in Stockholm, where it was made, because of ongoing litigation about lack of payments from the producer.

After making *The Day the Clown Cried,* Lewis appeared in no more films during the 1970s. In his autobiography, *Jerry Lewis in Person* (with Herb Gluck, 1982), he explained his action. Filmgoers were "crying out for happy entertainment," he wrote, but filmmakers were providing works "tainted by the grime of 'realism' and magnified on celluloid." The industry "was eroding under a heavy flood of X-rated films." Fed up, Lewis stayed away from the screen for a number of years.

He finally returned to movies by writing, directing, and starring in the comedy *Hardly Working* (1981). In it he played a circus clown who loses his job and tries various other lines of work, bungling them all. He also cowrote, directed, and starred in *Cracking Up* (1983, originally released as *Smorgasbord*), about a misfit recalling his failures. In *The King of Comedy* (1983) Lewis played his first straight dramatic role, as a TV talk-show host kidnapped by a deranged would-be comedian.

Jerry's Kids

One of Lewis's principal interests has long been his volunteer work as national chairman of the Muscular Dystrophy Association (MDA). He became formally involved with battling the disease in 1950 when he banded together with others to help raise funds to create a muscular dystrophy facility that opened at Columbia University in 1959. In 1966 he gave his first annual *Jerry Lewis Labor Day Telethon* in behalf of MDA. The first two telethons were broadcast in the New York City area only, but since 1968 the show has been networked to many other parts of the country. He publicly refers to the children suffering from the disease as "my kids."

In December 1982, just after he had completed his part in *The King of Comedy,* Lewis suffered a major heart attack, actually being clinically dead for several seconds. Emergency double-bypass surgery was performed, and he recovered well.

In the fact-based drama *Fight for Life* (TV, 1987) Lewis had another serious role. He portrayed a man fighting to make a special drug available to children with myoclonic epilepsy.

Jerry Lewis, more than any other comedian of his time, has generated a wide range of opinions about his abilities. Many American critics relegate him to the low end of the comic pole because of his mugging and sentimentality, whereas many European critics rank him near top because of his superior slapstick and his concern for the "little guy." The truth about the totality of his work probably lies between the extreme views of his unyielding disparagers and his fanatic followers. But for his gift of countless hours of laughter to millions of ordinary viewers around the globe, and for his courage to clown with compassion, Jerry Lewis deserves to be ranked as one of the greatest clowns and one of the funniest men in film history. ☆

JOE E. LEWIS
Comedian's Comedian

Joe E. Lewis parlayed his faults into a fortune. Joking about his gambling, drinking, smoking, laziness, and low comedy, he reigned for many years as one of America's major nightclub entertainers. He was more highly esteemed by his peers than he was by the general public. Other comics admired his ability to build successful routines with mediocre material through the sheer force of his timing, delivery, and personality.

Lewis was born in New York City, New York, on January 12, 1902. His original name was Joseph Klewan. Early in his career he was billed as Joe Lewis; but in the 1930s, to avoid confusion with the boxer Joe Louis, he inserted the middle initial *E.*, which stood for nothing, but *Joe E.* produced the sound of his nickname, *Joey.*

He began as a singer and comic in burlesque and vaudeville. The breakthrough in his career came when he was hired as the regular star at a Chicago nightclub called the Green Mill.

When a rival club offered him more money in 1927, he accepted. Angered, the owner of the Green Mill hired three thugs to attack Lewis; they bashed in his skull and cut his throat.

Hospitalized for six weeks, Lewis nearly died from his injuries. Suffering brain damage that affected his memory, he had to relearn the alphabet. In addition, his vocal chords had been severed, and he struggled long and hard to regain the use of his voice, which for the rest of his life sounded like two pieces of sandpaper being rubbed together.

Gradually he recovered and returned to show business. His progress was poor till 1933 when he purchased a novelty song called "Sam, You Made the Pants Too Long," based on "Lord, You Made the Night Too Long." The song had risqué lines, such as "I get the damnedest breeze through my BVDs. My fly is where my tie belongs. . . . Sam, you made the pants too long."

With that song as a springboard Lewis rose to prominence in nightclubs and casinos. Beginning in 1940 he headlined at New York City's famous Copacabana for twenty-six seasons in a row.

Nightclub audiences saw him dressed in a tuxedo, holding a microphone in one hand and a glass of liquor in the other, and wandering about the room while singing and talking. He typically began his act by raising a glass and saying, "Post time."

Lewis became principally known for sophisticated song parodies and for one-liners about his drinking and gambling. One of his songs was "I'm in Love with a Wonderful Rye," a parody of "I'm in Love with a Wonderful Guy (from Rodgers and Hammerstein's *South Pacific*). "I don't like to drink," he said. "It's just something I do while I'm getting drunk. . . . I broke my toe at a Christmas party. I saw a spider on the ceiling and tried to step on it. . . . If I had my life to live over, I wouldn't have the strength. . . . A race track is where the windows clean the people."

The Joker Is Wild

Lewis's life story was the basis for the movie *The Joker Is Wild* (1957), based on a book of the same name by Art Cohn. "Frank Sinatra had more fun playing my life than I had living it," Lewis quipped.

Nightclub Life

Refusing offers for a TV series and seldom making film or guest TV appearances, Lewis preferred to hang around nightclubs. He enjoyed the easy access to bookies, liquor, and women.

Afternoon Breakfasts

One of Lewis's favorite activities was having breakfast in bed at 2:00 P.M. while reading mail, newspapers, and a scratch sheet.

A Man of Many Vices

Joe E. Lewis bet heavily on race horses and dice games, drank a great deal (especially scotch), smoked three to four packs of cigarettes a day, and religiously avoided exercise.

On Drinking

When urged to quit drinking, Lewis would say, "I know more old drunks than I know old doctors."

Friar Lewis

Joe E. Lewis was abbot (head) of the Friars Club, a show-biz fraternal organization, from 1953 to 1971. He boasted that in his honor the members redecorated the bar: "They put new drunks around it."

Lewis was often hassled by hecklers. He would respond with such lines as this: "When you use your brain, it's a violation of the child-labor laws."

From the 1940s on, Lewis turned increasingly to satire. He poked fun at President Truman's piano playing, President Eisenhower's golf playing, and other subjects from the daily newspapers.

In 1966 Lewis suffered a stroke that temporarily impaired his speech. He died in New York City on June 4, 1971. ★

RICHARD LEWIS
Neurotic Comedian

Richard Lewis calls himself the most neurotic comedian in the United States. He says he inherited his condition: "My grandparents were depressed-again Jews." His grandmother "had a collection of antacids from around the world. Not to mention her antique dolls with angina." "My blood type is nega-

Lewis (left) with Louie Anderson in *The Wrong Guys*.

A thoughtful Lewis.

Tension Release

Since the early 1970s Richard Lewis had been in and out of psychological therapy of all kinds—private, group, marathon. He feels that comedy is a valuable emotional outlet for him and for his listeners.

Comedy "helps me get my problems off my chest" he says, "and it makes people feel better about themselves to let them know that other people have problems, too." "Someone actually came up to me and said, 'You're the wreck I can't be.'" "Maybe one day they'll say I died on the couch for them."

Three Influences

Lewis says three great comedians have had a profound influence on him: Woody Allen because of his neuroses, Buster Keaton because of his sad-sack poignancy, and Lenny Bruce because of his obsession with honesty and his manic intensity.

tive. My whole family—we're very negative. My grandparents had a bumper sticker: 'I'd rather be weeping.' And my grandfather used to take home movies and edit out all the joy. Then he'd put in a cry track."

Richard says his mother displayed the same dark temperament. "My only childhood pet, a collie named Phil, committed suicide because of my mother. I mean, she would toss Phil a bone and say, 'Don't fetch it. See what I care.' . . . The final blow was when mom told Phil, 'You can't go into the house, and you can't go out of the house.' So he shot himself with a handgun that he whittled out of a biscuit."

Richard's neuroses showed up early. "I've always been a hypochondriac. When I was a little boy, I used to eat M & M's one by one with a glass of water."

His stories about a guilt-ridden Jewish upbringing are largely fictional. But his onstage neuroses reflect real offstage anxieties. "I feel terrible," he said in 1985. "I don't understand why the doctors never find anything wrong." He keeps in constant touch with a network of therapists throughout the nation "in case of emergencies."

Richard Lewis was born in New York City, New York, in 1947. After earning a marketing degree at Ohio State University, he began to work for a New Jersey ad agency in 1972. In his spare time he wrote jokes for borscht-belt comics, including Morty Gunty.

Lewis in his *I'm in Pain* concert.

Soon Lewis himself was doing stand-up comedy in Greenwich Village.

In 1974 he appeared on *The Tonight Show*, but his style was deemed too frenetic. in 1976 he toured as the opening act for Sonny and Cher and then worked briefly in their TV series; but when he had to dress up as a banana and assorted vegetables, he quit. He then began to concentrate on performing in Los Angeles clubs.

The real breakthrough in Lewis's career resulted from his frequent appearances, beginning in 1982, on the popular TV talk-show series hosted by his good friend David Letterman. In 1987 Lewis had a key role in the prime-time TV sitcom *Harry*, as a hospital orderly who is bent both literally and emotionally; unfortunately for Lewis the series was short-lived. In the movie *The Wrong Guys* (1988) he had a leading role as a neurotic dentist.

In the spring of 1989 he starred as the neurotic journalist Marty Gold in the TV comedy series *Anything but Love*. "I feel guilty about everything," he said in one episode. "I have an extra G chromosome for that." ☆

Independent Mind

"I have a problem caring about things that everybody else does," Richard Lewis admits, "even rock groups and TV shows. I have never seen a *Bonanza* from beginning to end."

MARX BROTHERS
Madcap Comedy Team

The Marx Brothers remain unmatched in the range of their comedic accomplishments. No other team or individual has so well combined nonsense, slapstick, satire, pantomime, black humor, and witty dialogue. At the heart of their comedy was their refusal to be molded by the pompous powers of convention. The boys thumbed their noses at the Establishment (often personified on stage and screen by the stately actress Margaret Dumont, their favorite comic foil). A Marx Brothers performance was a wild conglomeration of pure madcap energy and anarchy.

The Groucho Wit

Groucho had one of the sharpest wits in the history of show business. When he quit the Friars Club, he sent a note: "Please accept my resignation. I don't want to belong to any club that will accept me as a member."

Groucho's Shyness

In real life Groucho Marx was shy, thoughtful, and kindhearted, much in contrast with his smart-alecky fictional character. But his fame as a caustic wit was so great that he felt obligated to live up to his reputation in real life as well. The conflict between his natural shyness and his desire to please others by insulting them often led him to experience great inner stress.

Groucho and Sports

In his early years Groucho was an expert tennis player. Later he became a baseball fan.

The Marx Brothers.

They began in vaudeville, where their ad-lib comical chaos pulverized their audiences. The Marx Brothers reached such heights of hilarity that they were "the one act I could never follow," admitted the great W. C. Fields. Later, on Broadway, they had to stay closer to a script, but they still ad-libbed frequently. Finally, in films, their spontaneity was further diluted, yet they nevertheless recorded the nearest thing to comic anarchy in the history of the screen.

All of the brothers were born in New York City, New York: Chico (originally Leonard) on August 21, 1887; Harpo (originally Adolph, later Arthur) on November 23, 1888; Groucho (originally Julius) on October 2, 1890; and Zeppo (originally Herbert) on February 25, 1901. Another brother, Gummo (originally Milton; born October 23, 1892), left the team in their early years.

Show business was in the family blood. Their maternal grandparents had operated a traveling theatrical troupe in Germany, their grandfather appearing as a magician and their grandmother as a harpist. One of their mother's brothers became Al Shean of the famous American vaudeville comedy team Gallagher and Shean.

Minnie Marx (originally Minna Schoenberg), the boys' mother, was determined that her sons would carry on the family tradition. The older boys left school

Literate Groucho

In his late years Groucho became a cult figure among many film enthusiasts. But his own interests were wide. A literate, articulate man, he corresponded with such notables as T. S. Eliot, James Thurber, and E. B. White. He was also a liberal activist, as in his support of George McGovern for the United States presidency in 1972.

Groucho read voraciously and became a skilled writer. He coauthored (with Norman Krasna) the play *Time for Elizabeth* (1948) and wrote the humorous books *Beds* (1930), a history of sleeping accommodations, and *Many Happy Returns!* (1942), an indictment of the Internal Revenue Service. He also wrote the autobiographical books *Groucho and Me* (1959), *Memoirs of a Mangy Lover* (1963), *The Groucho Letters* (1967), *The Secret Word is Groucho* (with Hector Arce, 1976), and *The Groucho Phile* (1976).

early to pursue separate careers in show business. Chico played the piano in nickelodeons, brothels, and vaudeville theaters. Harpo, whose principal musical instrument was the harp, also played the piano (though he knew only two tunes) in a nickelodeon. Groucho sang with various groups, including Gus Edwards's famous vaudeville kid act.

Then Minnie formed her own group of singers. It went through a couple of changes of membership before settling on Harpo, Groucho, Gummo, and Lou Levy, billed as the Four Nightingales. They toured from 1907 to 1910, and during that time they moved to Chicago, the center of the small-time vaudeville circuits that the group played.

The Four Nightingales remained basically straight singers till one memorable day in Nacogdoches, Texas. While they were performing in an outdoor theater, a mule caused a disturbance nearby. Most of the audience went out to watch the mule. When some of the people straggled back, the boys—furious at being upstaged a mule—hurled insults at the audience (Groucho, for example, quipped, "Nacogdoches is full of roaches"). The audience loved the "jokes" and laughed hysterically. Thus a new phase began for the team.

Soon they developed a comedy schoolroom show called *Fun in Hi Skule,* which they used from 1910 to 1913. At first they were billed as the Three Marx Brothers, and the cast consisted of Harpo, Groucho, Gummo, and several others. Then Chico joined the act, which became the Four Marx Brothers and Company. In 1913 the show evolved into *Mr. Green's Reception,* and in 1914 into *Home Again,* which was written by Al Shean. Later in their vaudeville career they performed other skits as well.

Before 1914 the boys were still known by their original given names (though Adolph had early changed his name to Arthur). During a 1914 poker game in Galesburg, Illinois, they were dubbed with the names by which they would become famous. They and their poker partner, a monologist named Art Fisher, noted how the popular comic-strip character Sherlocko the Monk had spawned such vaudeville names as Nervo, Henpecko, and Tightwado. Fisher applied the same naming system to the Marxes. He called Leonard, known for his success in chasing pretty girls, or chicks, Chicko (the *k* was later accidentally dropped by a typesetter, and the name became Chico, though the first syllable was still pronounced *chick,* not *cheek*). Arthur, the harpist, became Harpo. Julius, the moody one,

(Left to right) Harpo, Chico, and Groucho.

Harpo's Recreations
The mature Harpo led a quiet life. For many years he played golf and croquet till a heart problem forced him to give up those activities. He then spent much time painting in watercolors and casein.

Groucho in the Mikado
A long-standing fan of Gilbert and Sullivan's comic operettas, Groucho particularly enjoyed playing Ko-Ko, the Lord High Executioner, in *The Mikado* on TV in 1960.

The Marx Brothers involve themselves in their usual wild antics as Margaret Dumont looks on.

became Groucho. Milton, who wore gumshoes to help ward off colds, was henceforth Gummo.

During World War I Gummo was drafted into the army. He never returned to the act, choosing instead to become a businessman. His place was taken by the youngest brother, Herbert, who was named Zeppo when he joined the act.

In 1919 the Marx Brothers made it to the prestigious Palace Theater in New York City. Soon they were the biggest attraction in all of vaudeville.

Also in 1919 they performed in their first musical comedy, *The Cinderella Girl,* which lasted only three days in Battle Creek, Michigan. In 1920 or 1921 they made a silent movie, *Humor Risk,* which was so bad that they destroyed it.

But the musical revue *I'll Say She Is!* was a tremendous success. It opened in Philadelphia in the summer of 1923. After touring with the show for a year, they took it to Broadway, where it was also a hit. They followed up with two extremely successful Broadway musical comedies: *The Cocoanuts* (1925) and *Animal Crackers* (1928).

The Marx Brothers gained their greatest fame through movies, beginning with filmed versions of *The Cocoanuts* (1929) and *Animal Crackers* (1930). In the former the boys are involved in the Florida land boom. In *Animal Crackers* they are guests at a party where

Heavenly Harpo

In real life Harpo Marx was much like his fictional character—sweet, gentle, and puckish.

Groucho Marx (top) and Chico Marx (bottom).

Ultraconservative Groucho

Though he thumbed his nose at the Establishment in his movies, Groucho in real life yearned for the security of wealth. He was ultraconservative with money.

thieves covet a valuable oil painting. In one of his most memorable roles, Groucho portrayed Captain Jeffrey Spaulding, a bumbling African explorer.

Those two movies were shot on the East Coast. The Marx Brothers made the rest of their films in Hollywood. In *Monkey Business* (1931) the boys stow away on a ship, crash a party, and reluctantly catch some crooks. *Horse Feathers* (1932) is a spoof of college life, especially football. Groucho, as Professor Quincy Adams Wagstaff, played the newly appointed president of the school. In *Duck Soup* (1933) Groucho was Rufus T. Firefly, president of the mythical land of Freedonia, which wages war on its scheming neighbor Sylvania. A highlight of *Duck Soup* is the mirror scene, in which Harpo, who is being chased by Groucho, accidentally smashes a large mirror and then pretends to be Groucho's mirror image in a series of intricate and hilarious moves.

In the team's first five movies, plots were barely begun before the Marx Brothers began to destroy them by shifting attention to a series of tangential comedy routines showcasing the boys in various combinations.

The principal figure on the screen was Groucho, who wore an ill-fitting frock coat, a carry-over from his days as the schoolmaster in *Fun in Hi Skule* and a parody of the uniform of the society that he mocked. He also had a painted-on mustache, constantly smoked and flicked a cigar, insinuatingly twitched his eyebrows, and uttered savage wisecracks at virtually everyone and everything. Groucho would alternatingly romance and insult his favorite target, the pompous Margaret Dumont, who symbolized all of conventional society. In *Animal Crackers* he addressed her thusly: "You've got beauty, style, money—you've got money, haven't you? If not, we'll stop right now." "They're fighting for your honor," he told her in *Duck Soup,* "which is more than you ever did." In the same film, Dumont said to Groucho, "As chairwoman of the reception committee, I welcome you with open arms." To which Groucho replied, "Is that so? How late do you stay open?"'

Groucho was a master of verbal-humor delivery. He could raise laughter even with material that would fall flat coming from other comedians. For example, in his courtroom defense of Chico in *Duck Soup*, Groucho said, "Chicolini may look like an idiot, and he may act like an idiot, but don't let that fool you—he really *is* an idiot!"

Groucho sang comic songs with a unique nasal twang and outrageous, lovable mockery. He expressed the essence of the Marx Brothers spirit when he sang "(Whatever It Is) I'm against It" in *Horse Feathers.* In *Animal Crackers* he performed the nonsense song "Hello, I Must Be Going" and the self-descriptive "Hooray for Captain Spaulding," which became his theme song for the rest of his career.

Chico's screen humor was largely based on his use of a mock Italian accent and his misuse of the English language. In *The Cocoanuts* he confused *viaduct* and *why a duck.* In *Animal Crackers,* when asked the name of the first piece he was going to play on the piano, he answered quite sincerely, "Number One." In *Monkey Business* he confused *short cut* and *shortcake, vessel* and *whistle,* and *mutinies* and *matinees.* In *Duck Soup* Groucho asked, "Do you have a license [to sell peanuts]?" To which Chico replied, "No, but my dog—he's got millions of 'em." Chico was the "real" world's link with the silent Harpo, whom only Chico could understand. Chico, a fine instinctive pianist, provided the Marx Brothers films with many lighthearted melodious moments at the piano. He applied comedy even to his pianism, as in his technique of "shooting the keys," that is, pointing his index finger like a pistol, using his thumb as a "trigger," and striking a key.

Harpo portrayed a totally uninhibited childlike mute. His stage character became mute when Al Shean's script for *Home Again* accidentally left Harpo with only a few lines. Shean compensated for his oversight by asking Harpo to use pantomime. Thus was created one of the world's most beloved pantomimists.

In Harpo's wide-eyed innocence he gave himself over completely to his instincts, from simple exuberance (as in his wildly stamping and scattering documents at a passport inspection) to lechery (as in his literally chasing women and honking a rubber horn to attract their attention). His brothers frequently played straight men to his zaniness, as when Groucho, in *The Cocoanuts,* fed Harpo flowers and a telephone, and when Chico, in several films, deciphered messages that Harpo conveyed through charades.

Harpo's characteristic props included a fright wig, a bicycle horn, and an overcoat with enormous inside pockets, where he stored all sorts of bizarre objects (including a blowtorch, an ice-cream cone, a cup of coffee, and a ton of hardware). In vaudeville he had used a red wig, but the red showed up too dark on the screen in *The Cocoanuts.* Consequently, from *Animal Crackers* on, he used a blond wig.

In every Marx Brothers show, Harpo pulled a face called a Gookie, in which he puffed out his cheeks and crossed his widened eyes. The look was named after a

Groucho is shot out of a cannon as Harpo covers his ears and Chico makes a point.

Harpo Marx.

Zeppo Marx.

New York City cigar roller named Gookie, who unintentionally made the face as he worked in a cigar store, where Harpo, as a youngster, spotted and copied the expression.

Harpo created many beautiful moments on the screen with his harp playing. He had no formal lessons, and he tuned the instrument eccentrically; yet he became a highly admired harpist, being particularly adept at improvising on popular tunes.

Zeppo played the straight man to Groucho and generally supplied the romantic relief: he got the girl but not the gags. He also sang the romantic ballads.

After *Duck Soup* Zeppo left the team and opened what came to be one of the largest talent agencies in show business. At the same time, Gummo gave up his dress-manufacturing business to become Zeppo's partner, specifically as manager of the three remaining Marx Brothers.

The first five Marx Brothers films, made for Paramount Pictures, were dominated by the boys' comic anarchy at the expense of plot and of production values (such as direction and camera work). Their methods bordered on the surreal and appealed to a rather narrow urban audience.

Then they signed with the executive Irving Thalberg at Metro-Goldwyn-Mayer (MGM). Through his influence their next two films, at MGM, were made with firmer plots, stronger production values, and a broader audience appeal.

In *A Night at the Opera* (1935) the boys pave the way for the happiness of two young opera singers by deflating an unfair opera director and an egotistical tenor. A highlight of the film is the stateroom scene: the three Marx Brothers and a dozen other people are gradually squeezed into a tiny room; when Margaret Dumont opens the door to visit Groucho (as Otia B. Driftwood), the bodies pour out at her feet.

In *A Day at the Races* (1937) the Marx Brothers help a young woman to raise money for her sanatorium by assisting her boyfriend's horse in winning a big race. Groucho played Dr. Hugo Z. Hackenbush, a veterinarian who tries to pass himself off as a people doctor. In one scene, Chico pretends to be a tutti-frutti (in his lingo, "tutsi-frutsi") ice-cream salesman at a racetrack, while actually selling Groucho phony betting aids. In another scene, Harpo pounds a piano till it falls apart, leaving only the inside "harp," which he proceeds to play.

Thalberg died in 1936. His efforts had helped the Marx Brothers to reach the zenith of their career. But with Thalberg gone, their later movies never rose to the same plateau.

In *Room Service* (1938) they are penniless theatrical producers trying to find ways to stay in a hotel till they can find a backer. In *At the Circus* (1939) they save a circus from bankruptcy. Groucho played the shyster lawyer J. Cheever Loophole and sang the delightfully risqué "Lydia, the Tattoed Lady."

In *Go West* (1940) the boys tackle a western villain. The rousing finale is a train chase in which they literally tear their train apart to fuel the wood-burning engine. In *The Big Store* (1941) they save a department store from crooks.

In *A Night in Casablanca* (1946) they rout Nazi refugees in a North African hotel. Their last film as a team was *Love Happy* (1950), in which they search for a stolen diamond necklace. The story was conceived by Harpo, who, for the first time, had the limelight.

All three brothers were in the movie *The Story of Mankind* (1957) but not as a team; each appeared in scenes that did not include the two other brothers. The last time that all three appeared together on a screen was in the TV play "The Incredible Jewel Robbery" (1959) on *General Electric Theater.*

However, in their late years they did remain active in separate careers. In the 1950s Chico and Harpo had a dual act in nightclubs and at county fairs. Chico's solo work included guest-starring in the TV play "Papa Romani" (1950) on *The Bigelow Theater*, hosting the TV variety series *The College Bowl* (1950-51), and playing the piano in numerous engagements. Harpo's solo work included guest-starring in a 1955 episode of the TV comedy series *I Love Lucy,* in which he and Lucy recreated the famous mirror scene from *Duck Soup;* appearing in the dramas "The Red Mill" (1958) and "Silent Panic" (1960) on TV's *The Du Pont Show*; and playing the harp in numerous engagements. He also published his autobiography, *Harpo Speaks!* (with Rowland Barber, 1961). Harpo finally broke his professional silence in January 1963 when he announced his retirement just after giving a stage performance in Pasadena, California.

Groucho's fame continued to grow after the team broke up. He served as the wisecracking host of the quiz show *You Bet Your Life* on both radio (1947-51) and TV (1950-61, for which he grew a real mustache to replace the painted-on one that he had used on the stage and in movies). His quick-witted ad-libs made the show one of the legendary series in the history of television. One woman contestant went on and on

Chico disciplines the bellhop as Groucho looks on.

Chico the Charmer

In real life Chico Marx was an inveterate womanizer and gambler (especially on horse races and card games). He was very successful as the former, less so as the latter.

about how much she loved her husband and her children; finally a wearied Groucho stopped the flood: "I love my cigar, but I take it out of my mouth once in a while."

Groucho soloed in several movies, including *A Girl in Every Port* (1952) and *Skidoo* (1968). He also gave a number of one-night concerts, in which he told jokes, sang songs, and reminisced about himself and his brothers. In 1972 he performed a one-man show at Carnegie Hall in New York City.

He made many TV guest appearances, including some memorable moments on Dick Cavett's talk show. On one program, Groucho remembered a priest who had accosted him and said, "I want to thank you for all the joy you've put into this world." To which Groucho replied, "And I want to thank you for all the joy you've taken out of it."

Chico died in Beverly Hills on October 11, 1961. Harpo died in Los Angeles on September 28, 1964. Groucho died in Los Angeles on August 19, 1977. Gummo died in Palm Springs on April 21, 1977. Zeppo died in Palm Springs on November 30, 1979. ★

Chico's Recreations

Besides playing the piano, Chico could perform on the cornet, the violin, and even the zither. He was an excellent bridge player, a baseball fan, and a golf addict.

JACKIE MASON
Rabbi Turned Comedian

Jackie Mason is the hottest comedian in America today. But his climb to the top was unusually long and hard. For years he was kept out of movies and TV comedy roles by Jewish executives who felt that he sounded "too Jewish" to win a broad-based following. According to Mason, "what they really mean is that I remind them of where they come from, and they don't like that." Many other Jews were sensitive about the Jewish image he presented through his impudent manner and through such jokes as this: "Money is not the most important thing in the world. Love is. Fortunately, I love money." Mason, however, has steadfastly refused to give up the ethnic ambience of his monologues. "To give up your identity plays into the hands of anti-Semitism," he maintains. Furthermore, the difference between Jews and Gentiles are legitimate

fodder for humor: "If there wasn't a difference," he quips, "I wouldn't have an act."

His stature was rising steadily till 1964 when Ed Sullivan publicly (but erroneously) accused the comic of having made an obscene gesture on Sullivan's TV show. Mason's career was severely damaged by that charge, and for the next twenty-two years he labored to gain the respect that he deserved. Finally, in 1986 his one-man Broadway show *The World According to Me!* made him a star.

Mason does not just tell jokes; he creates oral essays couched in intelligence, understanding, and, of course, humor. His social commentary covers such subjects as sex, dating, hookers, money, politics, Israel, psychiatry, TV weathermen, and current events. He also mimics James Cagney, Ted Kennedy, Henry Kissinger, pop singers, and other personalities. His specialty is stories on the stereotyped differences among ethnic groups, including Jews, WASPs, Poles, Chinese, Japanese, Mexicans, Italians, and Puerto Ricans. Put-downs, aimed at himself as well as others, are a staple in his act.

Mason performs with a deadpan, bewildered expression on his face. As he speaks, he emphasizes points by jabbing the air with his right index finger or by using chopping movements with his delicate hands. His delivery is marked by rapid talking, stacca-

What You See Is What You Get

There is no essential difference between Mason's stage persona and his real-life personality. In private, too, he gesticulates constantly, turns statements into questions, and launches nervous, funny, opinionated attacks on any issue that arises.

That Crazy Hair

Before he had his hair "painted" a strange shade of orange, it was dark brown and graying.

Creature Comforts

Mason lives in Manhattan in a luxurious Fifth Avenue apartment containing high-tech telephones and large-screen television sets but almost no furniture or creature comforts. He does not own a car or expensive jewelry.

His one indulgence is clothing, which he buys in abundance, often off the rack. His wardrobe is low-key.

Confesses Egomania

"A normal person wouldn't become a comedian," says Mason. "The egomania, the neurosis, the need to overcompensate, the feeling that life is meaningless without stardom—it's too much suffering."

to articulation, a singsong cadence, and frequently a stress on the final word of a phrase or clause. He speaks with an overtly Jewish inflection, and he often uses Yiddish words.

Mason was born in Sheboygan, Wisconsin, on June 9, 1930 (by the consensus of best estimates, though in his autobiography the date is given as the "fourth year of . . . the 1930s"). His original name was Yacov Moshe Maza.

Yacov grew up on New York City's Lower East Side of Manhattan, to which his family moved when he was five. He came from a long paternal line of rabbis; his three older brothers followed that tradition. At eighteen Yacov became a cantor, and after taking a B.A. degree in psychology at the City College of New York and completing the seminary course at Yeshiva University, he was ordained a rabbi.

As a rabbi in Weldon, North Carolina, and in Pittston, Pennsylvania, he was uncomfortable, but he continued out of deference to his father. Yacov spiced up his services with humor, and after a couple of years he began taking jobs as a comedian in Jewish resorts in the Catskill Mountains, pretending to his father that this work was only a "hiatus."

After his father died in 1957, Yacov Maza became Jackie Mason, full-time comedian. He began on the borscht circuit, bouncing from hotel to hotel. When the summer seasons were over, he tried New York City nightclubs and strip joints, where his clean comedy and Jewish accent consistently flopped.

Feeling guilty about his career change, he sought help in psychoanalysis, an experience that inspired "neurotic" jokes before Woody Allen became famous for them. "When I went to a football game," Mason would say, "every time the players went into a huddle I thought they were talking about me."

He also began to experiment with routines that run listeners through a maze of stream-of-consciousness ironies and incongruities, notably his classic bit on psychiatry: "My analyst said, 'We have to search for the real you.' I said to myself, 'If I don't know who I am, how would I know what I look like? And even if I find the real me, how would I know it's me? . . . Besides, what if I find the real me, and I find that he's even worse that I am? I don't make enough for myself—I need a partner?' " When the psychiatrist asked for $75, "I said to myself, 'This is not the real me. . . . What if I find the real me and he doesn't think it's worth $75? Then I wasted my money for the real him.' . . . I said to the psychiatrist, 'What if you're the real me?

A Unique Personality

Some comedians fear having their jokes stolen. Not Jackie Mason. "The audience is buying our personalities," he says. "They get a kick out of you personally," not so much the jokes themselves.

A Jewish "Athlete"

"Moving your body around for health purposes" is understandable to Mason. But he thinks "torturing yourself" in sports is "stupid" and describes himself as "a Jewish athlete—always busy watching other people jumping and flying." He hated the golfing, swimming, and horseback riding that he had to do in *Caddyshack II.*

Then you owe me $75.' He said, 'If you promise never to come back, we'll call it even.' "

In 1960 Mason's stock rose sharply when his appearances at the Slate Brothers comedy club in Los Angeles led to engagements on Steve Allen's national television show. Soon he was working at top nightclubs, such as Manhattan's Copacabana and Blue Angel, and other TV programs, including those hosted by Perry Como, Garry Moore, and Jack Paar.

One of Mason's most popular routines in the early 1960s was his impersonation of Ed Sullivan, host of the TV show widely regarded as the pinnacle of prime-time exposure. Sullivan invited Mason to appear on *The Ed Sullivan Show* many times. On October 18, 1964, Mason was performing on the show when Sullivan, out of camera range, digitally signaled the amount of time Mason had left. The comic ad-libbed and began pointing too. Sullivan, mistakenly thinking that Mason had flipped the forbidden third finger, made a huge scene backstage and told him, "I'll destroy you in show business." Sullivan canceled Mason's contact and refused to pay him his fee for the night's performance. Later a New York State supreme court judge viewed a kinescope of the show and cleared Mason. Sullivan and Mason reconciled and the comic returned to the show in 1966.

Nevertheless, serious long-range damage had already been done to Mason's career. He was widely seen as a troublemaker, a censored comedian, and a bad representative of the Jewish community.

In 1966 and 1967 a series of events threatened his physical safety. His Las Vegas act included some jokes about Frank Sinatra's relationships with women. After receiving some anonymous threatening telephone calls, he was fired at and narrowly missed by three .22-caliber bullets in his hotel room on November 6, 1966. On February 13, 1967, he was attacked with punches as he sat in his parked car in Miami, Florida.

There soon followed some crucial career reversals. He formed his own production company, JaMa Productions, Inc., and starred in the Broadway play *A Teaspoon Every Four Hours* (1969) and the motion picture *The Stoolie* (1972). Both flopped.

Mason then returned to square one and retraced his original route to popularity. From the mid-1970s to the early 1980s he performed TV guest shots, worked hotels and nightclubs, and even did trade shows. On the screen, he appeared as the gas-station owner in the Steve Martin comedy *The Jerk* (1979) and as Jew #1 in Mel Brooks's *History of the World, Part I* (1981).

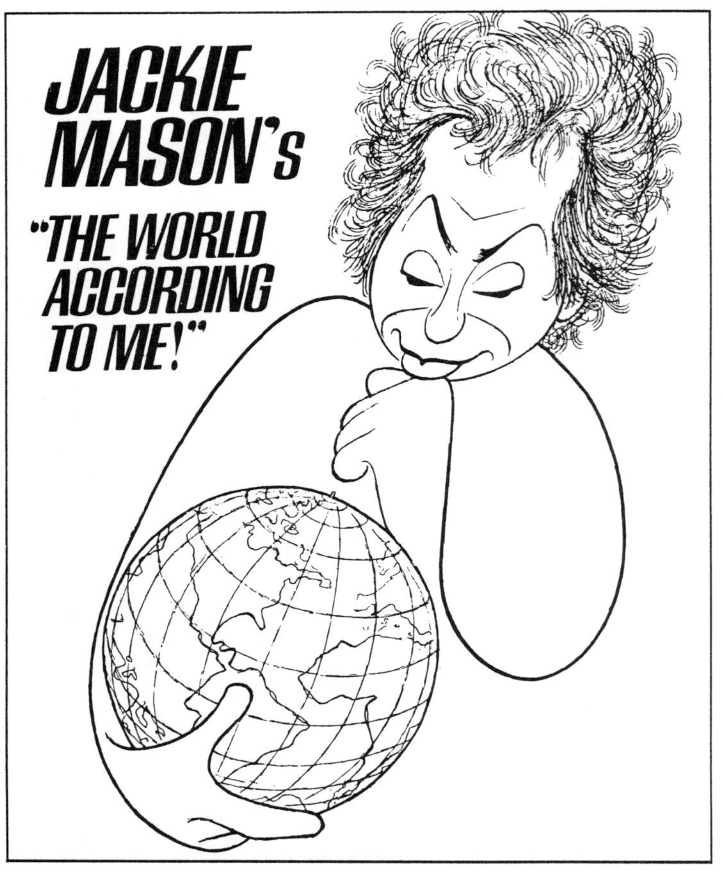

Jackie Mason's one-man show opened on Broadway in December 1986.

The springboard to Mason's current wave of success was his one-man show *The World According to Me!* After running for six months in southern California theaters (first in Hollywood, then in Beverly Hills), the show opened on Broadway in December 1986.

"I should have been a doctor," Mason says in his act. "In what other profession can a man tell a woman to take off her clothes and send the bill to her husband?" One of his favorite political targets is Richard Nixon: "People say I shouldn't pick on Nixon. He's got phlebitis. I say it's syphilis. You can't screw 200 million people and wind up with phlebitis." He has brought the house down with an eight-minute impression of President Ronald Reagan trying to explain his lack of complicity in the Iran-Contra covert-operations scam then under congressional investigation: "They say it was going on in my own basement. Why should I go to the basement? I'm the president. . . . "

Mason's act is loaded with jokes based on ethnic stereotypes. "My best friend is half-Italian, half-Jewish. If he can't buy it wholesale, he steals it." "I love the Puerto Ricans. I go to Puerto Rico all the time. I like to visit my hubcaps." "Every Jew loves food. What do you think Jews talk about for breakfast? Where to eat lunch. At lunch, where should we have dinner? Dinner, where should we have coffee? . . . The only people who never had a cockroach are white Protestant American Gentiles. There's no food in the house. After all, how much can a cockroach drink? . . . You never see a Jew in a bar, except if he gets lost looking for a piece of cake." "If a Gentile has a boat, he's out on excursions. There's no bigger schnook in the world than a Jew with a boat. All he wants is to show it to you. I know five thousand Jews with boats. I never saw one move yet."

The success of Mason's one-man Broadway show has brought him many other lucrative projects. He has come out with book, record-album, and cable-TV versions of the show. In 1987 he made a popular Honda TV commercial. He starred in the movie *Caddyshack II* (1988). In the summer of 1988 he reopened in his Broadway show after a hiatus for making the movie. And in the fall of 1988 he issued his autobiographical book *Jackie Oy! Jackie Mason from Birth to Rebirth* (with Ken Gross). ☆

On Building Jokes

"All my comedy is social and psychological commentary." Mason says. He wants to help people see through "the restriction of conventionality." His mission is rooted in the Talmud. "The Talmud is the study of logic," he explains. "Every time I see a contradiction or hypocrisy in somebody's behavior, I think of the Talmud and build the joke from there."

Mason's Metamorphosis

"The Jewish people took me for granted," Mason contends. "The young people saw me as an anachronism. Then I went to Broadway, where I *never* thought I'd succeed. For the longest time I'm considered some bum from the mountains by the same people who think I'm an art form now."

Loves Biographies

In his spare time Jackie Mason reads the life stories of such notables as Teddy Roosevelt and Gertrude Stein. "I like studying personalities and figuring out what drives people," he says.

BETTE MIDLER
Queen of Camp

Bette Midler, the self-styled Divine Miss M, rose to fame through her lively, sometimes bizarre, song-and-comedy stage shows. She used vulgar language profusely, wore odd or out-of-date clothing, appeared as a giant hot dog and as a female King Kong, and used such props as wheelchairs and mermaid tails. Breasts were one of her favorite topics; once she said that she had weighed her own breasts on a mail scale: "I won't tell you how much they weigh, but it cost $87.50 to send them to Brazil." She frequently boasted at being "the last of the truly tacky women" who do "trash with flash and sleaze with ease." Observers soon dubbed her the Queen of Camp.

Yet this "truly tacky woman" has recently proven herself to be capable of handling fully developed comedy roles. Her performances in *Down and Out in Beverly Hills* (1986), *Ruthless People* (1986), *Outrage-*

Bette in *Ruthless People.*

ous Fortune (1987), and *Big Business* (1988) have firmly established her as an outstanding film comedienne.

She was born in Honolulu, Hawaii, on December 1, 1945, not long after her parents had arrived from New Jersey. Her mother named the girl after the actress Bette Davis; but Mrs. Midler mistakenly thought that Davis pronounced her first name as "Bet" (instead of the correct "Bet-te"). Thus, Bette Midler's given name has always been pronounced "Bet."

As a youth she appeared in many school and community productions, and she dreamed of becoming a professional actress. While attending the University of Hawaii for one year, she studied drama.

In 1965 Midler got a bit part (as the seasick wife of a missionary) in the movie *Hawaii* (1966), which was being filmed on location. When the movie company traveled to Los Angeles to finish filming, she went with it.

After the movie was completed, she moved to New York City to begin a stage career. In 1966 she landed a job in the chorus of the hit Broadway musical *Fiddler on the Roof.* The following February she was promoted to the role of Tzeitel, one of the leading parts. She remained with *Fiddler* for three years.

Midler then decided to concentrate on a singing career. After having some minor engagements in Greenwich Village, she got her big break in 1970 when she was hired as a singer at the Continental Baths, a New York City Turkish bath for male homosexuals. There she sang songs from the 1930s-50s, often imitating the styles of the artists most closely identified with the tunes. To evoke the aura of those earlier years, she wore gold lamé gowns, garter belts, toreador pants, and platform shoes.

Her work at the Continental Baths led to request for her to appear on the David Frost and Johnny Carson TV shows. Soon she was in demand at leading nightclubs and theaters across the country.

Throughout the 1970s and early 1980s Midler combined song and comedy in her stage appearances. In 1979 she starred in the bawdy one-woman Broadway show *Divine Madness,* a performance that she recreated on film in 1980. She also issued albums, including *The Divine Miss M* (1972) and *No Frills* (1983).

Midler never abandoned her original ambition to be an actress. She appeared in the minor film *The Divine Mr. J.* (1974), a religious satire. In *The Rose* (1979) she starred as a hard-living, ill-fated rock singer.

Comedy, however, was her true calling. She appeared in the 1982 film comedy *Jinxed,* but friction with

Confession

"I wish I hadn't been so mean to some people in my name-calling days," Midler confessed in the mid-1980s, "and I wish I had been a better friend."

Favorite Comedian

Midler has a special admiration for Richard Pryor because he uses comedy to move people socially.

Avid Reader

Midler likes to read books on art and the theater, especially "stuff that has gone on before—circus acts, bubble dances, fan dancers."

Painful Childhood

"I was an ugly, fat little Jewish girl with problems," Midler has said. Performing helped to build her self-esteem.

Midler in *Jinxed.*

Bette Midler is the Divine Miss M.

others involved in the production soured her on an immediate return to movies.

In August 1983, while touring with her act *De Tour*, she fainted from overwork. When she recovered, she stated that she was ready to switch to a full-time comedy career, which she felt would be less exhausting than her music shows had been.

Soon she issued her first all-comedy album, *Mud WILL Be Flung Tonight!* (recorded live at a Los Angeles club in 1985). In it she hurled insults at celebrities, such as Madonna and Bruce Springsteen. She also defended her breast obsession: "Do they dump on the pope 'cause all he ever talks about is God?"

Midler returned to films in a series of comedies, beginning with *Down and Out in Beverly Hills* (1986), costarring with Richard Dreyfuss as a nouveau-riche couple who take in a transient in an effort to learn the meaning of life; in her performance, Midler parodies shallow, trendy women. In *Ruthless People* (1986) Midler played a screechy Bel Air heiress who is so overbearing that her kidnappers keep marking down the ransom money demanded from her husband, who does not want her back at any price. In *Outrageous Fortune* (1987) she played a brassy, vulgar, street-smart con artist. Midler gave a hilarious performance as a set

Old-fashioned Values

After many years of freewheeling single life, Midler, at the age of thirty-nine, married Martin von Haselberg (alias Harry Kipper) in 1984. Later she had a baby. Sophie.

"We're both old-fashioned," Midler says of herself and her husband. "In your young life, you rebel against values you think are square. After a while, you realize they are good values and there's a reason they've been around for thousands of years."

"Housefrau"

Since the birth of her daughter, Sophie, in November 1986, Midler has shifted the center of her life to her child. The belated mom sings and performs hula dances for the little one.

Midler also watches out for germs. "When I'm not working, I'm a real hausfrau," she declares. "I wash the floors; I wash the dishes; I wash *everything.* I'm insane about cleaning—absolutely obsessive."

of identical twins in the switched-body plot of *Big Business* (1988). In Disney's animated feature *Oliver and Company* (1988) she supplied the voice of the "world's most conceited pooch." In *Beaches* (1988) Midler expanded her range into a multidimensional role as a Bronx-bred Jew who blends comedy and pathos, egotism and vulnerability; while strutting her show-biz success, she realizes that she will never attain true personal happiness.

Through those six films, Midler has completely realized her childhood ambition to become a full-fledged movie star. And she may already have insured herself a niche in film history as one of the screen's greatest comediennes. ★

Public and Private Midler

In private life Midler is calm and gentle. But sometimes her onstage personality becomes so wild that she mentally stands aside and asks herself, "Who *is* that person?"

Simple Living

Midler lives unpretentiously. She spends much of her time in her house, which is full of gentle pastel colors and is decorated with flowers from her own garden. Midler and her husband like to cook and to visit art galleries together. Occasionally she joins friends for an afternoon to shop or to watch a movie.

RON MOODY
Fagin

Ron Moody, one of the world's greatest character comedians, has played a vast array of fantastic personalities on the stage, in films, and on television. His most notable characteristics are his lopsided face, his rubbery walk, and his nervous inquisitiveness. But he can mold himself into almost any kind of character, often with the aid of disguises and/or period costumes. His most famous role, which he has played on both stage and screen,is that of the thief Fagin in the musical *Oliver!*

Moody was born in Hornsey, London, England, on January 8, 1924. His original name was Ronald Moodnick.

Son of a master plasterer at Elstree Studios, Moody started working there as a wages clerk at the age of sixteen. He sneaked glimpses of Alastair Sim and other comic actors making movies, though at that time Moody had no thought of becoming an entertainer.

Later he spent four years in the Royal Air Force, where his duties as a current-affairs instructor led him to an interest in George Bernard Shaw's theories of socialism. Returning to civilian life, Moody began to study sociology at the London School of Economics, where he earned a B.S. degree in 1950.

But soon he also developed an interest in the

Moody in *Nobody's Perfect.*

Ron Moody (second from right) with Margaret Rutherford in *The Mouse on the Moon*.

theater. For a while his life was sociology by day and comedy sketches in theater clubs by night.

Eventually the theater won, and he spent several years performing in London revues, including *Intimacy at Eight* (1952), *For Amusement Only* (1956), and *For Adults Only* (1958). In 1959 he played the Governor of Buenos Aires in Voltaire's satire *Candide*. He made his film debut in *Davy* (1953), and he also had a small part in *Follow a Star* (1959).

His big break came when he was offered the part of the Jew Fagin, a crafty old thief who trains homeless boys to be pickpockets, in Lionel Bart's stage musical *Oliver!*, an adaptation of the Charles Dickens novel *Oliver Twist*. At first the role did not appeal to him. But then he saw a screening of the 1948 movie *Oliver Twist*, featuring Alec Guinness as Fagin. "I found [Guinness's interpretation] to be so anti-Semitic as to be unbearable," Moody later explained. "But Bart is as Jewish as I am, and we both felt an obligation to get Fagin away from a viciously racial stereotype and instead make him what he really is—a crazy old Father Christmas gone wrong." After he got into the role, Moody discovered that "there was something remarkable there: like Rasputin and Svengali, Fagin is a mesmeric figure."

Oliver! opened in London in 1960. He left the original run after one year to set up his own musical

Prefers Film Work

Partly because of his teenage experience on the sets of Elstree Studios, Moody developed a lifelong love of moviemaking. "Films still fascinate me more than anything else: concentration, pacing—it's all there."

Fagin Role

In December 1983, explaining why he was returning to his role of Fagin in *Oliver!* twenty-three years after the original production, Moody said, "I'm a lonely man. I never married, have no children. This seemed a great way to spend Christmas."

Favorite Roles

Moody's favorite roles include Pierrot (a mime) in the revue *For Adults Only* (1958), the Governor of Buenos Aires in *Candide* (1959), and Fagin in *Oliver!* (stage, 1960, 1983, 1984; film, 1968).

Not Motivated by Money and Fame

Moody lives modestly. He has turned down big money many times when scripts have failed to satisfy him. But "I don't have a mortgage or children to worry about," he says, "so I don't at all mind being left alone to get on with another novel for a year or so."

He admits that his career has not gone as well as it should have after reaching the heights of *Oliver!* But "I was never really intending to have a career in the professional theater in the first place. Considering that I set out to be a sociologist, I think I've really done quite well."

Straight Actor

"I think I'm a straight actor who occasionally does musicals," Moody observes. "Most people think I'm an eccentric comedian."

Moody as Novelist

When not acting, Moody writes intelligent, unusual novels, such as *Very, Very Slightly Imperfect* (1983).

Ron Moody in *The Twelve Chairs.*

Moody in *Dogpound Shuffle.*

(as book author, lyricist, composer, and star) about the famous clown Joseph Grimaldi; the show, entitled *Joey* (1962) failed. Moody reprised his Fagin role in the filmed version of *Oliver!* (1968).

His other stage work included *Peter Pan* (1966), as both Mr. Darling and Captain Hook; *Hamlet* (1971), as Polonius and the First Gravedigger; and, in the title role, *Richard III* (1978).

Moody's early films included the farce *A Pair of Briefs* (1962), as a cockney; the comedy *The Mouse on the Moon* (1963), as the prime minister of a mythical duchy; and the Dickens drama *David Copperfield* (1969), as the fawning clerk Uriah Heep. In Mel Brooks's comedy *The Twelve Chairs* (1970) Moody starred as a former member of the privileged class trying to find a treasure in early Communist Russia. In the Disney fantasy *The Spaceman and King Arthur* (1979) he played Merlin the Magician.

Moody's British TV work included the series *Moody in Storeland* (1961) and *Moody* (1968). In the American TV sitcom *Nobody's Perfect* (1980, aired in England as *Hart of the Yard*), he starred as Roger Hart, an urbane but klutzy Scotland Yard sleuth on loan to the San Francisco Police Department.

In late 1983 Moody starred in a London revival of *Oliver!* In early 1984 he headed a short-lived Broadway production of the musical. ☆

ZERO MOSTEL
Master of Slapstick and Subtlety

Zero Mostel possessed an unusually wide spectrum of comedic talents. He was a huge clown, yet he moved with balletic grace and Chaplinesque physical control. As a stand-up comedian, he mixed low comedy with subtle social and human observations. In his stage and screen roles, he proved himself to be a master of pure slapstick, yet could also act with insightful sensitivity.

Among his stand-up comedy routines was an impression of Charles Boyer: "Let me run through your hair, Hedy—barefoot." In another he gave a lecture as a nutty professor of ornithology; the punch line, delivered with a mad leer, was "Birds mate, you know!" Mostel also adopted the persona of a shy schoolteacher who had to give a sex lecture. Satirizing a senator making a speech on the Japanese bombing of Pearl Harbor, Mostel gave this brilliant concluding line to his blustering politician: "What the hell was Hawaii doing in the Pacific?"

In the stage (1962) and screen (1966) versions of the musical comedy *A Funny Thing Happened on the Way to the Forum,* he played Pseudolus, an ancient Roman slave conniving to gain his freedom. Mostel imbued the part with frenetic slapstick, including the traditional comic techniques of funny faces, double takes, and collapsing double-jointed knees. On the other hand, in the original Broadway production of the musical *Fiddler on the Roof* (1964), he gave subtle and sensitive humor to his role of Tevye, the poor Jewish milkman trying to marry off his daughters and to uphold tradition. And in the stage (1961) and screen (1974) versions of *Rhinoceros,* his transformation of a clerk into a wild animal was described by one critic as "sidesplitting and terrifying."

Mostel was born in New York City, New York, on February 28, 1915. His original name was Samuel Joel Mostel, an anglicization of his Hebrew name, Simcha Yoel Mostel.

He majored in art at the City College of the City University of New York (B.A., 1935). After graduating he

Zero Mostel played Leopold Bloom in *Ulysses in Nighttown.*

Art Collector

Peruvian textiles, Coptic art, and pre-Colombian figures were among the many kinds of works that Mostel collected.

He also liked to examine art works at museums. When he spent five months in London to appear in *Ulysses in Nighttown,* he went almost daily to the National Gallery.

Zero Mostel in ***A Funny Thing Happened on the Way to the Forum.***

traveled and worked at odd jobs. During that time he developed a strong interest in social causes.

Later he was hired by the federal Work Projects Administration (WPA) to teach drawing and painting in New York City. Mostel, however, was a natural-born zany, and his lectures soon turned into hilarious routines. When word spread about his lectures, he began to get calls to entertain at various local functions, where he would pick up extra money to help support his painting ambitions.

His first formal engagement as a professional comedian was at a nightclub called Café Society Downtown, where he debuted early in 1942. The club's press agent gave Mostel the name Zero, hoping to make people say, "Here's a man who's made something of nothing."

Within the next few months Mostel appeared on the radio series *The Chamber Music Society of Lower Basin Street*; made his Broadway debut, in *Keep 'Em Laughing;* and went to Hollywood to make his first movie, *Du Barry Was a Lady* (1943). But his work in the movie consisted only of a few of his nightclub routines, and he soon returned to New York City.

Mostel was then drafted into the army. After six months he developed an ulcer and was discharged.

In the late 1940s and early 1950s, Mostel's career moved slowly. He appeared in several movies, often as a villain, as in *Panic in the Streets* (1950) and *The*

Intellectual Comedian

Widely regarded as one of the theater's leading intellectuals, Mostel was invited to lecture at Harvard in 1962. He spoke of comedy as "a unifying force . . . clearly social in its meaning. . . . Comedy is rebellion against falsehood, . . . against all evil masquerading as true and good and worthy of respect."

Favorite Comedians

Among Mostel's favorite comedians were two with European music-hall origins: Charlie Chaplin (England) and Raimu (France). Mostel also admired W.C. Fields, whose American vaudeville background corresponded with Chaplin's and Raimu's music-hall experiences.

Gifted Artist

"Painting is a much more creative field than acting," Mostel claimed. "You take up an empty canvas; you fill it. In acting, you've got something to start with."

He continued to paint throughout his life, often working on several canvases at the same time. A gifted artist, he produced many works that were well received by art critics.

Offstage Antics

Mostel was an unpredictable character. He once shaved his good friend Sam Jaffe (the great actor) in a deluxe restaurant, using as shaving cream the whipped cream off Jaffe's strawberry shortcake. On another occasion he boarded a train, pretended to be blind, and groped his way through the aisles while randomly slapping people.

Enforcer (1951). But then the McCarthy-era blacklisting kept him out films because of his earlier involvement with progressive social causes.

He continued, however, to appear onstage, notably as Leopold Bloom in *Ulysses in Nighttown* (1958). Finally, in 1961, Mostel reached stardom when he played John in the stage production of *Rhinoceros.* That was followed by his memorable stage performance as Pseudolus in *A Funny Thing Happened on the Way to the Forum* (1962). He reached the peak of his career when he starred as Tevye in the original Broadway production of *Fiddler on the Roof* (1964); he repeated the role in several revivals in later years.

Mostel then turned his attention once again to movies, blacklisting having lost its effectiveness. He began with a filmed version of *A Funny Thing Happened on the Way to the Forum* (1966). In *The Producers* (1967) he played Max Bialystock, a seedy Broadway producer who devises an elaborate (but unsuccessful) scheme to cheat his backers out of their money. Later films included *The Great Bank Robbery* (1969), *The Hot Rock* (1972), and *Rhinoceros* (1974). He gave a fine performance in the *The Front* (1976), a re-creation of the 1950s witch-hunting for Communists, through which he had suffered in real life.

Mostel spent the first half of 1977 touring major American cities in *Fiddler on the Roof.* In September of that year he was in Philadelphia to try out the new play *The Merchant.* He deeply believed in the play because it addressed some important aspects of anti-Semitism. While he was in Philadelphia he suddenly died of a burst aorta on September 8, 1977. ★

Mostel as Tevye in *Fiddler on the Roof.*

JAN MURRAY
Game-Show Host

Jan Murray won his greatest fame as host of many TV game shows. But he is also an excellent nightclub comedian. In fact, it was his nightclub audience-participation routines that honed his skills in the light repartee characteristic of his work on TV shows.

He was born in New York City, New York, on October 4, 1917. His original name was Murray Janofsky.

High-School Dropout

Murray regretted having dropped out of school. He finally went back and earned his diploma in his forties.

Later he joked, "How old am I? How old could I be? I just finished high school in 1962!"

Man of Integrity

During the TV game-show scandals of the late 1950s, Murray's integrity was never in question, even after two employees of his *Treasure Hunt* had to be fired for misconduct (taking money to let contestants on the show). Once the program itself was cleared, it was canceled at Murray's own request.

A youthful Murray.

His Show-Biz Idol

Jan Murray's show-biz idol, Al Jolson, once told him to "fight for money and for billing. But before you lose the job, lose the fight. Nobody ever improved by laying off in a hotel room."

Murray still adheres to the spirit of that advice by working constantly, even in mosques, wrestling arenas, skating rinks, and high-school auditoriums.

A Favorite Joke

Murray likes to tell the story about a man jogging naked in front of the comedian's house. "I ask him, 'Why are you jogging naked in front of my house?' He asks me, 'Why did you come home so early?' "

Jan Murray (left) guest-starring on *The Practice*, the 1976 Danny Thomas TV series.

As a youth he learned the therapeutic value of comedy when his mother became very ill and he used to entertain her to make her laugh. He quit high school to work on the borscht belt.

Murray soon began to draw the audience into his act. In one routine he asked a customer to order chicken soup and then to change his mind. Murray, playing a waiter, then approached the man and announced, "We have two kinds of soup: chicken and pea." "I'll take the chicken soup," the customer ordered. "OK," Murray confirmed, "one chicken soup coming up." "Wait—I've changed my mind," the customer dutifully added. "I'll have the pea soup." Murray, to the offstage cook, shouted, "Hold the chicken—and make it pea!"

He continued his interplay, including much ad-libbing, with strangers during the 1950s and 1960s as host of innumerable TV game shows. Those programs included *Sing It Again* (1951), *Blind Date* (1953), *Dollar a Second* (1953-57), *Treasure Hunt* (1956-59), *The Jan Murray Show* (or *Charge Account*, 1960-62), and *Chain Letter* (1966).

Since then Murray has appeared as a guest on TV variety shows, and he is still going strong in nightclubs and casinos. He does not like the current comedy trend toward jokes on drugs and sex; and he prefers to put down himself rather than politicians, ethnic groups, and other categories of people. His staple topics, besides himself, are wives, airplanes, gambling, current news events, and other traditional fodder.

"Russia needs our wheat," begins one bit based on a topical news story. "After all, you can't expect them to invade a country on an empty stomach." Here is a wife story in which Murray himself is the target: "Sorry I'm late. That stupid wife of mine. She didn't shovel the snow from the driveway this morning. She also forgot to put on the snow tires. And halfway to New York I realized she hadn't dressed me."

Murray has acted in several movies. He made a fine dramatic impression in *Who Killed Teddy Bear?* (1965). His comedies included *The Busy Body* (1967) and *History of the World, Part I* (1981).

In 1988 Murray hosted a televised fund-raiser for the Chabad House drug-rehabilitation program. ☆

Matchbook Collector

Murray has collected matchbook covers from the many places where he has visited or entertained. He has spent much time cataloging the covers and filing them neatly into albums.

MIKE NICHOLS *and* ELAINE MAY
Improvisational Duo

Mike Nichols and Elaine May, in their prepared and improvised sketches, created humor by acting out characters. The duo was less concerned with telling jokes than with exposing the emotions and motives behind their characters' behavior. In the process of making those expositions, the team arrived at moments of deep, sometimes painful, seriocomic truth.

Mike Nichols was born in Berlin, Germany, on November 6, 1931. His original name was Michael Igor Peschkowsky. His grandmother Hedwig Lachmann

Hates Publicity

When she and Nichols were at the peak of their duo career, May hated publicity. To confound the media, she would give false information about herself. She told one columnist that her measurements were "24-35-127½."

Brief Reunions

In 1980 Nichols and May reunited to star together in stage a production of the explosive drama *Who's Afraid of Virginia Woolf?* And in 1985 they appeared in a Broadway fund-raiser for AIDS research.

Nichols and May were masters of improvisational comedy.

provided Richard Strauss with the German libretto for the opera *Salome*. His grandfather Gustav Landauer was leader of the German Social Democratic party and one of the earliest victims of the Nazi drive to exterminate the Jews. Nichols's father, Dr. Paul Peschkowsky, fled the Nazis and migrated to New York City.

After two years as a premedical student at the University of Chicago, Nichols studied acting under Lee Strasberg at the Actors Studio in New York City. He then returned to Chicago.

Elaine May was born in Philadelphia, Pennsylvania, on April 21, 1932. Her original name was Elaine Berlin. She was associated with the theater from her earliest days, her father, Jack Berlin, being a Yiddish stage actor. As a teenager she married and divorced Marvin May, whose surname she kept for professional use. She learned the Stanislavsky method of acting from the famed actress Maria Ouspenskaya. While in Chicago, May met Mike Nichols.

They both joined a group of improvisational players at the Compass, a Chicago nitery. After three years Nichols and May decide to form a duo.

In 1957 they reached New York City, where they played in cabarets and nightclubs. Some of their sketches were planned (though never written out, and others were suggested by audience members, who would provide two lines (which became the first and

Omnivorous Reader

Nichols reads everything from *Dog World* to contemporary fiction.

A Career Is Not Life

"When we are actually working, actually performing, I love it," Nichols said when he and May were at the height of their team success. "But in between, when there are all the meetings, the lawyers and producers, I don't know. It isn't that we don't realize that all of this stuff is necessary. Of course it is. It's just that if you're not careful, all you've got is a career—and no life."

last lines of the playlet) and the name of any author whose style the performers would imitate. Soon Nichols and May were in great demand on TV as well, appearing on the Steve Allen, Perry Como, Jack Paar, and Dinah Shore shows. From October 1960 to July 1961 they performed on Broadway in a show entitled *An Evening with Mike Nichols and Elaine May.*

One of their best-known routines was "Mother and Son," in which a manipulative mother forces guilt onto her adult son till he regresses into childhood. The son has failed to call home. "I sat by that phone all day Friday, all day Saturday, and all day Sunday," the mother wails. "Your father said to me, 'Phyllis, eat something; you'll faint.' I said, 'No, Harry, no, I don't want my mouth to be full when my son calls me.' " The mother claims that the nervous strain has made her ill; she will go to the hospital, where, she whines, "they'll X-ray my nerves." The son tries to defend himself. His mother stops him: "Someday, someday, Arthur, you'll get married and you'll have children of your own, and, honey, when you do, I only pray that they make you suffer! That's a mother's prayer. . . . I hope I didn't make you feel bad." "Are you kidding? I feel awful?" the son admits. "Oh, honey," exclaims the mother, "if I could believe that, I'd be the happiest mother in the world!"

Influencing People

"It's odd to think that you are going to impose or inflict something you have in your head on a large number of people," May observes, "and get paid for it, too!"

Country Squire

Mike Nichols lives in a spacious art-filled Connecticut farmhouse surrounded by sixty acres of farmland, a private lake, and stables for over ninety Arabian horses. He auctioned off thirty-one horses for $913,000.

Mike Nichols.

Elaine May.

She pleads with him to call: "Please, baby...." The son's voice becomes childlike and he says, "I promise. I love you, mommy." "Goodbye, baby." "Goodbye, mommy."

Other routines satirized quiz shows, funeral homes, telephone companies, political ghost writers, and show-business insincerity. In the depth of their characterizations and in the rawness of the nerves that they touched, Nichols and May broke new ground for later show-business satirists.

In 1962 the duo split up so that they could pursue careers suitable for their individual talents, Nichols's strength being direction and May's being invention. Nichols went on to become a major stage and film director. His stage credits include the original Broadway productions of *Barefoot in the Park* (1963) and *The Odd Couple* (1965). Among his films are *Who's Afraid of Virginia Woolf?* (1966), *The Graduate* (1967), and *Silkwood* (1983). May has worked as a writer, a director, and an actress for stage and screen. She performed all three functions for the film *A New Leaf* (1971), she scripted the popular movie *Tootsie* (1982), and she wrote and directed *Ishtar* (1987).★

Contrary Character

In the Nichols-May routines, she usually had the role with the hard edge to it. In real life, too, "I feel in opposition to almost everything," she once admitted. May has likened her works to those of the eighteenth-century writer Jonathan Swift, whose savage satire ridicules human pretensions and reveals the unthinking, self-indulgent basis of human behavior.

MOLLY PICON
Yiddish Variety Star

Molly Picon was the preeminent performer to emerge from the Yiddish variety theater. Her large eyes resembled Eddie Cantor's, her mime compared with Harpo Marx's, and her comic manner recalled Fanny Brice's. But Picon was Picon. The diminutive (five-foot-tall) star had a special versatility and dramatic-comedic depth (she has been called the Yiddish Helen Hayes). She acted in humorous sketches; wrote and sang songs, such as "A Day in the Life of a New York Woiking Goil"; and constantly surprised her audiences with new stunts and acrobatics, such as tap-dancing, roller-skating, entering on a horse, playing musical instruments, and performing dangerous feats while swinging from a rope. One of her trademarks was somersaulting, which she con-

Love of Audiences

"How can I tell you how much your love for me has gladdened my heart through a wonderful life?" Picon wrote at the end of her autobiography. "All I hope is that I have gladdened your hearts too, and brightened your lives as you have mine."

Athletic Performer

A performer is like an athlete, according to Picon. She had to watch her diet, exercise regularly, and limber up before every concert.

Benefits for Israel

Molly made many trips to Israel and raised huge sums of money for the nation through her benefit concerts.

tinued to do onstage till she was in her sixties. Picon not only headlined in the Yiddish theater, she also scored major success in the gentile worlds of vaudeville, Broadway, nightclubs, and motion pictures.

Molly Picon was born in New York City, New York, on June 1, 1898. When she was about three years old, she moved with her parents to Philadelphia.

At the age of five, billed as Baby Margaret, she began to win money for her singing and dancing at amateur contests. In 1904 she joined Michael Thomshefsky's Yiddish repertory company in Philadelphia, where she played juvenile roles for the next three years. Later she appeared in plays at the Arch Street theater (1908-1912) and then performed in cabaret (1912-15). She left high school after her second year so that she would have time to earn more money on the stage.

During 1918-19 she toured in a vaudeville act called *The Four Seasons.* that work took her to Boston, where she was hired in 1919 by Jacob Kalich, head of a Yiddish repertory company. Later that year she and Kalich, whom she nicknamed Yonkel, were married.

Picon rapidly became a major Yiddish star, especially in comic roles. She performed with her husband's troupe at the Boston Grand Opera House (1919-20) and then toured with the company in Europe (1920-22). Returning to the United States,

A Favorite Story

To help bring her autobiography, *Molly!* (with Jean Bergantini Grillo, 1980), to a close, Picon recounted this Jewish joke: "An old couple came to a rabbi for a divorce. They had been married for sixty-five years. The rabbi, astounded, asked the wife, 'Why, after sixty-five years, would you want a divorce?' And the old lady answered, 'Because enough is enough!' "

Her Teacher Yonkel

When Molly married Jacob ("Yonkel") Kalich in 1919, she was largely ignorant of Jewish culture. Yonkel, a highly literate man, taught her.

He also became the principal force in her career. An experienced writer, producer, and director, he guided her into the world of Yiddish theater and gave her the confidence—and the material—to succeed. "Yonkel started to groom me for stardom," Molly later said of their early days together.

Dog Lover

Molly and Yonkel had one dog, King, for eight years. Another dog, a collie, entered their home as a pup and became something special: "Prince grew old along with us."

Foster Parent

A pelvic problem prevented Molly from ever having children of her own, but she and Yonkel took many youngsters into their home as part of the Foster Parents' Plan for War Children.

she settled in New York City and appeared in such shows as *Yankele* (1923), *Shmendrik* (1924), *Rabbi's Melody* (1926), and *Hello, Molly!* (1928). With her husband she toured Europe, the Near East, South Africa, and Argentina in the early 1930s. She then returned to work in New York City.

With the decline of the Yiddish theater, Picon turned increasingly to Broadway, where she debuted as Becky Felderman in *Morning Star* (1940). In 1942 her husband's play *Oy is dus a leben* ("Oh, What a Life") became the first Yiddish work produced on Broadway. In that show Picon created her famous characterization of Shmendrick (whose name, also spelled Shmendrik, is traditional for a fool in Yiddish literature).

Perhaps the highlight of her stage career came with her role as Clara Weiss, an American looking for a husband in Israel, in the musical *Milk and Honey.* She starred in the play on Broadway in 1961-62 and then toured the United States with the show in 1963-64. Picon also received plaudits for her performances in *A Majority of One* (1960, 1965, 1966), as the Jewish widow Mrs. Jacoby, who finds companionship with a Japanese man. Later she appeared in the revue *How to Be a Jewish Mother* (1967); played Dolly Levi in *Hello, Dolly!* (1971); and gave a one-woman show in Yiddish, *Hello, Molly!* (1979).

Picon's film career began with two Yiddish musical-comedy pictures made in Poland: *Yiddle mit'n fiddle* (1936, released in America in 1937 with English subtitles as *Yiddle with His Fiddle*) and *Mamale* (1938, released in America in 1938 with English subtitles as *Little Mother*). Her first English-language movie was the comedy *Come Blow Your Horn* (1963), in which she played the Jewish mother of two fast-living sons. In the filmed version of the Jewish musical *Fiddler on the Roof* (1971) she played Yente the matchmaker. In *For Pete's Sake* (1974) she was a motherly madam. She also appeared in *Cannonball Run II* (1984).

In March 1985 she received one of the first ten Goldie Awards ever presented by the Congress for Jewish Culture (the awards are so named because they are statuettes of Abraham Goldfaden, father of the modern Yiddish theater). The honor was bestowed on Picon for her lifetime of contributions to the Jewish performing arts. ☆

Picon as Yenta the Matchmaker in *Fiddler on the Roof.*

Oasis in the Country

For nearly thirty years Molly and her husband, Yonkel, lived in a colonial-style country house in Mahopac, New York. She called it her "oasis," where she would retreat and refresh herself after each venture into the hectic world of show business.

Most of her earnings went into improvements for her home, which she and Yonkel called Chez Shmendrik. Molly particularly enjoyed their steambath and their swimming pool, where she often skinny-dipped.

Chez Shmendrik

Picon personally did much of the gardening at Chez Shmendrik. She liked being close to the earth and plants, but sometimes she faced unexpected side effects; for example, after buying $70 worth of shrubs to transplant, she discovered that she had "a sinister attraction for anything that bites or stings."

After her husband died in 1975, she literally attacked the gardens, pruning and weeding, in an effort to release emotion and avoid self-pity.

GILDA RADNER
Zany Sketch Comedienne

Gilda Radner rose to stardom through her daffy sketches on the TV comedy-variety series *NBC's Saturday Night Live* (1975-80). With her mass of tangled hair, her squawking voice, and her chickenlike walk, she created a gallery of eccentric characters, from the klutzy Lisa Loopner to the stately Baba Wawa.

Radner was born in a suburb of Detroit, Michigan, on June 28, 1946. After graduating from an all-girl high school, where she participated in plays, she enrolled at the University of Michigan as a drama student.

Leaving college without a degree, Radner moved to Toronto in 1969. There she had some minor parts in plays, spent one year in the religious rock musical *Godspell,* and then joined the Toronto offshoot of Second City, the Chicago-based improvisational comedy troupe.

Returning to the United States, Radner had a one-line part as a Buddhist in the movie *The Last Detail* (1973). In

Toucher and Hugger
Offstage, Radner earned a reputation for being kind, thoughtful, and nontemperamental. She was a compulsive toucher and hugger.

Joke Fest
During her final months, Radner spendt much of her time at the Wellness Community (Santa Monica, California), a cancer self-help group. One of her favorite activities there was the Joke Fest, where the patients cheered each other up with jokes, many of which openly made fun of their disease.

The Child in Radner
"I just never let go of my child self," Radner confessed. "Being a child is being impulsive. Keeping that part of me alive is very useful in comedy."

Gilda in *First Family.*

Gilda with Gene Wilder in *Haunted Honeymoon.*

1974 she participated in the weekly *National Lampoon Radio Hour.* The following year she was in *The National Lampoon Show,* an off-Broadway cabaret revue.

In 1975 she became part of the original cast on *NBC's Saturday Night Live.* Her character inventions on the show included Judy Miller, a bratty eight-year-old Brownie absorbed in her own fantasy world; Lisa Loopner, a sniffling teenage nerd; Roseanne Roseanadanna, a wisecracking newscaster who liked to elaborate on such topics as armpit hair and "that stoff you find in your eye"; Baba Wawa, a takeoff on the TV personality Barbara Walters; Rhonda Weiss, a gum-cracking Long Island Jewish "princess"; and Emily Litella, an eight-year-old who read confused editorial replies on such important matters as "Soviet Jewelry" and "Violins on Television."

In the summer of 1979 Radner took her personae to Broadway in the one-woman show *Gilda Radner—Live from New York.* The show was filmed and released as *Gilda Live* (1980).

In 1980 she left *NBC's Saturday Night Live* to concentrate on motion pictures. Among her movies were *The First Family* (1981), as a United States President's aging virgin daughter, who enthusiastically embraces her sacrifice to a pagan god of fertility; *The Woman in Red* (1984), as an ill-tempered secretary who has a crush on her boss; and *Haunted Honeymoon* (1986), as a radio actress who goes to her fiancé's spooky ancestral house, where she intends to be married but instead finds comical horror.

In 1984 Radner married the comic actor Gene Wilder, star of *The Woman in Red.* They had earlier worked together in *Hanky Panky* (1982), and later they teamed up in *Haunted Honeymoon.* In those films, she tended to play straight woman for Wilder.

In late 1986 Radner learned that she had cancer of the ovaries. Heavily involved with exhausting and painful treatments, she never worked again after her ailment was diagnosed. Radner died on May 20, 1989. Her best-selling biography, *It's Always Something,* was published posthumously ★

Changed Diet

Radner ate more wholesomely after the onset of her battle with cancer. For one thing, she no longer used artificial sugar (saccharin).

Her romance with her husband, Gene Wilder, was sparked by their shared passion for tuna fish. But during much of her illness, she had to give up tuna for chicken soup and crackers.

Quit Smoking

Formerly a constant smoker, Radner quit using tobacco after she developed cancer.

PAUL REISER
Star of "My Two Dads"

Paul Reiser's casual style of stand-up comedy sounds improvised but is actually carefully crafted. He pushes back the sleeves of his sweater and talks to his audience about everyday things that he observes or experiences. One of his favorite devices is the what-bothers-me line, as when he confesses his irritation at people who give directions like "the road curves, but you stay straight." On pets, he says that "dog is man's best friend because they think alike." Other topics include airlines, computers, philosophy, and being a New York native living in Los Angeles.

While successful at stand-up comedy, Reiser is best known for his comic roles in films and on TV. He rose to national attention with his part as the moocher in the movie *Diner* (1982). Since 1987 he has been a major TV star by virtue of his role as one of the fathers in the hit comedy series *My Two Dads.*

Reiser was born in New York City in 1956. As a child he was the class cutup. While in high school, he often went to Greenwich Village clubs to observe the comics. At the State University of New York at Binghamton he majored in music but also participated in theatrical productions. During the summers he divided his time between working in his father's

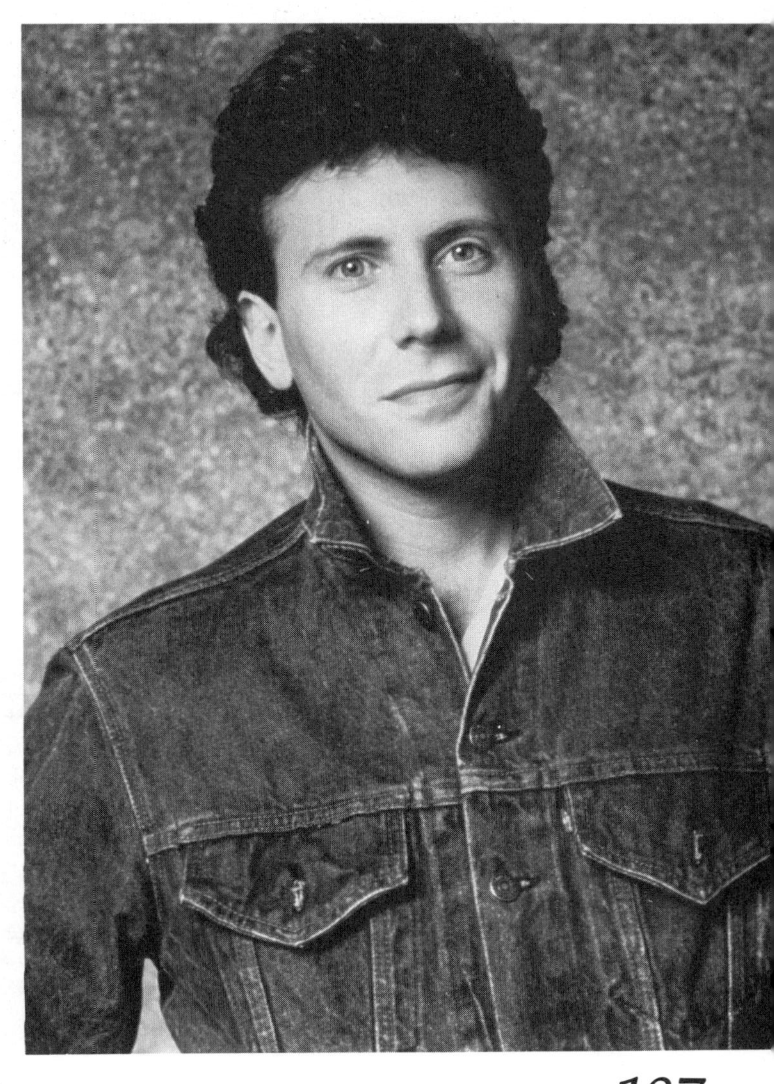

health-food business and performing as a comic in New York City comedy clubs.

After graduating form college in 1977 he continued to work both for his father and in comedy. His big break came in 1980 when he won a role in the movie *Diner* (1982), as Modell, who enters a diner but never orders anything, preferring to finish everyone else's food.

From that point on Reiser's career skyrocketed. He has continued to play clubs nationally, but since 1983 his home base has been Los Angeles, where he has been busy in films and on TV.

In the made-for-TV movie *Sunset Limousine* (1983) he had a leading role as the limo driver. in *Aliens* or *Alien II*, 1986) he played the evil Burke. Reiser starred in the film comedy *Odd Jobs* (1986) as Max, a confused but likable guy who bungles his way through life till he stumbles into heroism by capturing some car thieves; the role was an extension of his nightclub persona. He also appeared in *Beverly Hills Cop* (1984), *Beverly Hills Cop II* (1987), and *Cross My Heart* (1987).

On television Reiser has guested on *The Tonight Show* and *Late Night with David Letterman.* In 1987 he received high marks from fans and critics for his HBO special *Out on a Whim.*

In the sitcom *My Two Dads* (1987-) he appears as one of the two men who may be the father of a motherless girl. Reiser plays Michael Taylor, a conservative, business type, while the other man has a contrasting personality. Nevertheless, they raise the child as "tandem parents." Much of the show's success depends on Reiser's uncanny ability to deliver so-so lines with subtle facial expressions and vocal inflections that mark him as a young comic performer with extraordinary talent—and apparently unlimited potential.☆

Paul Reiser with Rick Overton (left) in *Odd Jobs.*

Typical Reiser

Among Reiser's what-bothers-me lines is his one about people who eat a bite of cheesecake from his fork and leave a disgusting residue.

One of his observations is about the Hearst castle in California, a popular tourist attraction. "If everybody stopped and looked at my house and gave me sixteen bucks, I could live like that too."

Talmud Study

Twice a month Reiser meets with his friends Larry Miller, Mark Schiff, Jerry Seinfeld, and Lotus Weinstock in their private homes to study liturgy and Talmud under the guidance of the two Hillel House rabbis from USC and UCLA.

Conversation

In casual conversation, Reiser speaks with the same kind of understated, half-joking analytical approach to subjects that he uses in his stage routines.

Private Life

Reiser is sensitive about his private life. He speaks freely up to a point but then will draw a line beyond which he will not go. Though easygoing, he exudes a slight sense of coolness and noncommitment.

DON RICKLES
Merchant of Venom

Don ("Mr. Warmth") Rickles creates heat. For years the debate has raged: does Rickles mock prejudice, or does he reinforce it? "People either love me or hate me," he admits.

The insult comedian par excellence, Rickles thrives on his reputation as the Merchant of Venom. "Are you Italian?" he asks a member of the audience. "You, the one with the flies all around." Or: "You're Chinese? You're not Chinese? Then get your eyes fixed." Again, "The Jew's laughing, and the black guy just picked his pocket." He calls a woman wearing an ostentatious fur coat "an old beaver in heat."

"My style is to rib people I like," Rickles explains. "If there's anger in it, it isn't funny. Audiences always know what I'm saying is, beneath it all, being done with a certain kind of love and respect. I think there's an element of catharsis in what I do. People laugh because they can see that ultimately it's all a satire of attitudes and prejudices."

Don(ald) Rickles was born in the borough of Queens in New York City, New York, on May 8, 1926. After navy service during World War II, he studied at the American Academy of Dramatic Arts in New York City. He wanted to be a dramatic actor, but the going was rough. So, on the side, he worked as a stand-up comic in strip joints. Customers heckled him, and he learned to create humor by insulting them in return.

An important event in his career took place in 1956 at the Slate Brothers Club in Los Angeles. Frank Sinatra was in the audience. Rickles, who had never met Sinatra, said, "Frank, I've seen you in nightclubs, I've watched you in movies, I've listened to you on records, and I say this from my heart—Frank, your voice is gone. It's all over for you. You're making a fool of yourself. You've got to find some other work." Sinatra loved the

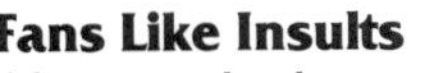

Fans Like Insults

Rickles says he has never had a serious run-in with an insulted fan. In fact, "people try to get seats up front where the odds are better that I'll get to them."

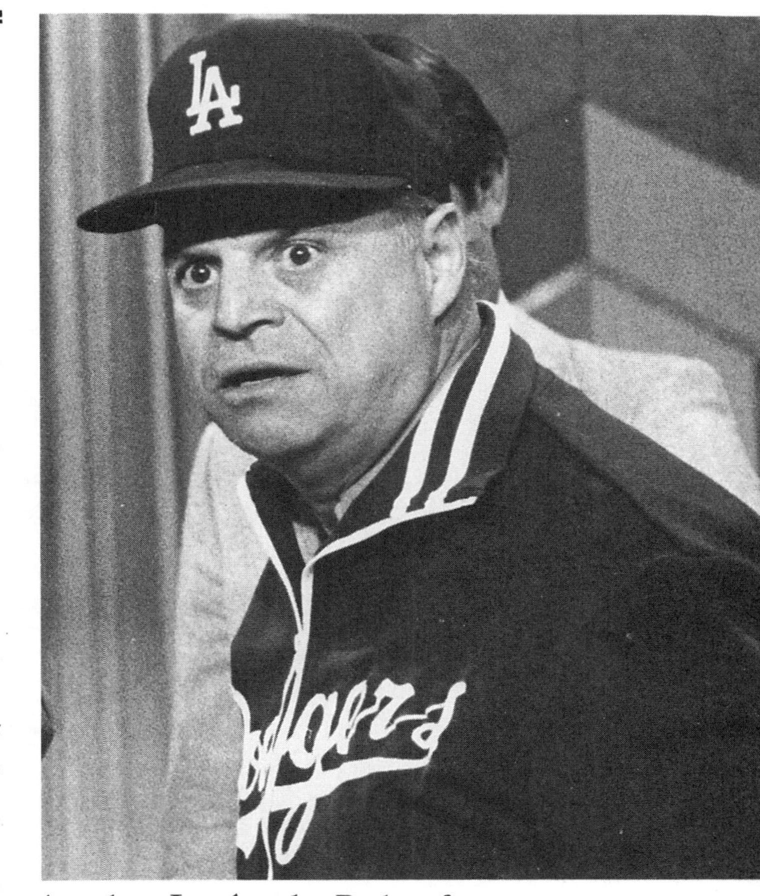

A zealous Los Angeles Dodger fan.

The Subject of Barbs

MILTON BERLE: "What can you say about Rickles that hasn't been said about hemorrhoids?"

PAT MC CORMICK: "Rickles will be a little late—he's out walking his rat."

Insult Humor

"My main problem," Rickles says, "is that my humor depends on my face. If you take a quote from me—in print it's different. I read it and say, 'Ouch!' It's what's not in print thats important—my honesty and my love for people."

Rickle Gems

To a fat person: "What do you eat for dinner? Furniture?"

To an elderly woman: "Hi ya, mom. I spoke to the home—you go in Friday!"

To Howard Cosell: "From the bottom of my heart, I say you're annoying and you should go away!"

To anyone: "You hockey puck! You dummy!"

Conscious of Jewishness

Raised in a strictly Orthodox household, Rickles says, "I'm still very pious, very conscious of being Jewish. I'm a serious man, serious about my work, my family."

performance, and Rickels began to gain notice from show-business insiders.

However, he struggled for nearly another decade before winning popularity from the general public. During that period he worked in nightclubs and played supporting roles in TV and film dramas, including the movies *Run Silent, Run Deep* (1958) and *The Rat Race* (1960).

It was the turbulent 1960s that finally provided the right backdrop for his abrasive brand of humor. Since then he has been one of America's leading stand-up comedians, working at major nightclubs, hotels, and casinos.

Rickles was featured in the popular beach-party movies of the mid-1960s, including *Bikini Beach* (1964) and *Beach Blanket Bingo* (1965). Among his later films were *Enter Laughing* (1967), *Kelly's Heroes* (1970), and *For the Love of It* (TV, 1980).

Rickles has also become a fixture on television. He has appeared as a guest on most of the important talk shows and variety programs. *The Don Rickles Show* of 1968-69 was a part-game, part variety program that he hosted. In 1972 *The Don Rickles Show* was a situation-comedy series with him as an advertising executive. More successful was *C.P.O. Sharkey* (1976-78), a sit-com in which he starred as Chief Petty Officer Otto Sharkey, a navy drill instructor.

In 1982 Rickles gave a fine seriocomic performance in an episode of the TV series *Archie Bunker's Place* as an obnoxious—but lonely and pitiful—roomer who dies. In 1984 he cohosted the TV comedy series *Foul-ups, Bleeps, and Blunders.* In 1989 he guest-starred as an insulting talk-show host on the TV sitcom *Newhart.*

With all of his success as the Merchant of Venom, Rickles is unlikely ever to follow his mother's advice to "tell nice stories like Bob Newhart."★

Rickles addresses the audience.

Feels Misunderstood

"People are wrong to think that I love to go to parties and insult the guests," Rickles maintains. "People are wrong to think that what I do on the stage is a hobby, that I get my kicks out of it. . . . I'm not some schmuck who goes around hollering rotten things about people because I got a vicious nature."

What is he really like? "I like to sit quietly, talking about the Dodgers or television programs. . . . I'm really Mr. Nice Guy."

RITZ BROTHERS
Unison Comedians

The Ritz Brothers, unlike most comedy teams (such as the wild Marx Brothers), performed largely in unison. Having begun their careers as precision dancers, they tended to apply that same

The Ritz Brothers: Al, Jimmy, and Harry.

sense of joint effort when they extended their act into singing and broad comedy.

All three brothers were born in Newark, New Jersey: Al(fred) on August 27, 1901; Jimmy (originally Samuel) on October 5, 1903; and Harry on May 22, 1906. Another brother, George, served as their manager. Their original surname was Joachim.

Al entered show business first when he began to win prizes for his dancing. In 1918 he had a bit part in the western movie *The Avenging Trail.* In 1925 Jimmy and Harry joined him, and they entered vaudeville as a comedy dance trio. Soon they added singing and slapstick comedy to their act, and by 1929 they were in big-time vandeville. In 1932 they hit Broadway in the *Earl Carroll Vanities.*

They performed complicated dance numbers. They sang (their theme song was "Collegiate"). And they clowned, mostly by mugging and by doing knockabout. Early in their career they wore baggy pants, red ties, and matching socks to parody the typical college clothing of the day. Another bit was to wear grotesque women's dresses, with rolled-up trousers clearly visible below their hemlines.

The Ritz Brothers, gentle compared with their famous rivals the Marx Brothers, performed little skits that spoofed well-known stories, such as monster movies, Snow White, and the Three Musketeers. One

Attitudes Toward Work

"Harry was a hard worker," reported Allan Dwan, director of *The Three Musketeers.* "I remember the other two wanted to get off early one day to go to the racetrack, and it was always hard to get them on." When Dwan threatened to drop Al and Jimmy from the movie, they began to cooperate.

Close to the Public

"Nobody knows what the public expects of funnymen," Al observed. "But we're pretty close to the public in our nightclub appearances. We never listen to the experts, just the people who see us perform. From their reaction we've learned that they like what we're doing."

The Ritz Brothers and Gloria Stuart.

Loyal Brothers

When the Twentieth Century-Fox executive Darryl F. Zanuck wanted Jimmy alone for the movie *On The Avenue*, Jimmy refused to work without the others; subsequently the whole team was hired.

Al said, "We're just like one person—one for all and three for one. We talk things out and don't keep business secrets from each other."

Comic Idol

The Ritz Brothers' comic idol was Charlie Chaplin.

All Hams

"We're all hams," Al confessed, "but Harry is the hammiest. That's why Jimmy and I put him in the center spot."

Perfect Timing

Harry Ritz's antics broke paths for later comedians: he encouraged Miton Berle's wearing of dresses, he introduced the scat singing emulated by Danny Kaye, and he employed some mannerisms that were adopted by Jerry Lewis.

Binnie Barnes spoke for many when she admitted having learned from the whole team: "They taught me a lot about comedy.... Their timing was so perfect."

of their best-known routines had Harry, the acknowledged leader, standing between his two brothers and singing "The Man in the Middle Is the Funny One" while Al and Jimmy berated him and tried to take his spot; as they yelled at him he would bellow, "Don't holler! Please don't holler!"

In 1934 the Ritz Brothers entered motion pictures with the excellent comedy short *Hotel Anchovy*. Soon they were playing secondary roles for comic relief in features, such as *Sing, Baby, Sing* (1936) and *On the Avenue* (1937), in the latter of which Harry first brought his drag act to the screen. Later they starred in a number of pictures. In *Life Begins in College* (1937) they played themselves wreaking havoc as college students. In *The Three Musketeers* (1939) they portrayed the Three Lackeys in a comedy version of the classic Dumas story. In *The Gorilla* (1939) they were bumbling private detectives hired to capture a killer who dresses as an ape; their efforts are complicated when a real gorilla shows up. In *Never a Dull Moment* (1943) they played the Three Funny Bunnies, nightclub comics who are duped into receiving stolen goods. Their other films included *You Can't Have Everything (1937), The Goldwyn Follies* (1938), *Argentine Nights* (1940), and *Behind the Eight Ball* (1942).

In the mid-1940s the Ritz Brothers returned full-time to live performances. For the next twenty years they were a major nightclub act in New York City, Chicago, Miami, and especially Las Vegas, where in 1945 they became the first "name" act to perform. They also appeared on TV in the 1950s.

On December 22, 1965, Al died in New Orleans, Louisiana. Jimmy and Harry then semiretired. They worked some TV and club dates, and they appeared in the films *Blazing Stewardesses* (1975) and *Won Ton Ton, the Dog Who Saved Hollywood* (1976). Harry alone had a small part in *Silent Movie* (1976). They formally retired in 1978.

Jimmy died in Los Angeles, California, on November 17, 1985. Harry died in San Diego, California, on March 29, 1986.☆

Entering Show Business
"It wasn't so much that we wanted to become actors," Harry Ritz explained, "as that we wanted to make money, to eat—and maybe to meet girls."

JOAN RIVERS
"Can We Talk?"

Joan Rivers is the most successful woman in the history of stand-up comedy. Among the first and few comediennes to use insult humor (traditionally a male province), she ridicules flaws and neuroses in celebrities, in herself, and in Americans at large. Her favorite topics are physical appearance, lifestyle, and sexuality. Rivers sets a tone of informality, as if gossiping with close friends, through her signature phrase, "Can we talk?"

She was born in New York City, New York, on June 8, 1933. Her original name was Joan Alexandra Molinsky.

While attending the Adelphi Academy preparatory school in Brooklyn, she participated in the drama program and placed second in a *Photoplay* acting contest. Shortly after her graduation, she landed a small role in the movie *Mr. Universe* (1951).

Under pressure from her mother, Rivers put aside her acting ambitions and studied English and anthropology at Barnard College in New York City. After graduating in 1954, she entered the business world, eventually becoming fashion coordinator for the entire chain of Bond clothing stores. She also married the son of the Bond stores' merchandiser. But her desire to return to performing led to the annulment of the marriage in 1958.

After a couple of years of struggling as an actress, she turned to comedy in 1960 with the initial aim of earning money to support her acting. She worked in strip joints, Catskill resorts, and dingy nightclubs.

During 1961-62 she performed with the Chicago-based improvisational acting troupe Second City. The group's stream-of-consciouseness comedy technique taught her, as she later recounted, "to short-circuit thought and hitch impulses directly to [her] tongue."

In 1962 she returned to New York City, where she discovered Lenny Bruce and admired the way he generated comedic material from personal pain and insight. Rivers, too, began to speak "directly and personally to the audience," releasing her hostilities and insecurities by telling jokes about herself as a nervous, unattractive loser whom her mother could not marry off.

Her first big break finally came in February 1965 when she appeared on *The Tonight Show.* She and the host, Johnny Carson, developed an instant rapport, and he pronounced her a future star. In July 1965 she married the producer Edgar Rosenberg.

Soon Rivers was being booked into the elite of the comedy nightclub circuit. She also began to record albums and to become a familiar face on TV. Throughout the 1970s she frequently guest-hosted *The Tonight Show.*

Some of her material was offbeat, such as her routine about her pet wig. She picked it out at a "wigpen" and taught it tricks ("Curl!"). When a motorist ran over it, he apologized for killing her dog. But most of her jokes were directed at herself ("My body is falling so fast my gynecologist wears a hard hat") and her married life ("If my husband didn't toss and turn in his sleep, we'd never have had a kid").

By the early 1980s Rivers was applying her acid wit to celebrities. On Elizabeth Taylor's weight problem: "This woman has more chins than a Chinese phone book!" On Bo Derek's intelligence: "She saw a sign saying Wet

The glamorous Joan.

Facing Adversity

In August 1987 her husband, Edgar Rosenberg, depressed over his failing health, committed suicide. "I don't know why I am being tested in this way," Rivers said, "but I have to go on because of my daughter [eighteen-year-old Melissa]." She decided that work was the best therapy. "I don't want sympathy audiences. . . .I don't want to turn my career into anything maudlin or sentimental. Besides, I'm too short to be a tragic figure."

Charities

Rivers has been the national chairperson of the Cystic Fibrosis Society since 1982, and she was the first major entertainer to headline fund-raising events for AIDS research. She is a former Hadassah Woman of the Year.

Vintage Rivers

"I'm having hot flashes. I went to my gynecologist. He didn't use rubber gloves—he used an oven mitt!"

"I'm Jewish. If God had wanted me to exercise he would've put diamonds on the floor!"

Floor so she did!" On the wardrobe of Queen Elizabeth II of England: "Gowns by Helen Keller." On Nancy Reagan's "bulletproof" hair: "If they ever combed it, they'd find Jimmy Hoffa."

Some critics accused Rivers of cruelty, but her aim was purely therapeutic. "If I thought I hurt anybody, I'd go crazy," she has said.

During 1981-82 Rivers went on an extremely successful tour with her antithesis, the mild-mannered and squeaky-clean David Brenner. From 1983 to 1986 she served as the first and only permanent guest host of *The Tonight Show.* From October 1986 to May 1987 she directly competed against her old friend Johnny Carson by hosting her own late-night variety program, *The Late Show Starring Joan Rivers.* Her unwonted mild manner did not go over well, and she was dropped from the show.

Rivers has been very successful as a writer. She cowrote the screenplay for the black-comedy movie *The Girl Most Likely to . . .* (TV, 1973); and she cowrote, directed, and acted in *Rabbit Test* (1978), a film about the world's first pregnant man. From 1973 to 1976 she wrote a nationally syndicated column for the *Chicago Tribune.* Her books include *Having a Baby Can Be a Scream* (1975) and *The Life and Hard Times of Heidi Abromowitz*(1984), the latter about "the most renowned tramp since Charlie Chaplin." In 1986 Rivers published her autobiography, *Enter Talking.* ★

Off and On

Publicly brash, Rivers offstage, according to intimates, is a shy, introverted, family-devoted woman.

Feeling Safe

As a child, Rivers was traumatized by her fatness and by her parents' constant fighting. Insecure in real life, she turned to the stage. Audiences, she has said, "made me feel I belonged, made me feel adored and . . . safe."

Offstage, however, even with all of her current success, she still believes tht everything could disappear overnight.

Suicide Attempt

In a moment of depression during the early years of her career, Rivers tried to commit suicide by taking a bottleful of aspirin tablets. Because she could never swallow pills with water, she pushed them down with Oreo cookies. "Never try to kill yourself with chocolate," she later advised (in her 1986 autobiography), "because after a while it makes you feel good again; and I began thinking, 'Oh, maybe things aren't so bad . . . .' "

Influence of Bruce

Lenny Bruce had the greatest influence on Joan Rivers. He "saved my life," she has said. While struggling to develop a comedic identity, she watched his act every night for three weeks in 1962. "I learned from Lenny that you could tell the truth onstage."

BENNY RUBIN
Bug-eyed Comedian

Benny Rubin was for many years one of the most familiar faces in motion pictures and on television. Few people knew his name, however, because the bug-eyed, rubber-faced comedian usually played secondary, even bit, parts. But professional entertainers knew who he was and admired his comedic talents. Indeed, in his early years he had been a top headliner as a tap dancer and comic dialectician in vaudeville. He also worked in tabloid shows, on showboats, in burlesque, in nightclubs, on Broadway, and on radio.

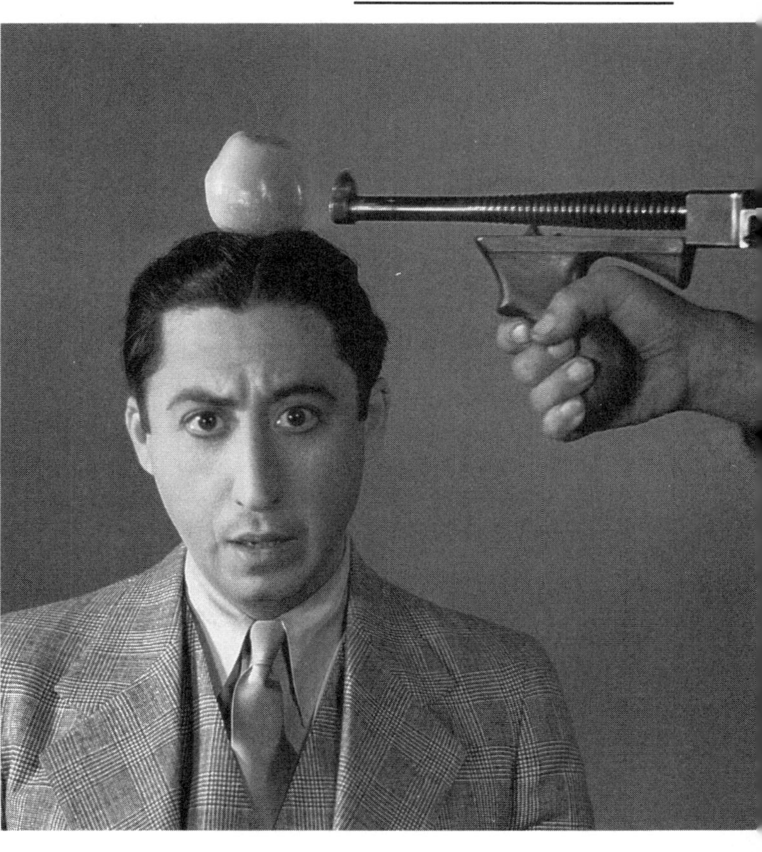

Rubin in *Lord Byron of Broadway*.

Rubin was born in Boston, Massachusetts, on February 2, 1899. In 1910 he began to appear in amateur shows as a tap dancer. In 1914 he quit school and entered show business professionally.

His first significant job was in a tabloid show, a condensed version of a Broadway production. Moving to New York City, he continued to get work onstage by developing whatever routines he could pick up—singing, doing Jewish monologues, tap dancing, playing the trombone, and juggling (which he learned from a young friend who later became a fair comedian himself, Fred Allen).

After working for a time in burlesque and small-time vaudeville, Rubin hit the major circuits in 1920. His stage appearances also included work on showboats, in nightclubs, and in book musicals, such as a Chicago production of *Girl Crazy* (1931).

In the late 1920s and early 1930s Rubin alternated work in vaudeville and in movies. During that time he was one of the most active Jewish comedians in films, often playing a recognizable Jewish type. In *It's a Great Life* (1930) he had a small part as Benny Friedman, a booking agent. In *Hot Curves* (1930) he starred as Benny Goldberg, a soda vendor who becomes a baseball hero. In *Sunny Skies* (1930) he had the lead as the shy, awkward Benny Krantz, a blend of pathos and comedy in an initiation story taking place on a college campus. Other early Rubin films included

Dancing with Roland

Rubin's favorite movie star in the days of silent films was Ruth Roland. One of the highlights of his life was when he had a chance to dance with her in a nightclub.

Sports Fan

From his early days as a street fighter in Boston slums, Benny Rubin developed a love of boxing as a way of staying in shape. He also attended boxing matches. Among his personal friends were the heavyweight champions Jack Dempsey and Max Baer.

Rubin enjoyed playing golf and baseball. Before major-league teams moved to the West Coast, he attended minor-league baseball games in California.

Naughty Baby (1929), *Leathernecking* (1930), and *George White's 1935 Scandals* (1935)

After the mid-1930s Rubin centered his activities in Hollywood, California, where he performed in films, on radio, and on TV. Among his movies were *Here Comes Mr. Jordan* (1941), *A Hole in the Head* (1959), *The Patsy* (1964), *Thoroughly Modern Millie* (1967), and *Won Ton Ton, the Dog Who Saved Hollywood* (cameo, 1976).

On radio Rubin worked for two years as one of Orson Welles's famed group of Mercury players. The comedian also frequently guested on Jack Benny's radio show.

When Jack Benny moved to television, Benny Rubin continued to work on the program. He made over four hundred appearances on Jack Benny's radio and TV shows. Rubin also guested on Milton Berle's early TV variety shows, the western *Gunsmoke*, and many other programs.

However, in his late years he found show-business jobs increasingly scarce. During slack periods he ran a dress shop or sold stocks and barbecues to old entertainment friends who now lived in Beverly Hills mansions.

Rubin died in Los Angeles on June 15, 1986. ☆

Skilled with Numbers

Quick and accurate in basic math, Rubin surprised business associates with his ability to make calculations without resorting to pencil and paper. He said he developed his skill from years of "playing horses, shooting craps, and paying commission."

Why Rubin Fell from Grace

In 1961 Benny Rubin explained why his star dimmed: "It wasn't a case of my giving up the business; it was the business that gave me up. Dialect comics were considered out . . . . Ethnic groups were becoming hypersensitive, and a section of the industry thought it knew what was best for the nation."

MORT SAHL
Pathbreaking Comedian

Mort Sahl, by successfully breaking some of the most basic traditional rules of nightclub comedy, opened the way for a whole new generation of entertainers. Before Sahl, a dress suit was standard attire; he wore slacks and a sweater. Before Sahl, jokes had punchlines; he introduced stream-of-consciousness monologues in which fragments of "jokes" were mixed in with hip jargon and sardonic social observations. Before Sahl, comedians were supposed to be inoffensive; he feared no taboos and, indeed, would often ask his audience, "Is there any group I haven't offended?"

Mort(on) Sahl was born in Montreal, Canada, on May 11, 1927. Early in life he was fascinated by the military. In high school he participated in the ROTC program and

A scene from *In Love and War*.

dreamed of attending West Point. But a stint in the air force changed his mind. Stationed in Alaska, he edited a newspaper, *Poop from the Group,* and printed such savage satire that he spent eighty-three consecutive days on KP.

When he returned to civilian life, Sahl, though he had abandoned the military mentality, still leaned toward other Establishment values. He enrolled at the University of Southern California, where he earned a B.S. degree (1950) in city management and traffic engineering.

That attitude began to change over the next few years. He wrote pieces for literary magazines, participated in experimental theater, and began to get comedy jobs on the West Coast.

In 1953 Sahl was hired at the hungry i (*i* for *intellectual*), a San Francisco beatnik hangout where he won his first fame. By the late 1950s he was one of America's most popular comedians at nightclubs in Los Angeles, Las Vegas, Chicago, and New York City. He also appeared on TV shows hosted by Steve Allen, Jack Paar, and others.

Some of Sahl's material played with intellectual jargon. For example, in one anecdote, a bank robber handed a teller a note saying to "act normal." The teller responded with another note: "Define your terms."

Some of his "jokes" seemed to be gratuitious attacks uttered merely for their shock value. Women were a favorite target, as in this twist on an old saying: "A woman's place is in the stove."

But by far most of his material consisted of biting social and political satire. His subjects came straight from the daily newspapers, which he carried onstage. On capital punishment, he said, "I'm for capital punishment. You've got to execute people. How else are they going to learn?" Senator Joseph McCarthy's loud, posturing witch-hunts for Communists inspired Sahl's suggestion for a new article of clothing: a McCarthy jacket with an extra zipper (or flap) to go over the mouth. On Richard Nixon's visit to Russia: "He can't call anyone a Communist over there and hurt their career." On Nixon's character: "He's been on the cover of every magazine except *True.*" "I'm not so much interested in politics," Sahl quipped, "as I am in overthrowing the government."

After President Kennedy's assassination in 1963, Sahl became obsessed with the conspiracy theory about the events in Dallas, and with his lack of faith in the Warren Report about the murder. For several years few TV shows and nightclubs would hire him.

Mort Sahl doing his stand-up routine.

Kenton a Hero

The intense monologist frequently pauses to relax with music. He enjoys classical music and jazz, particularly Stan Kenton, who was Sahl's hero because Kenton was defiant. "The band followed no rules except a greater allegiance than temporary popularity—the right of the artist to go his own way," said Mort.

Low-Key Clothing

Sahl prefers clothes that make a "minimal statement. Minimal and dapper. . . . When it's low-key, clothing recedes and the person emerges." For years he wore gray slacks, a blue buttondown collar, a black knit tie, loafers, and a blue blazer.

Razors, Watches, and Sports Cars

Mort likes to surround himself with electric razors, expensive watches, and sleek sports cars.

But in the late 1960s and early 1970s his stock rose as the behavior of Presidents Johnson and Nixon set a national tone of distrust and gave new grist to Sahl's mill. Since then he has been in steady demand, though his popularity has never approached the level that he enjoyed in the late 1950s and early 1960s.

Sahl has appeared in several movies. In *Inside the Third Reich* (TV, 1982) he played a Jewish cabaret comedian uttering anti-Nazi jokes in 1930s Germany. His other films included *In Love and War* (1958), *Johnny Cool* (1963), and *Nothing Lasts Forever* (1984).

In 1987 he appeared on the New York City stage in the one-man show *Mort Sahl on Broadway.*

Today Sahl has a strong following on college campuses and in Las Vegas. And he still attacks everyone, friends and enemies alike: liberals, conservatives, Democrats, Republicans, students, blacks, the press, homosexual cliques in the arts—is there any group he hasn't offended? ★

Irrelevant Comedians
The apoliticism of today's comics disheartens Sahl. "Their issues are so irrelevant," he laments.

Prolific Reader
Among Sahl's favorite authors are Mark Twain, Herman Melville, Tom Paine, Albert Einstein, and George Bernard Shaw.

SOUPY SALES
King of Corn

Soupy Sales rose to fame by hosting children's TV shows in the 1950s and 1960s. Masses of teenagers and adults also watched his slapstick programs, which featured puppets, jokes, and pies in the face. Today he is still the greatest proponent of having fun through pure silliness and corny gags: "You show me a sculptor who works in the basement and I'll show you a low-down chiseler!"

Sales was born in Franklinton, near Wake Forest, North Carolina, on January 8, 1926. His original name was Milton Supman. He acquired his nickname, Soupy, from his childhood playmates who punned it from his family name, Supman. (For a brief time early in his career he used the surname Hines, from which came the erroneous story that his nickname was derived by punning *Hines* with *Heinz,* the name of a well-known food-processing company.)

Sales grew up in Huntington, West Virginia. After graduating from high school, where he participated in dramatic productions, he served in the navy during

Soupy and friend on *The Soupy Sales Show*.

World War II. Returning to Huntington, he earned a B.A. in journalism at Marshall University.

In 1949 he took a daytime job as a script writer—later as a disc jockey—for a Huntington radio station. At night he performed as a nightclub entertainer.

In the early 1950s Sales went to Ohio to gain more experience as a TV entertainer. In 1953 he moved to Detroit, where he began to star in his own children's TV show. Later he broadcast out of Los Angeles and then New York City. Some of his shows were shown only locally, but he reached the peak of his popularity with his network telecasts from 1959 to 1962.

Wearing a sloppy black sweater and a floppy bow tie, Soupy Sales would admonish his viewers: "Soupy says don't bite your nails—your nails don't bite you. Be careful crossing streets—you might get that run-down feeling. Keep your chin up—it'll keep the milk from spilling on your clothes." He also interacted with other residents of his TV funhouse, notably two dogs represented only by hairy paws and offscreen growling and cooing: the giant White Fang and kindly Black Tooth. Among the other regulars were an irate neighbor (a hand in the doorway and an offstage voice) and several puppets (including Pookie the Lion). The host introduced the eccentric dance "The Soupy Shuffle" and not only took thousands of pies in the face but also induced many celebrity guests to do likewise, including Frank Sinatra and Jerry Lewis.

Idolized Harry Ritz

As a youth Soupy Sales liked to watch Ritz Brothers movies. He especially admired Harry Ritz, in whom Sales recognized a natural comedian, not an actor playing comedy roles.

A Favorite Joke

One of Sales's favorite jokes always flops with audiences. "If you want to drive a doctor crazy," the joke begins, "the next time he tells you to strip to the waist, take off your pants."

"When I did that joke, people would just sit there and look at me," Sales complains. "So I do it for spite."

Denigrators

Widely belittled by intellectuals and professional critics, Sales realizes that his name has become a generic term for low quality. But he feels his work has great value: "I'm a pioneer in television comedy. Because of me a lot of people are a little healthier, have a little better sense of humor, and are a little bit nicer."

Relaxes with Art

The frantic slapstick comedian slows down offstage. His favorite forms of relaxation are listening to jazz records and painting nonobjective pictures.

Since *The Soupy Sales Show* left the air in 1966, he has been a regular on *What's My Line* (1968-75), performed on other TV programs and commercials, had a daily New York radio show, acted in some plays, and performed stand-up comedy as a headliner in Atlantic City casinos, in comedy clubs, and at other venues. He also wrote the book *Soupy Sales' Greatest Jokes Ever Told* (1987).

Today he still has a big following among nostalgia buffs, lovers of camp and corn, and, of course, children, one of whom explained, "He's a nut, like us."☆

Pie-catching Champ

During his career, Sales has been hit in the face with over twenty thousand pies. They are filled, he says, with whipped cream or aerosol shaving cream, which is easier to clean up than custard.

AL SCHACHT
Clown Prince of Baseball

Al Schacht, known as the Clown Prince of Baseball, entertained fans in ballparks for over fifty years. He performed dozens of comical pantomine skits burlesquing baseball and other sports. His props included a baseball uniform, a battered silk hat, a red-lapelled tailcoat, and a five-foot baseball glove.

Al(exander) Schacht was born on November 12, 1892, in New York City, New York, in a Bronx district that later became the site of Yankee Stadium. As a child he ran errands for the New York Giants ballplayers, serving as the "special sandwich-bearer" for the great pitcher Christy Mathewson.

Nick Altrack (left) and Al Schacht, both baseball clowns, stage a pregame boxing match in the 1920s.

Heroes

Naturally enough, the people Schacht most admired were baseball players. He "idolized Christy Mathewson," the New York Giants pitcher, and "worshiped Sir Walter" Johnson, the Washington senators hurler.

Entertained Troops

Though suffering from fear of heights, Schacht made airplane trips during World War II to entertain USA and NATO troops in North Africa, Sicily, and the Pacific theater.

Restaurateur

In the early 1940s Schacht opened a restaurant in New York City. Thereafter he spent much of his time as a restaurateur.

Schacht, too, became a pitcher. By 1914, when he was playing for the Newark Bears of the International League, he had already developed a reputation for being a practical joker. Once he rode an old horse to the mound. Umpires frequently fined him or tossed him out of games.

In 1919, after a few years of bouncing from team to team, he landed with the big-league Washington Senators, on whose payroll he remained, with some interruptions, till 1934. Injuries abbreviated his playing career, and he ended with a major-league mark of fourteen wins and ten losses. He then became a coach for the Senators.

Soon after joining the team in 1919 he and Nick Altrock, a Senators coach, began to entertain fans between games of doubleheaders and just before the start of single games. In 1921 they were invited to give their first World Series performance.

Altrock played Schacht's straight man. One skit had Schacht throwing baseballs at Altrock, who caught every one till Schacht threw a soft rubber ball, which Altrock let go throught his hands and bounce off his head. (Once there was a mixup, and Altrock took a real baseball to the head. He was knocked out.)

They also performed pantomimes of golf, tennis, rowing, swimming, and tightrope walking. One of their most popular routines was a boxing match in which they used baseball mitts for boxing gloves; the big knockdown blow was preceded by a baseball-pitcher's windup.

In the 1922 World Series they brought the house down with their hilarious burlesque of Rudolph Valentino as a lover and a bullfighter in the movie *Blood and Sand.* Dressed as a toreador, Schacht conquered a goat and won the hand of Altrock, dressed as a senorita.

In 1933 Altrock dropped out of the act, and Schacht went on alone, often pantomiming multiple parts, as in the boxing routines. After leaving the Senators in 1934, Schacht coached elsewhere for a while. But in 1937 he gave up coaching, assumed the title Clown Prince of Baseball, and became a full-time comedian.

Schacht took his act on the road and in the following years played in every important major-league and minor-league ballpark. He performed at many World Series and All Star contests.

Schacht formally retired in 1968, but he continued to give occasional guest performances into his eighties. He died in Waterbury, Connecticut, on July 14, 1984, at the age of ninety-one. ★

Favorite Story

Al Schacht enjoyed the familiar story of a cocky young farm-belt player who was a big hitter in his home territory and was trying out for the majors. After the first week of spring training, the youngster wired his mother: "Dear mom. Leading all batters. These pitchers not so tough." A week later: "Looks like I will be regular outfielder. Now hitting .433." Early in the third week: "Dear mom. They started throwing curves. Will be home Friday."

Literary Bent

One of Schacht's favorite activities was writing. He produced several books, including the autobiographical *Clowning through Baseball* (1941, with "Grammar and Adjectives by Murray Goodman") and *My Own Particular Screwball: An Informal Autobiography* (1955, edited by Ed Keyes).

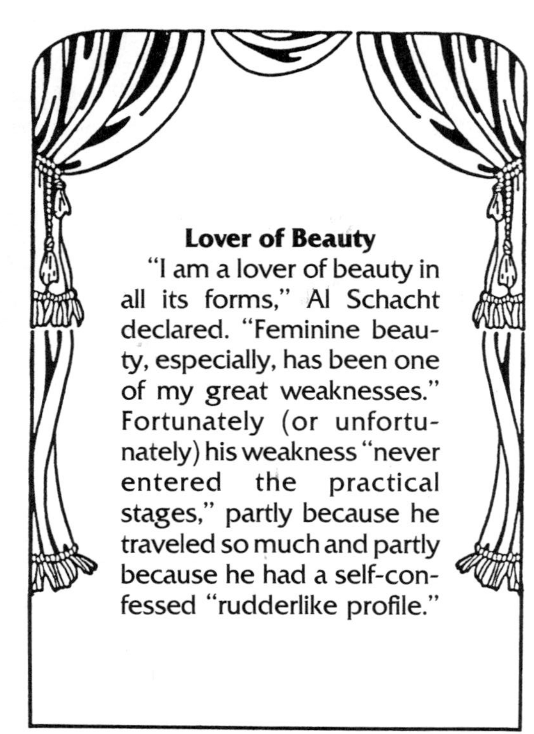

Lover of Beauty

"I am a lover of beauty in all its forms," Al Schacht declared. "Feminine beauty, especially, has been one of my great weaknesses." Fortunately (or unfortunately) his weakness "never entered the practical stages," partly because he traveled so much and partly because he had a self-confessed "rudderlike profile."

AVERY SCHREIBER
Lovable Bear

Avery Schreiber won his greatest fame early in his career when he performed sketches with Jack Burns. But Schreiber—with his rubbery features, woolly hair, and chubby, bearlike body—has also created many great comical moments as a soloist.

He was born in Chicago, Illinois, on April 9, 1935. After serving in the army (1954-55), he began a serious study of the theater. In 1960 he graduated in directing from the Goodman Theater School of Chicago.

While working as a member of the cast at Chicago's improvisational club Second City (1960-64), he met Jack Burns. Their satirical improvisations as a duo became a major attraction. During that time Schreiber developed his samurai-warrior shtick and his bit as a human computer (with attendant sound effects) sticking out his tongue with the answers.

After leaving Second City, Schreiber worked on his own for a couple of years. He appeared, for example, as

Strange Sense of Humor
Schreiber often finds humor where others do not. He regards the works of the Russian novelist Dostoyevski as funny. And once he was kicked out of a theater for laughing during a performance of Mozart's opera *Don Giovanni.*

Kermit on a Chain
In the 1970s Schreiber began wearing a neck chain holding a gold-colored replica of the puppet Kermit the Frog, one of the Muppets.

Jack Burns (left) and Avery Schreiber.

the evil Captain Manzini in the TV comedy series *My Mother the Car* (1965-66).

Soon, however, Burns and Schreiber reunited. In the late 1960s and early 1970s they frequently performed their sketches on TV, and in 1973 they hosted their own series, *The Burns and Schreiber Comedy Hour.*

Some of their improvisations turned into more-or-less set pieces. Most of them featured Schreiber as a cheerful Jewish cabbie, while Burns played a brash bigot. The obnoxious Burns character had the annoying habit of constantly repeating himself, especially by following a statement with repeated *huh*s despite Schreiber's *yeah*s: "Huh?" "Yeah." "Huh?" "Yeah." "Huh?" "Yeah." "Huh?" This huh-yeah dialogue became a national catchphrase.

Their skit called "The Cabdriver and the Conventioneer" was one of their most popular routines. Part of it centered on Schreibers's Jewishness. Looking at the cabbie's nameplate, Burns said, "You're of the Judeo-Hebraic tradition?" Schreiber replied,"You mean I'm a Jew." "Hey," objected Burns, "I don't go in for name calling! But lemme tell ya, pound for pound Hank Greenberg was one of the greatest ballplayers who ever lived." "What about Sandy Koufax?" "Don't tell me he's one of them, too!" Other skits focused on drugs, the Vietnam War, and similar high-tension topics.

During their 1973 TV series, Schreiber revealed a new talent for improvising extravagant characterizations, much in the manner of Jonathan Winters. Some sketches on that show had Schreiber imitating a machine that would say friendly things to a lonely customer (Burns).

Even while he was working with Burns, Schreiber continued to pursue an independent career. In 1967 he directed the Broadway production *How to Be a Jewish Mother,* and in 1969 he appeared in the movie *Don't Drink the Water.* Throughout the 1970s he was a hit in the comical TV commercials for Doritos corn chips (Schreiber produced earth-shattering crunches when he munched the chips).

After their TV series ended its brief run, Schreiber and Burns went their separate ways. Since then Schreiber has been a familiar presence on TV as a regular on the variety series *Sammy and Company* (1975-77) and *Sha Na Na* (1977-78), and as a guest on other shows. He had roles in the feature-length play *The Ascent of Mt. Fuji* (TV, 1978) and the two-hour pilot *Shadow Chasers* (TV, 1985).

Schreiber's Secret Ambition

Avery Schreiber sometimes laments being a funnyman instead of a leading man. Tapping his big belly, he confesses, "There's a Cary Grant in there trying to get out."

Influence of Marx Brothers

Schreiber regards the Marx Brothers as not only great comedians but also social critics. He says he sometimes draws ideas from their zany antics.

Passion for Food

Schreiber loves to eat. One of his favorite foods is a triple-decker club sandwich. And while making his Doritos TV commercials, he developed the habit of constantly munching on corn chips.

Schreiber played the community slob, Mendl, in the New York City stage production of the Jewish comedy *Dreyfus in Rehearsal* (1974). His later movies included *The Last Remake of Beau Geste* (1977), *Caveman* (1981), and *Cannonball Run II* (1984). In 1988 he appeared in a California Music Theater production of the Gershwin musical comedy *Strike Up the Band.*

JERRY SEINFELD
Clean Comedian

Jerry Seinfeld was voted America's Best Male Comedy Club performer in 1988 by a poll of nightclub regulars, even though by then he had already moved up to the large concert halls and amphitheaters for most of his performances. Part visual comedian and part lighthearted social commentator, Seinfeld characteristically builds his humor to a fever pitch by exploring a topic from all angles, as in this bit about a strand of hair in a bathroom:

> I don't like other people's showers. There's a problem with temperature adjustment. And there's always that little hair stuck on the wall. You want to get rid of it, but you don't want to touch it. You wonder how it got that high in the first place. Maybe it's got a life of its own. I don't want to get involved. So you have to aim the shower head at the hair, but then it always seems to just miss the hair. So you have to get a little water in your hands, go over there—[he throws imaginary water at the imaginary hair and watches it slither down the tile wall].

Child at Heart

"I wear sneakers every day," Seinfeld admits. "It's hard to picture myself as a grown-up."

Happy Comic

"This image of comedians as troubled souls gets irritating," Seinfeld complains. "People take comedy far too seriously." He says his happy childhood did not prevent him from becoming a successful comic.

Alertness

Seinfeld keeps his senses alert by neither smoking nor drinking.

In addition, he studies Eastern philosophy for enlightenment. "Zen," he explains, "is just looking at something from a different perspective, and that's what a lot of comedy is."

Talmud Study

Twice a month Seinfeld and his friends Larry Miller, Paul Reiser, Mark Schiff, and Lotus Weinstock meet at their private homes to study liturgy and the Talmud under the guidance of the two Hillel House rabbis from USC and UCLA.

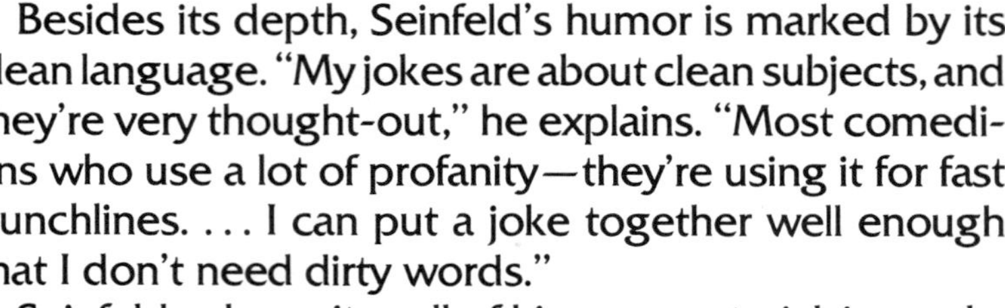

Comedic Influences

Seinfeld is not impressed by acting or actors, who speak other people's words. "I look up to people like Jay Leno and David Letterman," he says. "People who speak their minds." His other comedic influences include Bill Cosby and Robert Klein.

Home

Seinfeld spends little time at his home, which is barely furnished. It "looks like a hospital with a stereo," says his friend Jay Leno.

Academe

When he visits the Boston area, Seinfeld likes to walk through the Harvard University campus, looking around and saying, "I don't have to know any of this."

Talk Shows

Seinfeld dislikes TV talk shows because "they can be so dull. People don't have that much to say."

Besides its depth, Seinfeld's humor is marked by its clean language. "My jokes are about clean subjects, and they're very thought-out," he explains. "Most comedians who use a lot of profanity—they're using it for fast punchlines. . . . I can put a joke together well enough that I don't need dirty words."

Seinfeld, who writes all of his own material, is an observational humorist. When, for example, he watched the Winter Olympics, he thought about the meaning of the silver medal: "It means that of all the losers, you came in first of that group." He was baffled by the biathlon, which consists of cross-country skiing and rifle shooting: "How many Alpine snipers are into this? It's like combining swimming and strangling a guy. I don't get the sport."

Seinfeld has particular contempt for, yet fascination with, the grandiose, especially when it involves large numbers. For example, why does McDonald's continue to count its hamburgers? Sixty, eighty, ninety billion! "Do they want cows surrendering voluntarily?" he asks. "Showing up at the door? 'We'd like to turn ourselves in. We've seen the sign; we know we have no chance.'"

Here are a few more Seinfeld sidesplitters:

> Dogs are broke all their lives. You know why they have no money? No pockets. They see change on the street—there's nothing they can do about it.
>
> You go to the store and buy Grape Nuts. No grapes, no nuts. What's the story there?
>
> If he's the best man, why is the bride marrying the groom?

Jerry Seinfeld was born in New York City in 1954 and grew up in Massapequa, Long Island, New York. His father, who painted and sold business signs, "was always making people laugh," Jerry later said. "I watched the effect he would have on people, and I thought that was for me."

In 1976, shortly after graduating from Queens College with a major in theater and communications, Seinfeld began performing at small comedy clubs in New York City. "They weren't even clubs," he later admitted. "They were restaurants with a table missing."

In 1980 he moved to Los Angeles, where he struggled through some lean months. He did, however, manage to land a recurring, though short-lived, role on the TV sitcom *Benson*.

His big break came in 1981 when he made his first of many appearances on *The Tonight Show*. Subsequently he has become a favorite performer on *Late Night with David Letterman* and on Home Box Office.

Currently he is one of the busiest comedians around, being booked about three hundred times a year. "Four days is about my maximum to go without working," he says. "I took a vacation this year [1988], and I just hated it." ★

PETER SELLERS
Inspector Clouseau

Peter Sellers was a comedy chameleon. Not intrinsically a funny man, he nevertheless revealed a comic genius through a series of brilliant and hilarious screen characterizations of incredible variety. He frequently portrayed multiple roles in a single film. His best-known character, whom he played in the Pink Panther series of motion pictures, was the bumbling French detective Inspector Clouseau.

Sellers was born of a Protestant father and Jewish mother in the Southsea district of Portsmouth, England, on September 8, 1925. His parents were part of a theatrical touring company created by his maternal grandmother.

He began his own attempt at a show-business career in 1941 when he teamed up with a friend to form a song-and-joke act. Soon he took up the drums and played with various groups. From 1943 to 1946 he served in the Royal Air Force.

Returning to civilian life, Sellers worked up a variety act consisting of jokes, comic impersonations, and a little drumming and ukulele playing. He began to appear in music halls.

In 1948 Sellers telephoned a producer and impersonated the voices of two radio stars (Kenneth Horne and Richard Murdoch). Impressed, the producer hired him for some radio appearances. Sellers was an immediate hit, and soon he found himself inundated with offers for radio and concert engagements.

In 1949 he and a few friends, calling themselves Goons, made a recording of a comedy act and sent it to some radio officials. Two years later the recording finally led to the Goons' own radio series, *Crazy People*. In 1952 the program becme known as *The Goon*

Superstitions

Sellers geared much of his life around superstitions. For example, he avoided green as an "unlucky color." He believed in spiritualism and astrology, frequently consulting a medium or an astrological forecast before making decisions.

Favorite Hobby

Sellers rarely stayed with any recreation for very long, but he did develop a significant interest in photography. He even managed to take pictures of open-heart surgery without fainting.

Sellers in *Being There*.

Show. One of England's most popular radio programs, the zany, anarchic, surrealistic *Goon Show* lasted till January 1960 and made Sellers famous. His *Goon Show* characters included Bluebottle, a reedy-voiced bookworm; Grytpype Thynne, a cad and a takeoff on the suave actor George Sanders; William ("Mate") Cobblers, a timber merchant whose head was as thick as his product; and Major Bloodnok, a retired officer who had won the Military Cross for emptying trash cans during battle.

During his *Goon Show* years Sellers also made his first ventures into movies. He began with a spinoff of the Goon characters in *Penny Points to Paradise* (1951), appeared as one of the eccentric robbers in the classic *The Ladykillers* (1956), and made a good impression as the comical elderly movie projectionist in *The Smallest Show on Earth* (1957). But the first film that really showed what he could do was *The Naked Truth* (1958), in which Sellers played several different roles: a hypocritical Scottish quizmaster, an aging bureaucrat, a sportsman, and a genial policeman.

In *The Mouse That Roared* (1959), set in a mythical European duchy, Sellers played three parts: the wily prime minister, the aged Grand Duchess Gloriana, and the shy, lovesick commander of the army. In *I'm All Right, Jack* (1959), a brilliant satire of British labor and management practices, he portrayed the pompous, pathetically ignorant union leader Fred Kite.

Sellers's first American movie was *Lolita* (1962), in which he played the decadent playwright Clare Quiltz. After that, he periodically alternated his filmmaking between American and British companies, often with international casts and locations.

His first internationally flavored movie was *The Pink Panther* (1964), filmed in Rome with French, Italian, American, and British stars. In *The Pink Panther* Sellers created one of the most universally popular characters of the modern cinema: the inept French detective Inspector Jacques Clouseau.

Sellers derived his basic idea for Inspector Clouseau from a box of Captain Webb matches. The label on the box pictured Captain Webb, the first man to swim across the English Channel to France. He had a large mustache and a facial expression that Sellers associated with the ostentatious virility affected by some Frenchmen. The actor decided to give the foolish Clouseau a big mustache and a great dignity, feeling that "a forgivable vanity would humanize him

Favorite people

One of Sellers's favorite movies was *The Producers*, a Mel Brooks comedy starring Gene Wilder and Zero Mostel. Sellers often ran the movie when he needed cheering up.

The French comic actor Jacques Tati influenced Sellers's portrayal of Inspector Clouseau. Like Tati's screen persona, Clouseau was constantly harassed by inanimate objects, such as doors, couches, bathrobes, and globes of the world.

Sellers's favorite comedian was Stan Laurel, with whose on-screen childlike quality Sellers, in real life, had much in common. In one or another of his concurrent homes, Sellers always kept a huge picture of Laurel.

Extravagant Sellers

Obsessed with constantly buying new, expensive gadgets, even though he seldom used them for any length of time, Sellers purchased paintings, antique furniture, photography equipment, cars, yachts, a telex cabling machine, and extra homes. In the last year of his life, he spent nearly $250,000 on private air transportation. During the same period, he purchased a $5,000 pair of gold eyeglasses.

and make him kind of touching." Sellers also invented Clouseau's strange French accent, while the film's director, Blake Edwards, suggested the character's physical clumsiness, which would make his dignity even funnier.

Sellers played Clouseau again in *A Shot in the Dark* (1964), *The Return of the Pink Panther* (1975), *The Pink Panther Strikes Again* (1976), and *Revenge of the Pink Panther* (1978).

One of Sellers's most memorable achievements came in *Dr. Strangelove; or, How I Learned to Stop Worrying and Love the Bomb* (1964). He played three roles: the liberal-humanist president of the United States, the captive English military officer, and the mad German nuclear scientist Dr. Strangelove, whose right arm uncontrollably reasserts its inbred violence (by attempting to strangle him) and Fascism (by giving the Nazi salute).

Later came roles in the film comedies *The World of Henry Orient* (1964), as a lecherous and lousy concert pianist; *What's New, Pussycat?* (1965), as a nutty psychiatrist; *I Love You, Alice B. Toklas* (1968), as a Jewish lawyer who becomes a hippie; *There's a Girl in My Soup* (1971), as an aging playboy; *Murder by Death* (1976), as the Chinese sleuth Sidney Wang; and *The Prisoner of Zenda* (1979), as both the cockney hansom cabdriver and the monarch of a mythical kingdom.

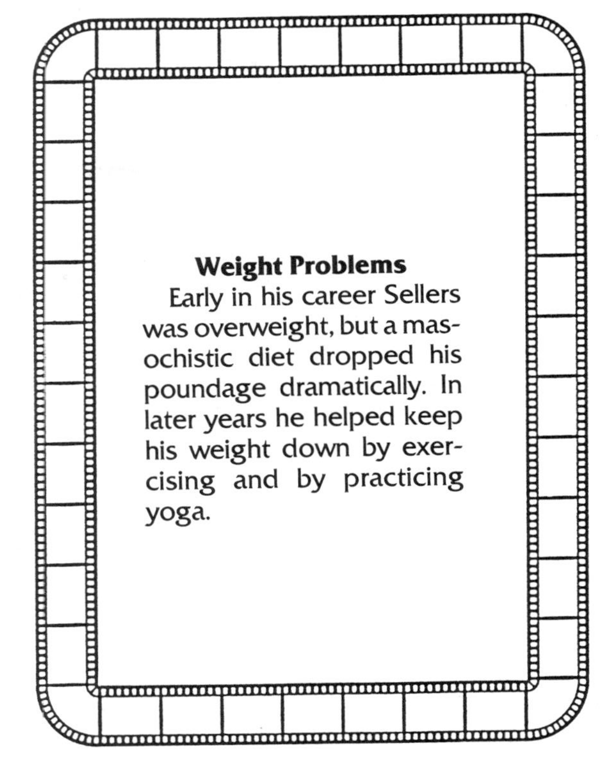

Weight Problems

Early in his career Sellers was overweight, but a masochistic diet dropped his poundage dramatically. In later years he helped keep his weight down by exercising and by practicing yoga.

Car-swapping Mania

Sellers loved to buy and trade automobiles. His first post-World War II car was a Rover I, which he kept only four weeks. Over the next twenty years some ninety cars—including Jaguars, Cadillacs, and Rolls-Royces—passed through his hands. Once he even rented an ambulance.

Hypochondria

Sellers constantly feared illnesses of all kinds. He consumed medicines the way some children devour sweets.

Recurring Depression

Afflicted with recurring depression and suicidal inclinations, Sellers nevertheless rejected psychiatric help because, he said, "psychiatrists only talk common sense to you"; that is, he feared that they would make him become aware of even more and deeper problems within himself.

Peter Sellers.

Sellers's greatest achievement was his performance as Chauncey Gardiner (or Chance the gardener) in *Being There* (1979), an allegory of American society's worship of the appearance of things rather than their substance. Chance has spent his entire life inside the home and walled garden of the millionaire whose plants he tends. All he knows of life comes from what he has seen of it on TV. When the millionaire dies, Chance is turned out into the world. Through other people's illusions about him, he comes to be seriously thought of as a candidate for the presidency of the United States.

The role of Chance required a naive character who had been tranquilized against the harsh realities of the world and benumbed into a permanent passivity by his overexposure to the slick packaging of TV. In creating the part, Sellers felt that the key was the voice, which he eventually derived as an offshoot of the childlike, innocent voice of Stan Laurel. Then came the leisurely walk and the rest of the passionless character.

Sellers's last role was in *The Fiendish Plot of Dr. Fu Manchu* (1980). He was preparing to do another Inspector Clouseau movie, *The Romance of the Pink Panther*, when he died of a long-standing heart ailment (he had had attacks in 1964, 1977, and 1979) in London, England, on July 24, 1980.

In 1982 the movie *Trail of the Pink Panther* was created from outtakes and previously unused sequences originally filmed for earlier comedies in the Pink Panther series. ☆

Comics Are Children
Shawn claimed that he, like most comics, was "basically shy. The reason they try to be funny is to get attention . . . . Comics are basically children."

Baseball Dreams
In his youth Shawn wanted to be a professional baseball player. He was signed by the Chicago White Sox, but he was drafted into the army before he could join the club.

DICK SHAWN
Hip Comedian

Dick Shawn derived his humor by adopting a self-absorbed, excessively hip stage persona. He was "hard to classify," he admitted. "I don't do mother-in-law or ugly-girl jokes. In fact, I hardly tell jokes at all."

He was born in Buffalo, New York, on December 1, 1924. His original name was Richard Schulefand.

He began his comedy career while serving in the army during World War II. Back in civilian life, he briefly

attended the University of Miami (Florida), where he developed comedy routines, including one about a schizophrenic named Joe Phreenie and Sam Schizo. Later he moved to New York City, won an amateur talent contest, and appeared on Arthur Godfrey's *Talent Scouts* TV show.

Turning to straight acting, he made his New York City stage debut in *For Heaven's Sake, Mother!* (1948). He billed himself as Richy Shawn.

Comedy, however, remained his principal interest. He toured in cabaret, and in 1953 he appeared at New York City's famed Palace Theater as the chief comic in the revue *Betty Hutton and Her All-Star International Show.* Soon he was performing on Ed Sullivan's TV show and in Las Vegas nightclubs with Marlene Dietrich, Zsa Zsa Gabor, and other headliners.

After making it big as a comedian, Shawn frequently took time off for straight acting roles. His stage credits included *A Funny Thing Happened on the Way to the Forum* (1964) and *The World of Sholem Aleichem* (1976). In the 1970s and 1980s he guest-starred in many TV series, such as *St. Elsewhere.*

A highlight of his film career was his role in *The Producers* (1967), as a hippie actor playing Adolf Hitler in the campy musical *Springtime for Hitler.* Shawn also appeared in *Wake Me When It's Over* (1960); *It's a Mad, Mad, Mad, Mad World* (1963); *Love at First Bite* (1979);

Comedy Therapy

"I was quiet on the outside, and ready to explode inside," Dick Shawn said of his youth. "If I hadn't learned to do comedy, or find a way to express myself, my hair would've blown off.... The only way I could express myself when I was younger was through my body. That's why my comedy is so physical."

A Private Person

"The fact that I'm not a household name never bothered me," Shawn asserted. "I don't really care. My ego doesn't need it. I never owned any jewelry. Rolls-Royces never fascinated me. I just took a little house by the beach in Santa Monica—away from the Beverly Hills crowd. I live my own private life."

Pell-Mell Quality

Offstage, Shawn was tense. He tended to speak in short bursts and to bounce quickly from one topic to another.

His Santa Monica home reflected his pell-mell quality. The furnishings came from Italy, Egypt, and Japan. An American Indian blanket covered a huge petrified goatskin coffee table. And he kept a monkey in a birdcage.

Shawn muses on the banana.

The Secret Diary of Sigmund Freud (1984); and other movies.

Meanwhile, his comedy career was flourishing. In the 1970s and 1980s Shawn frequently performed the one-man show *The Second Greatest Entertainer in the Whole Wide World*. He showed the eccentric range of his talents by tap-dancing, playing scenes from *Othello*, and creating comic characters.

His stand-up comedy act was also popular. He appeared on TV, in nightclubs, and at benefits. But his hilarious hipness went over especially well on college campuses.

During a performance at the University of California in San Diego, he collapsed onstage. Because he was known for such falls during his act, the audience at first mistook the move as a joke. Soon a doctor was called. Shawn died at a nearby La Jolla hospital on April 17, 1987. ★

The Perfect Fruit

Shawn was fascinated by the banana. The attraction began when he ended a song in *The Producers* while eating that fruit. Soon he put banana-eating into his solo comedy act. The banana is "funny" and "pure," he said. "There isn't a *seed* in a banana. You see, I'm talking about perfection."

AL SHEAN
Gallagher's Partner

Al Shean teamed up with many straight men during his years as a burlesque and vaudeville comic, but today his name is irrevocably linked with that of Ed(ward) Gallagher. During their two stints together (1910-12, 1920-25), they formed one of the most popular comedy teams of their time.

Their most famous routine was their theme song, "Mr. Gallagher and Mr. Shean" (introduced in the early 1920s), the lyrics of which varied on different occasions; here is part of one version:

BOTH: There are two funny men, the best I've ever seen.
One is Mr. Gallagher, the other Mr. Shean.
When these two cronies meet, it surely is a treat,
The things they say and the things they do,
And the funny way they greet.
SHEAN: Oh, Mr. Gallagher!
GALLAGHER: Oh, Mr. Shean!
SHEAN: Oh, Mr. Gallagher! Oh, Mr. Gallagher!
GALLAGHER: Hello. What's on your mind this morning, Mr. Shean?
SHEAN: Everybody's making fun of the way this country's run.
All the papers say we'll soon live European.
GALLAGHER: Why, Mr. Shean, why, Mr. Shean,
On the day they took your old canteen
Cost of living went so high
That it's cheaper now to die.
SHEAN: Positively, Mr. Gallagher?
GALLAGHER: Absolutely, Mr. Shean!

Shean was born in Dornum, Germany, on May 12, 1868. His original name was Adolf Schoenberg (or Schönberg).

Before migrating to the United States in about 1876, his parents were beergarden performers, his father as a magician and ventriloquist and his mother as a harpist. Adolf had three siblings, including Minna, whose own children became the famous Marx Brothers comedy team.

He grew up on New York City's Lower East Side.

Helped the Marx Brothers

When the Marx Brothers, Shean's nephews, were in their early, strugggling years, he provided them with financial support and theatrical advice. He also wrote some material for their vaudeville act.

Kids Loved Shean

When he visited his sister Minna and her family, Shean always gave money to his little nephews, later famous as the Marx Brothers. And when he left their home, he would toss a hundred pennies into the air and let the neighborhood children scramble for the coins.

A Potent Combination

According to Groucho Marx, Shean had a strong liking for Limburger cheese, which combined with Shean's bay-rum cologne to give Groucho an unusual odoriferous memory of his uncle.

Kept Two Homes

Besides owning a comfortable house in Mount Vernon, New York, Shean had a fishing camp at Haines Landing, Maine.

Al Shean (fourth from right) in a scene from *The Great Walty.*

After working for a while as a pants presser in a garment factory, he became a member of the Manhattan Comedy Four, a group of singers and knockabout clowns. They toured dime museums and cheap burlesque houses till they finally made it to vaudeville theaters. After that team disbanded in 1900, Shean spent several years with Charles L. Warren in a burlesque of the famous *Quo Vadis* story.

In 1910 Shean formed his famous comedy duo with Ed Gallagher. The tall, slim, mustached straight man (Gallagher) contrasted with the short, stocky, clean-shaven comic (Shean). They performed in vaudeville and in the Broadway revue *The Rose Maid* (1912) before ill feeling developed between them and they split up.

Shean worked on his own in vaudeville and on Broadway till 1920, when, under pressure from his sister Minna, he and Gallagher reunited. Their new act was initially called *Mr. Gallagher and Mr. Shean in Egypt*, and therefter Gallagher wore a straw hat and Shean a fez. In vaudeville the following year they introduced their theme song, "Mr. Gallagher and Mr. Shean," which helped to propel them to enormous popularity in the 1922 edition of the *Ziegfeld Follies* Broadway revue. However, despite their great success together, they permanently parted in 1925.

Fight Fan

In his late years Shean liked to watch boxing matches on TV.

Liked the Ladies

Shean, though married, frequently had casual affairs, even late in life. When he was sixty-nine years old, he appeared onstage as a virtuous priest in *Father Malachy's Miracle*. The playwright George S. Kaufman went backstage to congratulate Shean and caught the old man with a female. Later Kaufman quipped, "I just saw a priest buttoning his fly."

For several years Shean continued to work in vaudeville with other straight men. But increasingly he turned to character-acting roles on the stage and in films. His stage credits included *Betsy* (1926), *The Prince of Pilsen* (1930), and *Father Malachy's Miracle* (1937), in the last of which he had the title role as a simple priest. Among his many movies were *San Francisco* (1936), *The Prisoner of Zenda* (1937), *The Great Waltz* (1938), *Ziegfeld Girl* (1941), and *Atlantic City* (1944).

Shean died in New York City on August 12, 1949.

☆

ALLAN SHERMAN
Musical Parodist

Allan Sherman attained overnight fame in October 1962 with the release of his album *My Son, the Folksinger*, a folksong travesty in Jewish style. Over the next several years he enjoyed enormous success with more albums, stage performances, and TV appearances. The staples in his act were song parodies, consisting of familiar tunes combined with Sherman's own hilarious lyrics. His satire frequently targeted urban Jewish mores, as in his twist on Meredith Willson's "Seventy-six Trombones": "Seventy-six Sol Cohens in the country club, / And a hundred and ten nice men named Levine."

He was born in Chicago, Illinois, on November 30, 1924. His original name was Allan Copelan. When he was six his parents divorced, and later he took his mother's maiden name, Sherman.

Short-lived Hobbies

In his spare time the singing parodist engaged in a series of brief hobbies: model railroading, photography, filmmaking, antique collecting, golf, and art collecting.

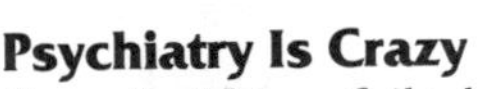

Psychiatry Is Crazy

When hobbies failed to reduce Sherman's stress, he tried psychiatry. "Four times I looked for psychiatric help," he complained, "and each time I arrived at the inescapable conclusion that the psychiatrist was crazier than I was."

Most Moving Moment

In January 1963, at the Pasadena (California) Civic Auditorium, Sherman shared the bill with Harpo Marx, who was giving his last performance. Sherman, who idolized Harpo, tried to make the retirement announcement, but he broke down and wept onstage. The old pro Harpo had to go onstage and bail out Sherman, who later wrote that in his entire career the Harpo episode was "the thing that moved me most deeply."

"Comedy is gentle and sweet and good and intelligent and honest, and that is what Harpo Marx was," Sherman concluded.

In 1945 he moved to New York City, where he wrote jokes and songs for comedians and TV shows. In 1951 he and a friend created the idea for *I've Got a Secret*, a TV game show. For several years Sherman produced the program. Later he produced other TV shows, but the work became sporadic.

In the fall of 1962, out of work and desperate for money, Sherman recorded and released his first album: *My Son, the Folksinger.* It sold over half a million copies in the first month. Soon he came out with two more albums: *My Son, the Celebrity* (1962) and *My Son, the Nut* (1963). He also began to work in major nightclubs, to appear on TV programs (including a stint as host of *The Tonight Show*), and to make concert tours (including two legendary shows with his friend Harpo Marx, who was giving his farewell performances).

In his concerts Sherman sang parodies of Broadway show tunes, which he could not use in his albums because of copyright problems. He irritated many songwriters. Richard Rodgers, for example, detested Sherman's changing "There Is Nothin' like a Dame" (from Rodgers and Hammerstein's *South Pacific*) into "There Is Nothin' like a Lox."

In his recordings Sherman drew from folk tunes, classical melodies, and other public-domain music. For example, in his first album "Frère Jacques" became "Sarah Jackman." "The Battle Hymn of the Republic" was transformed into the story of a cutter's heroic stand during a fire in Irving Roth's garment factory; the saga concluded with the cutter, Harry Lewis, "trampling through the warehouse where the drapes of Roth are stored. . . . Glory, glory, Harry Lewis."

The second album featured the Israeli folksong "Hava Nagila" as "Harvey and Sheila." "Bill Bailey" was parodied with "Won't you come home, Disraeli?"

The third album contained Sherman's biggest hit, "Hello, Muddah; Hello, Fadduh" (the key words are variously printed as *Muddah . . . Faddah* and *Mudduh . . . Fadduh*; Sherman himself, in his autobiography, *A Gift of Laughter* [1965], spells the words *Muddah . . . Fadduh*). It is cast in the form of a complaining letter from a child in summer camp to his parents: ". . . Now I don't want this should scare ya / But my bunk mate has malaria. / You remember Jeffrey Hardy? / They're about to organize a searching party . . ." The melody is the "Dance of the Hours" from Ponchielli's 1876 opera *La Gioconda.*

The country became saturated with Sherman's parodies, and by 1966 his popularity began to decline sharply.

Books and Music

Books and music were lifetime passions with Allan Sherman. He especially liked the stories of Horatio Alger, who "taught me that nothing is impossible."

"Lousy" Voice

A critic once said that Sherman's voice sounded like that of "a strangling myna bird." In his autobiography Sherman himself called his singing "lousy."

He died of respiratory failure in Los Angeles, California, on November 20, 1973, a few days short of his forty-ninth birthday.

Recent years have seen a renewed appreciation of Sherman's unique comedic gifts. ★

SAMMY SHORE
Warm-up

Sammy Shore has been for many years the most sought-after warm-up comedian in show business. He has opened shows for such stars as Elvis Presley, Sammy Davis, Jr., Tom Jones, and Ann-Margret.

Shore's trademark has long been his bit as Brother Sam, a preacher-healer ("You people up there in the balcony, you wanna be saved?" "Yeah!" "Jump, you mothers!"). But his range has deepened and broadened in recent years, so that he has become a kind of besieged Everyman, much in the manner of Woody Allen. With his shaggy-dog appearance and his blend of Jewish humor and pathos, Shore complains about his hip transplants, his problems with women, and his strained relationships with family members. He makes cogent observations about TV commercials, frequent-flier programs, parking meters, and TV evangelists. Among his longer routines are those on bullfighting, on the resemblance between the behavior of a mouse with only a few hours to live and our own

Comedy Heals
Comedians are "divine healers," Shore asserts, "put on earth to spread the word of joy and laughter."

Health Conscious
Since the late 1970s, when he joined Alcoholics Anonymous, Shore has worked out regularly, eaten healthfull, lost weight, and given up smoking. He relaxes by meditating.

Revises Priorities
In recent years Shore has tried to reduce his tension and depression previously caused by overwork and endless worry. "Now when I work, I work at my comedy one hour a night. The remainder of my time is for resting and simply being a person."

Not a Laugh Machine
"People seem to forget that comedians are not always comedians," Shore says. "We are human beings first," doing something onstage that is basically unnatural. "We can't be that way all the time. Yet many people think that at any given moment they can turn us on for an instant laugh."

Sammy Shore.

frantic lives, and on playing a trumpet (a regular part of his act) while his piano accompanist constantly interrupts to correct him. He draws great poignancy by playing an aging father at a retirement home waiting for his son to visit him.

Sammy (or Samuel, originally Semelah) Shore was born in Chicago, Illinois, in 1925. He took trumpet lessons as a child and wanted to enter show business. But he spent many years working in his father's rooming house and then in a men's store (where he was the unofficial resident clown).

In 1949 he got his first show-business job, as a comedian and social director at a Wisconsin resort. There he briefly teamed up with another comedian who would later hit the big time, Shecky Greene.

During the next twenty years Shore had a few shining moments, such as opening for Barbra Streisand at the New York City nightclub Bon Soir in 1963. But most of the time he struggled in obscurity in small clubs and third-class resorts.

His big break came in 1969 when he was asked to open for Elvis Presley in Las Vegas. Shore did so well that he stayed with Presley in Las Vegas and on tours till 1972.

In 1972 Shore opened the Comedy Store, a Los Angeles nightclub with entertainment provided solely by comedians. Most of the performers were unknowns looking to be seen by big-time agents and producers. Among the comics discovered at the Comedy Store were Freddie Prinze, Gabe Kaplan, and David Brenner.

In 1974 Shore gave the Comedy Store to his ex-wife, Mitzi. The format of the club has since been widely copied.

During those years, the early 1970s, Shore's long-standing drinking problem became so acute that his career virtually came to a halt. However, in 1976 he joined Alcoholics Anonymous, and in 1977 he opened for Ann-Margret in Las Vegas.

Since then his career has moved steadily forward, especially at casinos in Las Vegas and Atlantic City. In 1984 he published his autobiography as *The Warm-up*. The following year the book was adapted into the play *Hard Laughs*, staged in Santa Monica, California, with Shore appearing as his own father. In the spring of 1988 he proved that he could not only play second banana but also headline when he held the stage himself in a series of performances at the Santa Monica Playhouse.☆

Governed by Fear

Shore says his "fear, insecurity, and neediness" have caused him many unhappy love experiences. "I chose disturbed ladies to fix things for me," he confesses.

Favorite Comedian

The comedian Buddy Hackett, known for his spontaneous interplay with audiences, is Shore's idol. Sammy has called Hackett "a comedic genius."

PHIL SILVERS
Hilarious Manipulator

Phil Silvers delighted in portraying fast-talking swindlers, through whom he satirized the haste and deception that characterize so much of modern materialistic civilization. His career reached its peak during his four seasons (1955-59) as the manipulator par excellence Master Sergeant Ernie Bilko in the TV sitcom *You'll Never Get Rich* (later known as *The Phil Silvers Show* or *Sergeant Bilko*). By then Silvers had already paid his dues through years of apprenticeship in vaudeville, burlesque, nightclubs, musical comedy, and films.

He was born of Russian immigrants in New York City, New York, on May 11, 1911. His original name was Philip Silver. He added an *s* to his surname because several other performers named Silvers had already become successful in show business, such as Lou Silvers (Al Jolson's conductor).

Before reaching the age of five, Phil Silvers was already singing at family weddings and bar mitzvahs. Later he sang at a stag party, a movie theater, a beer hall, and elsewhere.

Lived for the Stage

"I know, when I am in front of an audience, doing my best, nothing can stop me," Silvers avowed in 1973. "I *exist* onstage. . . .The pain I've endured, the waste I've made of years of my life, have made me a more serious, deeper comedian."

Emotional Instability

An admitted neurotic and compulsive gambler (especially on horse races), Silvers went through many years of torment both professionally (worrying about his performances) and personally (suffering from insomnia and going through two divorces). Several times he nearly lost touch with reality. But in the early 1970s he found the return ticket: "I've gone back to people—I don't see how I can withdraw into my cocoon again."

Phil Silvers in the Broadway musical *A Funny Thing Happened on the Way to the Forum.*

In 1923 he was invited to join Gus Edwards's famous troupe of vaudeville youngsters. With that group, Silvers played in New York City's Palace Theater and elsewhere. However, within a few months the boy's voice began to change, and he was out of work.

When he was fourteen he got a job playing a juvenile in a comedy routine with the adult vaudevillians Joe Morris and Flo Campbell. Silvers stayed with the act for six years. Then, after a brief time spent in other vaudeville work and on the borscht circuit, he entered burlesque and performed in obscurity there for seven years (1932-39).

In 1939 Silvers was asked to play a small role in the Broadway musical comedy *Yokel Boy.* One of the male leads was Jack Pearl, a Dutch-dialect comedian. When Pearl left the show at an early stage, Silvers replaced him. Pearl's role as a Dutch-dialect film director was rewritten to make Silvers a sharp Hollywood press agent who speaks New Yorkese. The role thus created, Punko Parks, became the prototype for the kind of comic character that Silvers played to perfection many times during the rest of his career: the aggressive, smiling manipulator.

He then turned to films. His early movies included *You're in the Army Now* (1941), *My Gal Sal* (1942),

Admired Merman

A chronic worrier himself, especially on opening nights, Silvers greatly respected Ethel Merman's steely nerves: "She plays the best opening night of any musical-comedy performer."

Favorite Recreations

Taking steambaths and playing the clarinet were two of Silvers's favorite recreations.

For most of his life he feared water. But in his late years he took up swimming, awkwardly. "It's exercise," he said, "and ultimately relaxing, because I end up exhausted."

Sports Figures

Silvers enjoyed the company of boxers, jockeys, ballplayers, and sportswriters.

Coney Island (1943), *Cover Girl* (1944), and *Don Juan Quilligan* (1945).

In the late 1940s Silvers worked principally in nightclubs. He also performed on Broadway in *High Button Shoes* (1947) and hosted the TV variety series *Welcome Aboard* (1948) and *The Arrow Show* (1948-49).

In 1951 he made a tremendous impression in the Broadway musical comedy *Top Banana.* He played Jerry Biffle, a burlesque comic whose whole life centers on getting laughs at any cost. Silvers, who modeled his performance of the role after the real-life comedian Milton Berle, also starred in the filmed version of the show (1954).

In 1955 came the hit TV comedy series *You'll Never Get Rich,* starring Silvers as the army's Master Sergeant Ernie Bilko, a cardsharp, promoter, and master swindler who covered his evil cunning with a mask of outraged innocence. By the end of its four-season run, the series had become known as *The Phil Silvers Show*; it was later syndicated as *Sergeant Bilko.*

In the 1960s he had another TV series: *The New Phil Silvers Show* (1963-64), in which he played the factory worker and con artist Harry Grafton. Silvers also performed in the stage musical *Do Re Mi* (1960) and appeared in several movies, including *It's a Mad, Mad, Mad, Mad World* (1963) and *A Guide for the Married Man* (1967).

He was offered the lead in Stephen Sondheim's Broadway musical *A Funny Thing Happened on the Way to the Forum* (1962), based on ancient Roman comedies by Plautus. But Silvers rejected the offer because he felt the work was "too artsy." Later, however, he changed his mind and played the secondary role of Lycus, the procurer, in the filmed version (1966). In a 1972 stage revival of the play, he took the starring role of Pseudolus, the conniving slave.

In the early 1970s Silvers suffered a stroke, and for a time he had to reduce his activities. Among his later performances were roles in the movies *Won Ton Ton, the Dog Who Saved Hollywood* (1976); *The Cheap Detective* (1978); and *Goldie and the Boxer* (TV, 1979).

Silvers died at his apartment in the Century City section of Los Angeles on November 1, 1985.★

Silvers as Jerry Biffle in *Top Banana.*

Avid Reader

Silvers read widely, and he could converse well on many subjects, including politics, drama, and literature.

Haphazard Eating Habits

For most of his life, Silvers's meals were "catch-as-catch-can." To avoid sluggishness onstage, he tried to eat at least 3½ hours before a show. If he had to eat nearer the opening, he would limit himself to a malted milk or a pastrami sandwich. ("That delicious, lethal deli food is an occupational hazard," he said.) After a show, he liked to eat late at night, especially with friends. If he had to eat alone, he would have a hurried sandwich or omelet.

YAKOV SMIRNOFF
Russian-American Comedian

Yakov Smirnoff, a Russian immigrant in the United States, bases his comedy act on jokes that confirm Russian stereotypes and poke fun at American customs and language:

> The Russian Express Card. Don't leave home.
>
> I have no relatives left in Russia, except for some cousins twice removed—from their apartments.
>
> On the Fourth of July in Russia we had fireworks, too. They'd put you up against a wall and fire. It works!
>
> The waitress said, "We have cheesecake for dessert. I said, "I don't like cheesecake. Do you have Jello?" And she said, "Yes, we have lots of Jello, Jello coming out of our ears." I said, "No, thanks, I'll have the cheesecake."

Yakov Smirnoff was born in Odessa, the Soviet Union, on January 24, 1951. His original surname was Pokhis.

At the age of fifteen he made his debut as a professional stand-up comedian. In 1969 he was drafted into the Soviet army, where he spent two years entertaining the troops. He then began to tour the country as a civilian comic.

However, Smirnoff soon tired of having his material censored, and in 1975 he applied for permission to emigrate. He was promptly fired from his job. After two years of being constantly interrogated, he was finally allowed to leave, probably because the Soviet government, to pave the way for a wheat deal by appeasing the United States, had slightly eased emigration for Russian Jews.

Memories of Russian Circuses

While growing up in the Soviet Union, Smirnoff loved to attend Russian circuses. He especially enjoyed the clowns. The Soviet people, he says, desperately need "to get those laughs from circus clowns because, unlike Americans, they don't have political candidates and TV evangelists."

Russian Through and Through

"I'm Russian, and I'll be Russian probably for the rest of my life in people's eyes," Smirnoff admits. "But it doesn't matter, because I could play an attorney from Russia or anything else."

Hollywood Hills

Smirnoff has settled into a Hollywood Hills mansion once owned by Lenny Bruce.

In 1977 Smirnoff arrived in the United States. While he was learning English, he held a few odd jobs, including one as a bartender at Grossinger's in the Catskills. There he studied the comics and eventually got his first American job as a comedian.

Soon Smirnoff was appearing at New York City comedy clubs, including the Comic Strip. In Los Angeles he became a regular at the Comedy Store. He also began to work throughout the United States in nightclubs, at colleges, on TV talk shows, and in theater concerts.

Smirnoff is best known to millions through the Miller Lite beer commercial in which he says, "What a country. In America, you can always find a party. In Russia, party always finds you."

He has had bit parts in several movies, including *Moscow on the Hudson* (1984) and *The Money Pit* (1986). In 1986 he starred in the syndicated TV sitcom *What a Country!*, about a group of immigrants studying English and hoping to find big success in the United States. Smirnoff published a collection of his jokes in the book *America on Six Rubles a Day* (1987).☆

New Homeland

When American friends tell Smirnoff that the United States wants people to believe that it is better than it really is, he replies, "It's hard to see bad stuff when you're in love, and I'm still in love with this country."

On July 4, 1986, Smirnoff became a naturalized American citizen.

Luxury Cars

By the mid-1980s Smirnoff had acquired three luxury cars: a Mercedes 450SL, a Rolls-Royce (with a personalized license plate reading COMRADE, and a Ferrari (license plate, EX-RED).

JOE SMITH *and* CHARLIE DALE
Sunshine Boys

Smith and Dale kept America laughing for over sixty years—from the early 1900s in vaudeville to the 1960s on television. Using Jewish dialect, they performed humorous sketches that poked fun at doctors, chefs, tax consultants, and others. Smith delivered most of the punch lines, while Dale played the deadpan straight man. Their endless onstage arguing provided the principal inspiration for Neil Simon's comedy *The Sunshine Boys*, which examines the strained relationship between two elderly ex-vaudevillians.

Joe Smith was born in New York City, New York, on February 16, 1884. His original name was Joseph Sultzer. Charlie Dale was born in the same city on Septem-

Smith and Dale in *Two Tickets to Broadway.*

ber 6, 1881. His original name was Charles Marks.

In 1898 they literally ran into each other on bicycles. Soon they became fast friends and entered show business together. They joked, sang, and danced wherever they could get jobs—in cafés, saloons, and theaters.

They arrived at their stage names by accident. A printer had a hundred "Smith and Dale" cards left over when a duo of that name canceled the order. To take advantage of the bargain price for the cards, Sultzer and Marks became Smith and Dale.

Just after the turn of the century, they created a school act, a forerunner of similar acts later formed by Gus Edwards and by the Marx Brothers. "Give me a sentence with the word *delight*," the teacher would demand. To which the pupil would respond, "De wind blew in de window and blew out de light."

Soon thereafter Smith and Dale joined two singing waiters from the Avon Café in New York City to form a group called the Avon Comedy Four. Over the next few decades the other two members would change many times, but the name of the quartet would remain the same, as would the four characters portrayed: a Hebrew, a German, a tough, and a sissy. Eventually the team came to be called Smith and Dale and Their Avon Comedy Four.

By 1906 they had become top vaudeville comedians. They were also big hits in Europe, especially in London. In 1929 they headlined for the first time at the London Palladium.

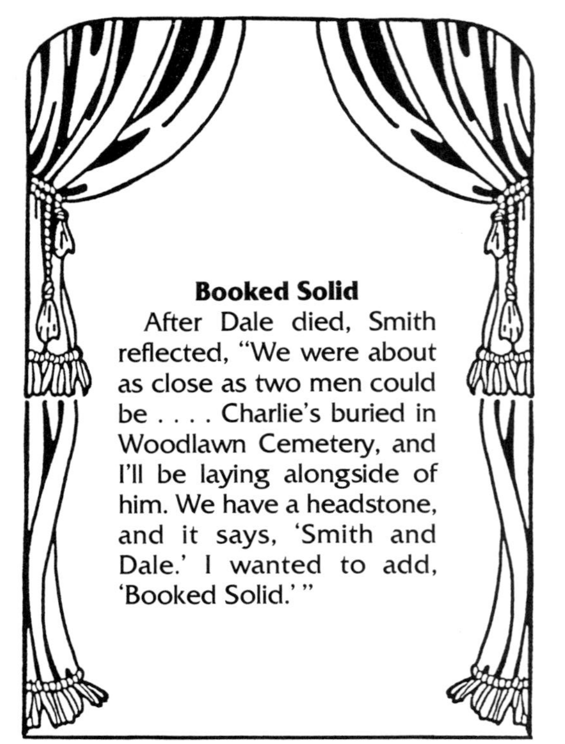

Booked Solid

After Dale died, Smith reflected, "We were about as close as two men could be . . . . Charlie's buried in Woodlawn Cemetery, and I'll be laying alongside of him. We have a headstone, and it says, 'Smith and Dale.' I wanted to add, 'Booked Solid.' "

No Arguing Offstage

Asked if he and Dale fought as much privately as they did publicly, Smith replied, "We do so much arguing onstage that we don't have anything left to argue about offstage."

Hobbies

In his later years, Smith painted watercolors and read voraciously, his favorite authors being Montague Glass, Ben Hecht, and Octavus Roy Cohen.

Their most famous routine was *Dr. Kronkhite* [also spelled *Kronkheit*; *kronkheit* is Yiddish for "sickness"] *and His Only Living Patient*:

SMITH: Are you a doctor?
DALE: I'm a doctor.
SMITH: I'm dubious.
DALE: I'm glad to know you, Mr. Dubious.
SMITH: I'm still dubious.
DALE: Mr. Dubious, are you a married man?
SMITH: Yes and no.
DALE: What do you mean, yes and no?
SMITH: I am but I wish I wasn't!

• • •

DALE: Mr. Dubious, what's your complaint?
SMITH: Before you I saw another doctor. He said I had snoo in my blood.
DALE: Snoo? What's snoo?
SMITH: Nothing. What's snoo with you? But doctor, I'm sick. Every time I eat a heavy meal I don't feel so hungry after.
DALE: Maybe you don't eat the right type of vitaminees! What type of dishes are you eating?
SMITH: I should eat dishes? What am I—a crock-odile?

• • •

DALE: So when you drink, vat kind of drinks, liquids—.
SMITH: Doctor, (wiping face) don't speak so fluidly!
DALE: Please, my time is liniment.
SMITH: Don't rub it in.
DALE: I have no patience!
SMITH: I shouldn't be here either.

• • •

DALE: You owe me $10.
SMITH: For what?
DALE: For my advice.
SMITH: Well, doctor, here's $2. Take it. That's my advice!
DALE: You cheapskate! You come in here—you cockamamie—.
SMITH: One more word and you only get a dollar.
DALE: Why—.
SMITH: That's a word! Here's the dollar!

Besides starring in vaudeville, Smith and Dale appeared in many New York City shows, such as *The Whirl of New York* (1921), *The Sky's the Limit* (1934), and *Bright Lights of 1944* (1943). Their movies included

The Laugh Was on Charlie

Even though Joe Smith delivered most of the punch lines in their act, he admitted that Charlie Dale often broke him up.

Charlie once got a big laugh without even being present. The two partners were together so much that people sometimes mistook one for the other. "One time a fellow gave me $10. He owed it to Charlie," Smith confessed. "I laughingly took it."

Jabbing and Spitting

In Neil Simon's comedy *The Sunshine Boys*, Al Lewis constantly jabbed his finger into the chest, and accidentally (with certain letters) spit into the face, of his partner, Willie Clark. In reality, according to Smith, he would point his finger at Dale and sometimes poke him gently. But it was Dale who spit with his *t*'s.

Smith liked *The Sunshine Boys*. He said that in the play, he and Dale had been "Simonized."

Manhattan Parade (1931), *Nob Hill* (1945), and *Two Tickets to Broadway* (1951). They also made recordings in the 1920s, worked on radio in the 1940s, and later performed on TV variety programs. They retired in 1968.

In their last years, after their wives died, Smith and Dale both lived at the Actors Fund Home in Englewood, New Jersey. They often staged shows for visitors.

Dale died in Teaneck, New Jersey, on November 16, 1971. Smith died in Englewood on February 22, 1981. ★

DAVID STEINBERG
Taboo Breaker

David Steinberg rose to fame in the late 1960s when he broke a long-standing taboo against religious humor on television. Later he diversified his material. His informal manner and intellectual style have given him a unique comedic personality.

He was born in Winnipeg, Canada, on August 9, 1942. Son of a rabbi, young Steinberg himself studied theology in Israel and in Chicago.

Controversial Role

"My presence is controversial," Steinberg says. "I like the tension that I create with an audience . . . . I'm leading them into areas of *honesty* that you don't normally get on television."

A comedian, he believes, should "sniff out all that's really rotten in those areas we've become lazy about," such as politics.

Favorite Comedians

Steinberg likes Bill Cosby's stand-up routines. He also appreciates Bette Midler and Carly Simon because they "have a specific sense of humor."

New Art Form

"I think commercials are great art forms," Steinberg observes. In 1984 he began to direct TV commercials, his first being one for NCR Corporation computers.

Recreations

Among Steinberg's favorite recreations are watching and playing basketball. He also plays the guitar and reads avidly.

Favorite Dish

Steinberg's favorite dish is any dish holding fish.

Turning from the spiritual to the mundane, he earned an M.A. in English literature at the University of Chicago. While there he began to experiment with comedy. In 1964 he joined the Second City, an improvisational group with whom he worked for a couple of years.

Steinberg then tried serious dramatics, appearing on Broadway in *Little Murders* (1967) and *Carry Me Back to Morningside Heights* (1968). But the shows had short runs, and he returned to comedy.

His big break came when he was engaged for some guest appearances on the Smothers Brothers TV series in 1968. Steinberg's religious satires shocked and angered some people, but delighted many others. "And God looked down," begins one bit, "and saw that the land and the people were bad. If He didn't look down so much maybe things would pick up." When God tells Moses, "I am that I am," Steinberg's Moses coughs politely and says, "Thanks for clearing that up." Steinberg formulated memorable one-liners, such as "The Gentiles grabbed the Jews by the Old Testament."

His career skyrocketed after his Smothers Brothers appearances. He began his long-standing role as frequent guest-host of *The Tonight Show*, and in 1972 he hosted his own TV variety series.

Soon his material broadened. Sex became a favorite topic: "Imagine you have attained undreamed-of horizons of virtuosity. You have devised and executed maneuvers that would mystify even Masters and Johnson. You have become to sex what Julia Child is to a chicken. And as you're lying there in the afterglow of a moment that poets devote their whole lifetimes to describe, she turns to you and says, 'Hey—that was cute.'"

Steinberg's literary education frequently surfaces in similes. "President Nixon," for example, "has a face that looks like a foot." And an old man's wrinkled neck "looks like the escalator at Bloomingdale's."

In recent years Steinberg has continued to work as a comedian on TV and in nightclubs. But he has also shown an increasing interest in moviemaking. He acted in *The End* (1978) and several other films. His credits as a director include *Going Berserk* (1983). ☆

David Steinberg with Burt Reynolds.

JERRY STILLER
Meara's Mate

Jerry Stiller has achieved his greatest success in two-character comedy sketches with his wife, Anne Meara. The team explores the battle of the sexes through ordinary people. The comically deadpan Stiller portrays a narrow-minded but vulnerable lost child, while Meara is strong or fragile as the skit demands. Though their sketches sometimes reach climaxes of extreme hostility, the duo always manages a denouement of warm humor.

Stiller was born in New York City, New York, on June 8, 1927 (1926, 1928, and 1929 have also been listed). After earning a B.S. degree in speech and drama at Syracuse University (1950), he began to act in summer stock and other stage productions.

In 1954, he married Anne Meara, a struggling young actress of Irish descent. For the next several years they acted, sometimes alone and sometimes together, in

Jerry Stiller and Anne Meara.

How Stiller and Meara Met

While waiting for a job interview, Stiller heard a woman's scream coming from the agent's office. The office door flew open, and a tall, pretty redhead dashed out. She said the agent had chased her around the room. Stiller confronted the man, who thereupon chased *him* around the room. Neither Stiller nor Meara found a job that day—but they found each other.

Two Concerned Citizens

The comedy couple do charity work, and they show fervent concern for big issues (such as nuclear freeze) and small ones (such as their local New York City block association).

Yearns for Dramatic Roles

His role as Tamkin, the greedy, street-smart con man, in the 1986 made-for-TV film *Seize the Day* forced Stiller to rethink the direction of his career. "It can be a painful process to discover who you really are," he said. "We're all greedy, but Tamkin's greed is close to what I have felt—wanting too much and not being connected to what really makes you happy."

Stiller feels that his original idealistic image of acting became blurred by commercial considerations when he turned to comedy. Though he wants to continue as a comedy team with Meara, he would also like to explore more dramatic roles.

the New York City area. They appeared in Shakespeare Company productions staged in Central Park, Meara usually as the leading lady and Stiller as the fool or comic foil.

To make more money, Stiller and Meara decided to become a comedy team and began to play in cabarets, in nightclubs, and at benefits. They broke new ground by directly, but humorously and touchingly, addressing the issue of mixed marriage. Other sketches satirized movies and various absurdities of daily life. A typical routine went like this:

STILLER: I hate you.
MEARA: You hate me? I hate you!
STILLER: You don't know what hate is—the kind of hate I have for you.
MEARA: Listen, my hate for you is such a hot hate—I hate you with hot heaping hunks of hate!
STILLER: The heat of your hot hate could not begin to approximate the hateful hatredness with which I'm hatefully hating you right now.
MEARA: If it was possible to write the word *hate* on each grain of sand in the Sahara Desert, all that hate on each of those hateful grains wouldn't equal one one-millionth of the hate that I'm hating you with right now!
STILLER: You know how much you hate me? Double it! That's my hate for you! (pause) I'd like to ask one question. Do you think this marriage can be saved?

Soon Stiller and Meara were playing major clubs in New York City, London, and elsewhere. In the 1960s they frequently performed on Ed Sullivan's popular TV variety program. Since then they have often appeared on TV specials and talk shows, and they have won high praise for their creative and comical radio commercials for Blue Nun wine and other products.

They have also continued their acting careers. Stiller had a regular role on the TV sitcom *Joe and Sons* (1975-76), and he has guested on many TV series, including *Alice*, *Private Benjamin*, and *Archie Bunker's Place*, on the last of which Meara was a regular. Stiller had an important role in the Broadway play *Hurlyburly* (1984), and he appeared in the movies *Airport 1975* (1974), *Seize the Day* (TV, 1986), and others.

Today Stiller and Meara are still happily married and still perform their stand-up routines to delighted audiences. ★

Stiller in *Those Lips, Those Eyes.*

Offstage Manner

In real life Jerry Stiller has a quiet demeanor. He seems perpetually pensive, with a constant crease in his forehead.

Annie as Crutch

"I didn't realize it for a long time," Stiller admitted in the mid-1970s, "but Annie was a crutch for me, a Rock of Gibraltar." She had a great creative mind, and he trusted her instincts. When he was preparing for one role, she offered him advice: "She told me to speak more clearly," he reported sheepishly.

In recent years his solo acting success has given him more confidence.

LARRY STORCH
Corporal Agarn

Larry Storch is a gifted nightclub comedian and impressionist. He is also a dependable light-comedy actor in motion pictures and stage productions. But his principal fame has come through television, particularly as Corporal Agarn in the farcical TV western series *F Troop* (1965-67), which enjoys a kind of cult following among many TV buffs.

Lawrence Samuel Storch was born in New York City, New York, on January 8, 1923. After serving as an entertainer in the navy during World War II, he won success as a nightclub comic. His act was based on humorous impressions of film stars, such as Jack Benny and Ronald Colman.

In the late 1940s Storch began to receive invitations to appear on TV. He hosted the summer variety show *Cavalcade of Stars* in 1952. The following year Jackie Gleason picked him to serve as Gleason's sum-

Storch as Corporal Agarn in *F Troop*.

Fond Memories

"We were a great team," Storch says of the *F Troop* cast, "and we had great fun. . . . I'm proud to have been on that show, and I don't mind a bit if people only remember me for that."

Nature Boy

Storch has a strong interest in nature. He loves gardens and has at times created a gardenlike atmosphere in his bedroom. In the 1970s he liked to explore the Hollywood canyons behind his home.

Recreations

Larry Storch enjoys cooking, swimming, skin diving, and playing the guitar and the saxophone. His favorite music is jazz.

Innate Goodness

Storch has a strong concern for the well-being of all creatures. For example, while filming *F Troop* he would look out for the welfare of the animals, as by insuring that dogs had water and by shooing flies away from horses' eyes. When his house cat brought home still-kicking prey (such as mice and lizards), Storch would gently rescue them and put them safely outside.

His concern extends to humans as well. If, for example, he thinks his gardener is overloaded with work, Storch will go out and help. He has exasperated his wife by such spontaneous acts as inviting a cab-driver in for dinner.

mer replacement; the program was called *The Larry Storch Show*, another variety series.

During the 1950s Storch performed on the New York City stage in *Red, White, and Blue* (1950); *The Littlest Revue* (1956); and *Who Was That Lady I Saw You With?* (1958). The last show was made into a movie with the shortened title *Who Was That Lady?* (1960), in which he also appeared.

During the next several years Storch had supporting roles in many film comedies and comedy-dramas. Among them were *Forty Pounds of Trouble* (1962); *Captain Newman, M.D.* (1963); and *Sex and the Single Girl* (1964). In *The Great Race* (1965) he played the comical western villain Texas Jack.

From 1965 to 1967 Storch worked in the TV sitcom *F Troop*. He played Corporal Randolph Agarn, a wheeler-dealer cavalryman in the Old West. To execute various profit-making schemes, Agarn and his cohorts keep up a pretense of hostility toward the Indians. Through syndication *F Troop* remains one of the most popular shows on TV.

Later Storch appeared in the short-lived TV sitcom *The Queen and I* (1969). In *The Ghost Busters* (1975-76) he starred as Eddie Spenser, who fights the ghosts of historic villains.

Storch was also busy in the 1960s and 1970s as a guest star on TV comedy series. Among the 1960s shows were *Get Smart* and *Gomer Pyle*. His 1970s guest spots included roles on *All in the Family* and *Love American Style*.

Storch has acted in many made-for-TV movies, both comedies and dramas. His comedy roles were highlighted by appearances in *The Incredible Rocky Mountain Race* (TV, 1977), as Eagle Feather, a daffy Indian who helps Mark Twain in a race, and *The Adventures of Huckleberry Finn* (TV, 1981), as Dauphin.

Storch also continued to act in theatrical films. Among them were *The Great Bank Robbery* (1969), *Airport 1975* (1974), and *S.O.B.* (1981).

Still a magnificent impressionist, Storch likes to borrow elements from famous personalities when he creates roles. For example, when he portrayed Dr. Einstein in a 1987 stage production of the comedy classic *Arsenic and Old Lace*, he used Marlene Dietrich as a model.

Today Storch plays about two dozen nightclub dates a year as a comic impressionist. He mimics such personalities as Muhammad Ali, Cary Grant, Jackie Gleason, Laurence Olivier, James Mason, and Orson

Contemplative Person

"I'm always in a quandary over things," Storch laments. "I guess it's my dark Russian soul."

He is disturbed by the misery in the world and spends much time contemplating ultimate meanings. He has studied everything from astrology to Yoga.

Traveler

Storch travels frequently. Among his favorite places are Morocco and Tuscany.

Welles. Besides duplicating their voices, Storch improvises dialogue that captures their essential characteristics.☆

THREE STOOGES
Slapstick Comedians

The Three Stooges—whose trademark was violent slapstick clowning in the old burlesque-vaudeville tradition—made nearly two hundred short films from the early 1930s to the late 1950s. Subsequent showings of the films on TV have made the team world famous. Though widely held in contempt by many observers because of their low comedy, the Three Stooges at their best were masters of comedic flow and timing.

Two players were members of the trio throughout its existence: Moe Howard (originally Moses Horwitz; born June 19, 1897, in New York City, New York) and Larry Fine (originally Louis Fineberg [sometimes spelled Fineburg/Feinberg]; born October 5, 1902, in Philadelphia, Pennsylvania). The third spot was filled at various times by one of four different men, principally Shemp Howard (originally Samuel Horwitz; born March 17, 1900, in New York City, New York) and Curly Howard (originally Jerome Lester Horwitz; born October 22, 1903, in New York City, New York), both of whom were Moe's brothers.

Sourpussed Moe was the leader, typically barking out orders, pretending to know more than he really did, and initiating the violence, which often backfired on him. Childlike Curly (or dopey Shemp) was usually the fall guy, while the blandly idiotic Larry generally found himself caught in the middle. Their regular mode of communication was to slap, poke, and hit one another. When no obvious pain resulted, the slapstick worked. When pain was apparent (as it was in many of their later films), the humor flopped.

Moe explained the starting point for all of their stories: "Where would we be most out of place?" The answer was in high society, on a hospital medical staff—in any place where wild fools would create havoc.

The genesis of the team was based on Moe's child-

Screen Character

In real life Curly Howard resembled his screen persona: an overgrown child wandering through life and caring little about anything except having fun. He even used some of his on-screen language and gestures.

Played Baseball

In his youth Moe was a good baseball player. In the early 1920s he made twelve two-reel silent sports comedies with the baseball great Hans Wagner.

Moe's Hair

Moe did not wear an on-screen wig. For everyday life he combed his thick hair back, and it looked perfectly normal. Just before filming a scene he would shake his head, and his hair would fall down to its familiar bowl shape.

Mild Mean Moe

Though violence was his on-screen hallmark, Moe Howard in real life was gentle. He seldom vented his emotions.

For many years he served as president of the Spastic Children's Guild, and every Christmas he would play Santa Claus for the kids.

Last-Minute Larry

Larry Fine in real life had a devil-may-care attitude. He drove the fanatically punctual Moe crazy by nearly always arriving at the last possible instant for appointments and performances. Often Moe and Curly were already on-stage, ready to give their partner's entrance cue, when Larry would finally arrive just in the nick of time.

The Three Stooges: (left to right) Larry, Moe, and Curly.

hood friendship with Ted Healy. Moe and Ted went into vaudeville together, with Ted as the star onstage and Moe as the heckler in the audience. Later Shemp and then, in 1925, Larry joined the act, which worked under several billings, including Ted Healy and His Gang, Ted Healy and His Racketeers, and Ted Healy and His Stooges. Soon they were one of vaudeville's top acts.

In 1930 the ensemble (with the Stooges billed as the Racketeers) made their film debut, in the feature *Soup to Nuts*. In 1932 Shemp left the team, and he was replaced by Curly. In 1933-34 Healy and his underlings made minor appearances in some features and starred in several Metro-Goldwyn-Mayer (MGM) shorts. In 1934 Healy and the Stooges parted.

The trio then signed with Columbia Pictures, which released 190 Three Stooges shorts between 1934 and 1959. The shaved-headed Curly was the principal funnyman in the early films. His funny little "nyuk-nyuk" expressed a sarcastic self-satisfaction that never lasted long. He spent most of his energy expressing fear, anger, and frustration by "woo-wooing," running in place, repeatedly slapping the front of his own face, and snapping doglike at his enemies. Curly conveyed frustration with particular conviction, as in *Dutiful but Dumb* (1942), in which he tries to eat a bowl of clam soup but is thwarted by a live clam that squirts him and steals his crackers.

Never Late

Fanatically punctual, Moe would routinely pay bills long before they were due and would arrive an hour early for appointments.

Bald Pate

Larry lost most of his hair after years of Moe's yanking it out.

Versatility

Curly was a fine singer and an accomplished ballroom dancer.

Shaved Head

Curly naturally had a full head of wavy brown hair. When he joined Ted Healy and His Stooges, he shaved his head at Healy's insistence. Throughout the rest of his career, Curly had his hair clipped to the nub once a week.

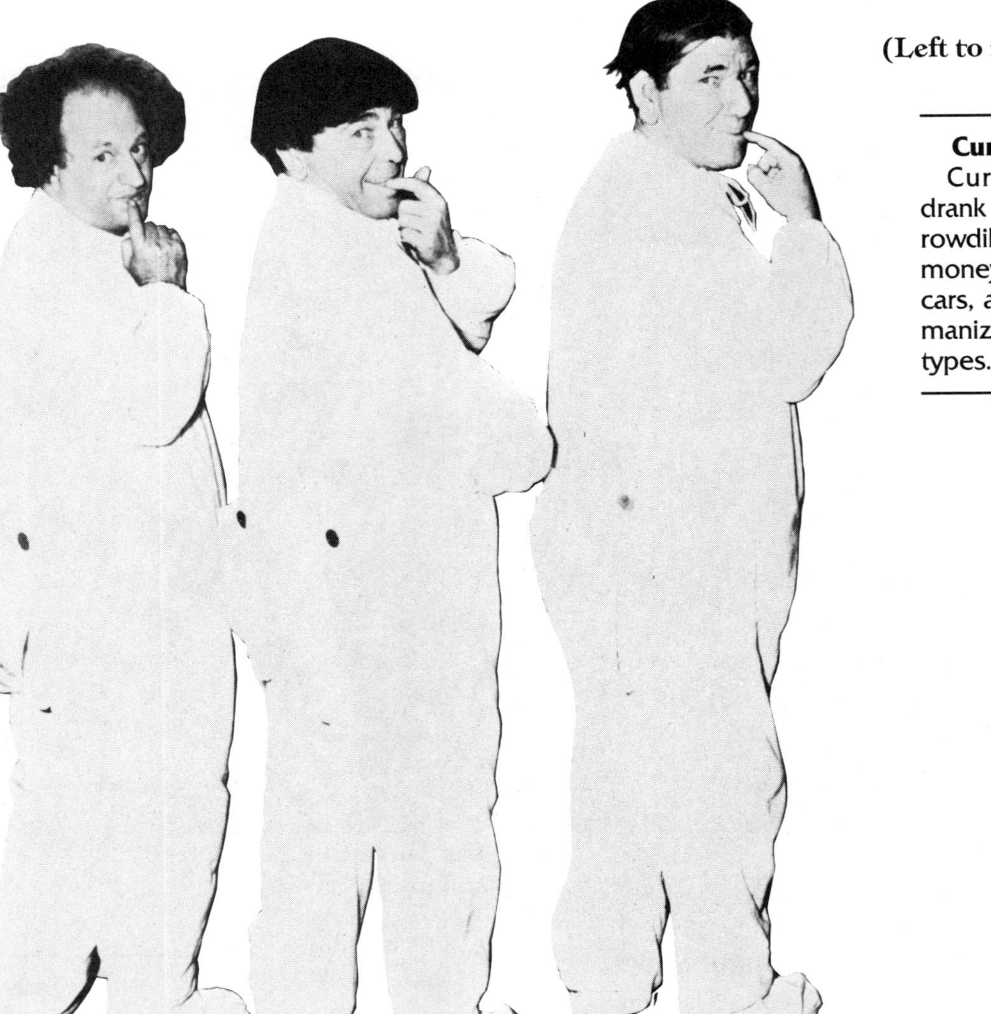

(Left to right) Larry, Moe, and Shemp.

Curly's Compulsions

Curly ate too much; drank too much; behaved rowdily in nightclubs; spent money recklessly on dogs, cars, and houses; and womanized with uncultured types.

Schlemiel Shemp's Shtick

Shemp distinguished himself from the other Stooges by speaking with a gravelly voice and by combing his hair straight back and parting it in the middle. He was also the only member of the team who felt the need for an independent career, which he pursued for fourteen years (1932-46).

Recreations

In his youth Larry boxed to strengthen injured arm muscles. He also played the violin, using the instrument in his pre-Stooge nightclub and vaudeville acts.

On-Screen Limp

Curly's funny little on-screen limp was real. In 1916 he accidentally shot himself in the foot while cleaning his rifle. Thereafter he was in constant pain, which may have accounted for his excessive drinking.

Feared Obesity

Standing only 5′4″ and loving to eat, Moe always feared getting fat. He walked a lot to burn up calories, and he watched his diet.

In 1946 illness forced Curly to retire. His last Stooges film was released in 1947.

Shemp thereupon rejoined the team. On his own he had effectively appeared in many movies, notably the W.C. Fields classic *The Bank Dick* (1940). But his films with the Stooges were a letdown from the Curly-dominated pictures, partly because Shemp's facial appearance and gruff manner paralleled, rather than contrasted with, Moe's. The films also began to show an overindulgence in violence with little redeeming humor.

In 1955 Shemp died. He was replaced by the veteran comic Joe Besser, with whom the Three Stooges completed their Columbia series of shorts.

In the 1960s the team made several feature films, with Joe De Rita in the third spot. The pictures included *Snow White and the Three Stooges* (1961) and *The Outlaws Is Coming* (1965).

Curly died in San Gabriel, California, on January 18, 1952; Shemp, in Los Angeles on November 22, 1955; Larry, in Woodland Hills, California, on January 24, 1975; Moe, in Los Angeles on May 4, 1975.

JOE WEBER *and* LEW FIELDS Dialect and Burlesque Comedians

Weber and Fields, low comedians par excellence, began as a German-Yiddish dialect act and eventually became masters of true burlesque. Weber, short and rotund (because of heavy padding around his middle), played the innocent dupe. Fields, tall and lanky, played the bossy, violent member of the team.

Both were born of Polish immigrants in the Bowery section of New York City, New York, Weber on August 11, 1867, and Fields on January 1, 1867. Joe Weber's original name was Moisha Weber; later his name was recorded as Morris Weber and Joseph Morris Weber. Lew Fields's original name was Moisha Schanfield; later his name was recorded as Lewis Maurice Schanfield and Lewis Maurice Fields.

They met in elementary school, and by the time they were ten years old they were already appearing together on the professional stage. With a slapstick comedy act in German-Yiddish dialect, as well as with Irish and blackface song-and-dance routines, they served a long apprenticeship in dime museums, beer gardens, amusement parks, and cheap theaters.

By the early 1890s they had achieved stardom with their dialect bits as Mike (Weber) and Myer (Fields).

Weber (right) and Fields.

Lew's Offspring

Lew Fields's children had a major impact on the American theater: Dorothy as a lyricist, Herbert as a librettist, and Joseph as a playwright.

Different Strengths

Between the two, Weber had the better business mind, while Fields had the better artistic vision.

Two Became One

"Every time I saw Fields's name on a show poster after our separation I thought of a one-legged man," Weber said. "Lew and I have answered either to Weber or to Fields for forty years. 'Glad to meet you, Mr. Weber,' a man says on shaking my hand, and 'Goodbye, Mr. Fields,' when he leaves. . . . Lew and I sometimes wonder if they'll get our names straight on our tombstones."

Mike would open their acts offstage by shouting, "Don't poosh me, Myer!" A typical exchange went like this:

WEBER: I am delightfulness to meet you.
FIELDS: Der disgust is all mine.
WEBER: I receivedidid a letter from mein goil, but I don't know how to writteninin her back!
FIELDS: Writteninin her back! Such an edumuncation you got it? Writteninin her back! You mean rotteninin her back. How can you answer her ven you don't know how to write?
WEBER: Dot makes no nefer mind. She don't know how to read.

But what audiences most enjoyed was the duo's physical humor. As Weber himself admitted, "All the public wanted to see was Fields knock the hell out of me." In their routine called "The Poolroom," Fields would introduce Weber to the basics of pool, cheat him as much as possible, and, when Weber protested, chase him around the table, beating him with a pool cue. Audiences also saw choking, eye-gouging (later imitated by countless comics), and pie fights (long before pies flew across silent-movie screens). Sometimes Weber would retaliate by kicking Fields in the shin. But Fields's pièce de résistance was literally to plant a hatchet in Weber's head (protected by a steel-plated wig and a cork cushion). Despite their slapstick, Weber and Fields were actually creating a new kind of vaudeville comedy, one based not on presenting pure nonsense but on poking fun at some aspect of the real world (such as human behavior in a poolroom).

In the mid-1890s Weber and Fields, sensing that ethnic groups were becoming sensitive about the use of dialect humor, turned to true burlesque (mock imitation). In 1896 they opened their own Broadway music hall, where they rose to the peak of their career by not only continuing the development of their knockabout sketches but also establishing themselves as brilliant parodists. Their 1897 variety show, entitled *The Glad Hand,* contained "Secret Servants," their comic version of William Gillette's play *Secret Service.* Later that year the duo staged "Pousse Café; or, The Worst Born," burlesquing Anna Held's performance in *La Poupée* and David Belasco's production of *The First Born.* Weber and Fields presented Edmond Rostand's classic *Cyrano de Bergerac* as "Cyranose de Bricabrac" (1898). Their 1899 burlesque of *Catherine* was so devastating that Annie Russell, star of the drama, admit-

Classic Joke

From about 1887 comes this classic Weber and Fields joke:

WEBER: Who was that lady I saw you with last night?
FIELDS: She ain't no lady—she's my wife!

Influence on Others

Many later comedy teams have learned from Weber and Fields. Smith and Dale employed the older duo's constant arguing. The Three Stooges used Weber and Fields's violent slapstick.

Laurel and Hardy, as well as Abbott and Costello, borrowed their predecessors' famous "Drinking Routine." Here is the way Weber and Fields originated it:

FIELDS: I have only five cents. Remember, when we go into the saloon, I'll have a beer and you say you don't want any. Say, in a sort of careless way, "Oooh, I don't care for anything." Now let's try it. What are you gonna have?
WEBER: I don't care for anything.
FIELDS: Something in my heart tells me you're not gonna do this right. Come on, be a sport.
WEBER: No, no.
FIELDS: Take something small.
WEBER: Well, I'll take a small bottle.
FIELDS: What! A small bottle with my poor five cents?
WEBER: Well, what do you wanna coax me for?
FIELDS: I wasn't coaxing. I was only making a bluff.
WEBER: Well, I don't take bluffs!

• • •

FIELDS: What did you say in there?
WEBER: Oh, I don't care if I do.
FIELDS: So the bartender gave *you* the glass, and I had to say I don't care for any, and I have a thirst that would sink a battleship!

ted that she and her fellow players "never again were able to give a completely serious performance of the original for recollection of the counterfeit."

Early in 1904 new fire laws forced Weber and Fields to close their music hall. Later that year a rift came between them and they broke up. They reteamed in 1912, but the glory days of true burlesque were gone. Their later years, as performers and producers, were spent in musical comedy, vaudeville, and motion pictures. Sometimes they worked together, sometimes apart. The movies in which they both appeared included *Friendly Enemies* (1925) and *Lillian Russell* (1940).

Both men moved to Beverly Hills, California, in 1930. Their work thereafter was limited to a few film and vauderville appearances.

Fields died in Los Angeles on July 20, 1941. Weber died in the same city on May 10, 1942. ★

MARC WEINER
Kaleidoscopic Comedian

Marc Weiner presents a kaleidoscope of comedy. Within a single performance he may be a stand-up comic, a clown, a juggler, a mime, a magician, and a puppeteer. Nearly half of his act is improvised. He involves his audience as much as possible, as in a skit where Sea Captain Weiner asks for help in finding his lost dog Schooner.

Weiner was born in Far Rockaway, New York, in 1952. When he was in the second grade, he developed a leg disease that put him on crutches for two years. He also had undiagnosed dyslexia, which made him hate read-

Breaking the Shell

Like many entertainers, Marc Weiner is not naturally gregarious. "I was always a shy, private person," he says. Performing helped him to break out of his shell.

Purpose in Life

Weiner has explained his increasing involvement with Judaism. "If you're young and single," he says, "the road is a party and, when you don't have any morality, it's a lot of fun. But for me life was very empty." He found himself caught in a vicious cycle of constantly looking for higher levels of success. "Being a comedian is totally consuming: you never know when you're going to think of a joke, so you're always working. I thought there had to be more of a purpose than that. I felt the only reason I was living was to perpetuate my puppets; it was really sick."

Leaving the System

The principal reason that Weiner left college in 1973 was the attitude of his sociology professor. "He convinced us to hate the Establishment by saying we were just leeches living off our parents," Weiner recalls, "and in order not to be sucked in, we had to get out of the system."

Sea Captain Weiner
Weiner's routine as Sea Captain Weiner is partly based in fact. While working on the sloop *Clearwater,* he earned his captain's license in 1975.

ing. The boy became hyperactive, and his clowning in school covered up his physical and psychological pain.

In 1973 Weiner dropped out of college in his third year. He opened a campus coffeehouse, where he entertained the customers. "I would study people's idiosyncracies and exaggerate them until they became more insane and laughable."

Later he became a cook and first mate on the folksinger Pete Seeger's sloop *Clearwater,* an environmental boat that sailed up and down the Hudson, promoting ecology. On the *Clearwater* he also performed as a juggler and magician to entertain the passengers.

Leaving the boat, Weiner moved to Boston, where he worked for several months as a street clown. He then returned to New York City, where he broadened his repertory on the streets and began to appear in showcase clubs.

His first big break came in 1978 when Robin Williams improvised with him on a New York City street. Soon Weiner's career soared. During the late 1970s and early 1980s he was one of the most popular college and comedy-club acts in the country. He also appeared many times on TV shows, including *Sesame Street* and *NBC's Saturday Night Live.*

The zany, bulbous-eyed Weiner broke audiences up by transforming himself into a human vacuum cleaner, a microwave oven with a sarcastic personality, and a Jewish alarm system that makes people feel guilty and asks them to wipe their feet. The most popular part of Weiner's act was his finger-size puppets, the Weinerettes, featuring Rocko, a gravel-voiced rock star.

In 1984 Weiner's meteoric rise came to an abrupt halt when he began to observe the Jewish Sabbath, which prevented him from working on Friday nights or Saturdays. Most comedy clubs dropped him even though he had been a major factor in the fantastic growth of such clubs (from about 10 paying clubs in 1980 to about 250 several years later). TV jobs also stopped coming. By 1986 his career was at a crawl.

Recently, however, some TV executives and club owners have begun to call again, relalizing that Weiner's comic ability has not been affected by his adoption of religious Orthodoxy. Employers now book him around his observance of the Sabbath. ★

LOTUS WEINSTOCK
Split Personality

Lotus Weinstock bases much of her humor on her split personality, which is reflected in her name. Originally named Marlena Weinstock, she replaced her first name with *Lotus* to stand for her spiritual aspirations, while she retained *Weinstock* to admit her earthly, Jewish realism. "The Lotus in me wants to be totally free," she says; "Weinstock will settle for a discount."

Both of her were born in Philadelphia, Pennsylvania, on January 29, 1943. She studied dance at the Philadelphia Academy of Music and theater arts at Emerson College in Boston. Weinstock left college to join a musical-comedy repertory company. Later she studied dancing and acting in New York City, where she became a hostess at the Bitter End, joined a comedy act billed as the Turtles, and then flopped as a soloist in Greenwich Village in the early 1960s.

Her life and career changed when she moved to the West Coast. There she met the uninhibited comedian Lenny Bruce, who became her mentor and fiancé. His death in 1966 prevented their marriage, but from him she learned to provoke thought as well as laughter in her act. "Lenny was the turning point of my life," she recalls. "Never again would I play beneath my intelligence or be anything less than honest onstage."

During the 1970s her career moved steadily forward. She became a regular on the nightclub circuit and began to appear on TV talk shows, such as Merv Griffin's.

Split Personality

Weinstock's telephone answering machine carries this message: "Lotus is here, but Weinstock is out pursuing her earthly goals. Please leave your number, and we'll call back when we are at one."

Tongue-in-Cheek Humility

Weinstock's goal is someday to be able to say, "Fame and fortune didn't bring me happiness."

Lenny Bruce Influence

"He was like a prophet, a seeker," Weinstock says of Lenny Bruce. "He knew comedy had to have substance," and because of him she dropped what she calls her "little phony tricks" of comedy and began to talk honestly to audiences.

Talmud Study

Twice a month Weinstock meets with her friends Larry Miller, Paul Reiser, Mark Schiff, and Jerry Seinfeld in their private homes to study liturgy and the Talmud under the guidance of the two Hillel House rabbis from USC and UCLA.

Lotus Weinstock.

Weinstock tells audiences about her split personality and about the problems it presents in raising her daughter, Lili Haydn. As Lotus, she is confident that the child will be guided by the One Presence and Power; but as Weinstock, a typical JAM (Jewish-American mother), she constantly worries.

Weinstock also tackles a wide range of important topical issues. Combining busing and astrology, she made this satiric suggestion: "Too many Geminis at one school? Bus them! Let them mingle with a Taurus or a Sagg! Get to know the other half of the zodiac!" She gathered many of her stories into the book *The Lotus Position* (1982), which addresses health, food, reincarnation, fidelity, sex, gun control, and other topics.

In recent years Weinstock has made her daughter, Lili, part of her stand-up act. In 1988 they appeared together in a Los Angeles stage production of the comedy play *Molly and Maze.* ☆

Gene Wilder.

GENE WILDER
Deadpan Comic Actor

Gene Wilder's fame rests largely on the wild contrast between his deadpan expression and his madcap behavior. That contrast reflects the real man. "My quiet exterior used to be a mask for hysteria," he says. "After seven years of analysis, it just became a habit."

Wilder is one the truly outstanding comic talents in contemporary motion pictures. He likes to draw humor from characters who are essentially sad, perhaps reflecting his early experiences in creating comedy for his invalid mother. His performances in Mel Brooks's frenetic films *The Producers* (1967), *Blazing Saddles* (1974), and *Young Frankenstein* (1974) are comic gems.

Gene Wilder was born in Milwaukee, Wisconsin, on June 11, 1935. His original name was Jerome Silberman.

When he was six, his mother had a heart attack that left her a partial invalid. He used to cheer her up by improvising comedy skits, thus developing an early awareness of the coexistence of laughter and pain.

His parents sent him to the Black Fox Military Institute in Los Angeles. "I was the only Jew in school," he later

Wilder in *Quackser Fortune Has a Cousin in the Bronx.*

said, "and I got either beaten up or insulted every day." He soon returned to his native city, where he began acting lessons in 1947 and graduated from high school in 1951.

While attending the University of Iowa (B.A., 1955), Wilder acted in school plays and worked in summer stock. During 1955-56 he studied at the Old Vic Theater School in Bristol, England.

Returning to America, he was drafted for two years of service in the army (1956-58), where he was assigned to the Valley Forge Hospital in Pennyslvania. He requested duty in the neuropsychiatric ward because he felt that the experience would be helpful in his acting studies.

In 1961 he joined the Actors Studio (in New York City), where he began to study with Lee Strasberg. That same year saw Wilder's first Broadway role, as the confused valet in *The Complaisant Lover.* Over the next several years he appeared in more plays, including *One Flew over the Cuckoo's Nest* (1963), and some TV programs, such as *The Defenders.*

Wilder's film debut was in *Bonnie and Clyde* (1967), in which he played a neurotic undertaker kidnapped by a gang of outlaws. The turning point in his career came when his friends Mel Brooks invited him to take an important role in *The Producers* (1967); Wilder por-

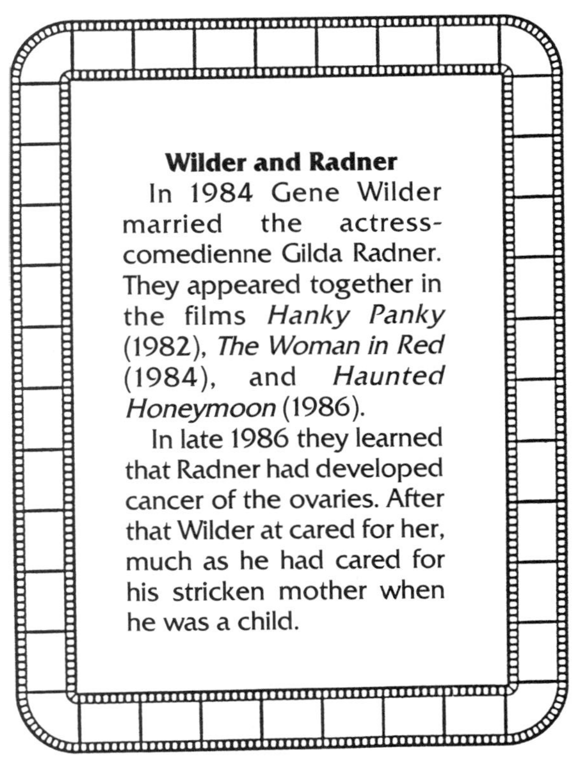

Wilder and Radner

In 1984 Gene Wilder married the actress-comedienne Gilda Radner. They appeared together in the films *Hanky Panky* (1982), *The Woman in Red* (1984), and *Haunted Honeymoon* (1986).

In late 1986 they learned that Radner had developed cancer of the ovaries. After that Wilder at cared for her, much as he had cared for his stricken mother when he was a child.

trayed the neurotic accountant Leo Bloom, who is drawn by a crooked producer into a wild scheme to cheat theater investors. There followed several movies in which Wilder's comic acting far outshone the scripts, as in *Start the Revolution without Me* (1970) and *Willy Wonka and the Chocolate Factory* (1971).

But when he turned once again to Brooks's films, comic magic resulted. In *Blazing Saddles* (1974), a spoof of Hollywood westerns, Wilder portrayed a brazen alcoholic gunslinger. In *Young Frankenstein* (1974), a gothic-horror parody whose script he cowrote with Brooks, Wilder played the title role, a brain surgeon who tries to live down the scandal of his infamous ancestor (partly by changing the pronunciation of his name from "FRANKenstein" to "FRAHNKensteen") but who finally succumbs to the temptation to follow in his forebear's footsteps by creating a monster from dead human parts; breaking tradition, however, he teaches the creature to dance in top hat and tailcoat.

Encouraged by his successful collaboration on *Young Frankenstein,* Wilder began to write, direct, and star in his own movies. Following Brooks's lead, he has constructed spoofs of distinct film genres, though Wilder's style has tended to be gentler than Brooks's. First came *The Adventure of Sherlock Holmes' Smarter Brother* (1975), a parody of the Holmes detective movies. *The World's Greatest Lover* (1977) is a takeoff on the Rudolph Valentino romantic films of the 1920s. In *Skippy* (1981) Wilder spoofed sex comedies, the hero signing himself into a mental hospital to overcome a sex problem. *The Women in Red* (1984) is an American comedy version of the myriad French films on casual adultery; here the would-be adulterer (Wilder) bungles all of his carefully planned efforts to seduce a beautiful model. In *Haunted Honeymoon* (1986) Wilder tipped his foolscap to all of the old haunted-house movies.

Among the other films Wilder has appeared in are *The Frisco Kid* (1979), a comedy about an Orthodox rabbi (Wilder) traveling from Poland across the United States to San Francisco in 1850; *Stir Crazy* (1980); and *Hanky Panky* (1982); and *See No Evil, Hear No Evil* (1989). ★

Wilder in *The Woman in Red.*

Off-Screen Manner

In real life Wilder is serious but calm and cheerful, in contrast with his usually frantic on-screen image.

Silent-Screen Comedians

In his own films, Wilder gives tributes to the silent-screen comics whom he admires. For eample, early in *The World's Greatest Lover,* there is a sequence in which a baker (Wilder) gets trapped on a cake-conveyer belt; the scenes bring to mind some of the great screen moments of Charlie Chaplin, as in *Modern Times.*

Recreations

Wilder likes to play bridge and tennis.

ED WYNN
Perfect Fool

Ed Wynn, more than any other stage comedian, made himself resemble the traditional image of a circus clown. He whitened his face to set off his grease-painted eyebrows, horn-rimmed glasses, prominent nose, and red-lipped mouth. And he clothed his pear-shaped frame with zany hats (eight hundred of them), misfit clothes (including three hundred jackets and coats), and oversized, flapping shoes.

As a performer, he had many trademarks, including a lisp, a high nasal voice, a squeaky giggle, fluttering hands, and a constant look of surprise and wonderment. He loved puns. In the variety show *Ed Wynn Carnival* (1920) he introduced his ball-juggling routine by asking the orchestra conductor to "play something in a jugular vein." In a sketch in *Boys and Girls Together* (1940) he played a showboat impresario

Gray Panthers

"This business of involuntary retirement is a crusade with me," Wynn declared in 1959. "What this generation is doing to people my age is a crime against humanity, and sooner or later society will pay for it!"

Fantasy World

"I never wanted to be a real person," Ed Wynn confessed. He was truly happy only in the fantasy world that he created during his performances. In real life he tended to be morose and withdrawn. "Maybe I used up all my happiness on the stage," he once mused.

Wynn in *The Absent-minded Professor.*

Ed Wynn with son Keenan.

who said, "I bred my cast upon the waters." His celebrated exit line was "I'll be back in a flash with more trash."

He also became famous for his preposterous inventions, such as a pole over eleven feet long "to use on people you would not touch with a ten-foot pole." Other inventions included a silent soup spoon, a baited mousetrap sealed shut so that the frustrated mice will move to another house, a typewriter whose moving carriage is equipped with corn on the cob so that a diner's head need not move, windshield wipers for eyeglasses when a person eats grapefruit, and a pianocycle, a combination piano and tricycle that he pedaled around the stage while a girl sat on the piano and sang.

Ed Wynn was born in Philadelphia, Pennyslvania, on November 9, 1886. His original name was Isaiah Edwin Leopold.

His father was a moderately prosperous manufacturer and retailer of women's hats. As soon as the boy could walk, he was putting on ladies' hats and drawing laughs from his father's customers.

Young Leopold desperately wanted to become a professional comedian, but his parents objected. Hence, in the summer of 1902, at the age of fifteen, he ran away from home and joined a repertory company as a backstage helper and occasional onstage player. Soon, however, the company went bankrupt in New England and he returned home.

After selling hats for a while, he ran away again. To avoid embarrassing his father, he formed a stage name by splitting the two syllables of his middle name: Edwin became Ed Wynn.

In 1903 he began his long, successful vaudeville career. For a while he and Jack Lewis performed together under the billing of Win and Lose. However, Wynn worked principally on his own as one of the top vaudeville comedians of his time.

In 1910 he made his Broadway debut by appearing in the short-lived musical comedy *The Deacon and the Lady*. But it was through the *Ziegfeld Follies of 1914* that Wynn became a Broadway star. In the 1915 edition of the *Follies*, Wynn was in the show with W.C. Fields. During the latter's famous pool-table act, the audience kept laughing at the wrong times. At last Fields discovered Wynn under the table—comically catching flies. The two great comedians did not speak to each other for several years, but peace was eventually restored.

Wynn went on to star in many other Broadway revues and musical comedies. His most successful appearances were in his own variety shows, which he preferred to call "entertainments" rather than revues. Besides starring in the shows, he often had a hand in producing, directing, writing books and lyrics, and composing music for them. *Ed Wynn Carnival* (1920), *The Perfect Fool* (1921), *The Laugh Parade* (1931), *Boys and Girls Together* (1940), and *Laugh, Town, Laugh* (1942) were some of his entertainments. Beginning in 1921 he billed himself as the Perfect Fool. He also wrote a book called *Philosophy of a Fool* (1933).

Wynn was the first entertainer to broadcast a full-length Broadway show to a radio audience, performing *The Perfect Fool* on a New York City station in 1922. In his first radio series, *The Fire Chief* (1932-35), he introduced the technique of combining his comedy with the sponsor's commercial messages. He also starred in *Happy Land* (1944-45), as King Bubbles, ruler of a mythical kingdom of happiness. His shows were popular, but Wynn was essentially a visual comedian, working in costume even for his radio broadcasts.

The arrival of television in the late 1940s gave him a much more appropriate medium. He hosted the

Wynn's Winners

Many of Ed Wynn's original jokes and stories have become classics, retold and varied by generations of comedians. Here are two of his one-liners: "A husband is what is left of a sweetheart after the nerve has been taken out"; "A bachelor is a man who never made the same mistake once."

independent variety program *The Ed Wynn Show* (1949-50) and then another program with the same title (1950-51) on a rotating basis with other shows as part of the *Four-Star Revue* series.

However, by the mid-1950s his brand of humor had become dated. He feared that his career was over.

Then, in 1956, Wynn surprised everyone and opened a whole new facet to his career when he performed straight dramatic roles in the movie *The Great Man* (released in 1957) and in the live TV play "Requiem for a Heavyweight" (1956) on the *Playhouse Ninety* anthology series. During the rest of his career, he concentrated on being a film actor in both dramatic and comedic roles. Among his serious parts were roles in *The Diary of Anne Frank* (1959) and *The Greatest Story Ever Told* (1965). On the light side, he played Jerry Lewis's fairy godfather in *Cinderfella* (1960); the toymaker in *Babes in Toyland* (1961); Uncle Albert, who floats to the ceiling whenever he laughs—and he cannot stop laughing!—in *Mary Poppins* (1964); and Rufus, the 1,100-year-old gnome king, in *The Gnome-Mobile* (1967).

Wynn died in Beverly Hills, California, on June 19, 1966.☆

A Favorite Story

In one of Wynn's favorite stories, he owned a horse that liked to sit on eggs. When a man bought the horse, Wynn told him about the animal's peculiar habit. The man praised Wynn for his honesty, said he did not foresee any problem, and took the horse anyway.

Later Wynn's phone rang. "What do you mean selling me a crazy horse?" the buyer screamed over the phone. "I'm riding him home and when he comes to the bridge he won't cross it, but wades into the river with me and sits down."

"Oh, I forgot to tell you," Wynn replied innocently. "He likes to sit on fish, too.

HENNY YOUNGMAN
King of One-Liners

Henny Youngman has broken up audiences for over fifty years with his blatantly unsophisticated brand of stand-up comedy. His style is based on compact wording, simple phrasing, rapid-fire delivery, and quick transitions between topics. Other than his use of the derogatory Polish joke, he avoids offensive and controversial subjects, including politics and X-rated sex.

Youngman's most famous jokes are conceptual one-liners, especially those based on a pun, such as "Take my wife—please!" But he also uses easily visualized "cartoon" jokes, as in this classic: "A fellow walked up to me. He said, 'You see a cop around here?' I said, 'No.' He said, 'Stick 'em up!'"

Henny (originally Henry) Youngman was born of

Dial-a-Joke

When the New York Telephone Company set up its Dial-a-Joke service in 1974, Youngman was the first comedian enlisted to tape material. He recorded about 250 jokes covering thirty minutes.

American citizens in Liverpool, England, on January 12, 1906. He grew up in the Bay Ridge section of Brooklyn, New York City, New York.

As a youngster he took violin lessons, and in his teens he formed a band, the Syncopaters. After several years of playing in and around Brooklyn, he and his group began to appear regularly at the Jewish resorts in the Catskill Mountains.

Gradually he worked comic bits into his act, and in 1932 he switched to solo comedy. Over the next four years Youngman struggled in the borscht belt and at small nightclubs in New York City and elsewhere.

He finally hit the big time with his regular appearances on Kate Smith's popular network radio show from 1936 to 1938. Walter Winchell, the gossip journalist, dubbed Youngman the "king of the one-liners."

Since then the comedian has been one of America's busiest traveling entertainers, often averaging over two hundred engagements a year. Besides being a fixture on the banquet circuit and appearing at nightclubs, casinos, hotels, and theaters, Youngman—perhaps more than any other big-name comedian—performs at private sales meetings, trade shows, business openings, fraternal roasts, and even an occasional bar mitzvah or wedding party. Beginning in the 1950s he also widened his popularity with TV appearances, notably on *The Tonight Show.*

Often teased for using old jokes, Youngman replies that "no joke is an old joke to people who haven't heard it." After purchasing and polishing jokes for over half a century, he has a repertory of about 1,600 "gems," as he calls them. "I play for the masses," he explains. "I tell easy jokes. You don't have to think. My jokes happen to everybody. Some people get embarrassed because my jokes are corn. They're plain. They make people laugh." ★

Violin Prop

In his early years as a comedian Youngman, following a common vaudeville tradition, used a cigar as a prop. But on Kate Smith's radio show, he started playing the violin between jokes. Since then the violin has been part of his in-person act as well.

TV Fan

"I've always been a television fan," Youngman admits. "I'm either watching it or on it. Sometimes both, watching me being on it."

To Youngman, "The greatest invention in the world was videotape. it made it possible for me to go home and watch myself and see what I did wrong. I get pretty sick of *that*! But I'll never stop watching. It's so much fun to see when I do something right."

Launched Abbott and Costello

When Youngman decided to leave the *Kate Smith Show*, he found two former burlesque comedians, Bud Abbott and Lou Costello, to replace him in 1938. The duo quickly attained national popularity and went on to movie stardom

A Youngman Potpourri

"I was so ugly when I was born—the doctor slapped my mother."

"Things were rough when I was a baby—no talcum powder!"

"I've been married for forty-nine years, and I'm still in love with the same woman. If my wife ever finds out, she'll kill me."

"Last night I baited a mousetrap with a picture of cheese. I caught a picture of a mouse."

His Most Famous Joke

Youngman was preparing for a broadcast of the *Kate Smith Show.* "At the last minute, my wife came in for some tickets," he later explained. "I said, 'Take my wife—please! Get rid of her!' It stuck." It is the only joke in his repertory for which he claims authorship.

THUMBNAIL SKETCHES

Literally hundreds of Jewish comic performers can be added to the list of personalities detailed in the main section of this book. The following is a sampling.

BERNIE ALLEN is a fine comedian who struggled for many years before attaining show-business success. After serving in World War II, he ran a restaurant till 1956. Then he drove a cab. One day he picked up the boxer Rocky Graziano and floored him with jokes. Graziano introduced Allen to the comedienne Martha Raye, through whom Allen began to get jobs as a stand-up comic, becoming a favorite in Las Vegas. In the 1970s he briefly teamed up with Steve Rossi.

RABBI ROBERT A. ALPER delighted his Temple Micah (Wyncote, Pennsylvania) congregants by illustrating his sermons with humor. Now his stand-up comedy delights audiences not only at synagogues, churches, and organizational events but also on radio and TV programs and at top comedy clubs in Manhattan and Philadelphia. Here is a typical Rabbi Alper story: "A woman whose husband had just died called, asking, 'Rabbi, how long after the funeral must I wait before I can start dating?' Suddenly my other phone rang. 'Just a minute,' I said. 'Thank you,' she said and hung up."

SANDY BARON, an excellent stand-up comedian, won renown for his portrayal of Lenny Bruce in a 1972 Los Angeles stage production of the play *Lenny.* He has also acted in films, such as the comic horror flick *Vamp* (1986).

BELLE BARTH (originally BELLE SALZMAN) began her career by performing popular-song standards as a singer-pianist. But in the 1950s she switched to ribald songs and X-rated jokes, often translating English four-letter words into Yiddish slang. A regular at Catskills resorts for decades, she also issued bawdy albums and worked at clubs and hotels in Miami and Las Vegas. For stage purposes, she kept the surname of the first of her three husbands. She died in 1971.

BEN BERNIE (originally BERNARD ANZELEVITZ) was known as the Eccentric Violinist in vaudeville, where he developed a style of comical bantering with the audience. Later he became famous as an orchestra leader on radio, where he uttered wry comments and gags between selections. He died in 1943.

MEL(VIN) BLANC is the voice of the cartoon characters Bugs Bunny, Daffy Duck, Porky Pig, the Road Runner, Tweety Pie the canary, Sylvester the cat, Woody Woodpecker, Yosemite Sam, and many others. For the TV cartoon series *The Flintstones* (1960-66) he supplied the voices of Barney Rubble and Dino the dinosaur. From the late 1930s on, he was a regular on Jack Benny's radio show, where Blanc played many roles, including Benny's temperamental Maxwell automobile; Carmichael, the ill-tempered polar bear who guarded Benny's underground vault; and the laconic railway conductor who intoned the names of such California towns as "Ana-heim, A-zuza, and CUC-amunga." When Benny moved to TV in 1950, Blanc continued to work on the show. Blanc had on-camera supporting roles in several movies, including *Neptune's Daughter* (1949), and supplied voices for many others, such as the live-action film *Champagne for Caesar* (1950, as the voice of Caesar, a talking parrot) and the animated features *Gay Purr-ee* (1962) and *Hey There, It's Yogi Bear* (1964). He died in 1989.

BEN BLUE (originally BENJAMIN BERNSTEIN) was a deadpan, sad-faced, rubber-limbed mime and comedian. He began in vaudeville and later worked

in nightclubs, in films, and on TV. Among his early movies were *College Rhythm* (1934) and *My Wild Irish Rose* (1947). His cameo appearances stood out in several later pictures, such as *The Russians Are Coming, the Russians Are Coming* (1966). He died in 1975.

STAN(LEY) BURNS, one of the world's finest ventriloquists, divides himself into countless characters through the use of his "woodniks" (talking dolls). Also a renowned stand-up comedian, he creates sustained hilarity at every performance with his audience-participation sketches.

EMIL COHEN is an American humorist who uses his mastery of the Yiddish idiom to bring alive the folklore, satire, and humor of earlier, persecuted, poverty-stricken generations of East European Jews.

JACK EAGLE, a gifted stand-up comic, is now best known for his role as Brother Domenic in the lighthearted Xerox TV commercials. He began the role in 1975 and soon was making about 150 personal appearances a year for the company. "I'm probably the most famous monk of all time," Eagle quipped, "and I'm Jewish."

HERB(ERT) EDELMAN is a bald, lanky character actor who specializes in comic roles. He made his Broadway debut in Neil Simon's *Barefoot in the Park* (1963). His films have included *The Odd Couple* (1968) and *The Front Page* (1974). He is a frequent guest star on TV, notably in a recurring role as Dorothy's ex-husband on *The Golden Girls.*

BENNY FIELDS (originally BENJAMIN GEISENFELD) starred with his wife, Blossom Seeley, in a duo act in vaudeville, in nightclubs, at hotels, and on TV. She was a brassy singer, while he assisted in the singing (he pioneered the crooning style) and provided comedy relief. He died in 1959.

HERSCHEL and **JUDY FOX** are a rising young husband-and-wife team who intersperse comedy bits into their vocal acts, which consist of contemporary music, Broadway tunes, Jewish novelty songs, and traditional Yiddish, Israeli, Hasidic, and cantorial material. Herschel has also starred in musical comedies.

MICKEY FREEMAN is fondly remembered as Private Zimmerman on the classic TV sitcom *You'll Never Get Rich* (or *The Phil Silvers Show,* 1955-59; syndicated as *Sergeant Bilko*). He now captivates live audiences as a stand-up comic at major nightclubs. Freeman also conducts a nostalgic, hilarious combination of lecture and question-and-answer session about the *Sergeant Bilko* show and about making TV programs in general.

JACKIE GAYLE (originally JACK POTOVSKY) was a fast-talking, wacky saloon comedian for many years. In 1973 he was named Lounge Star of the Year in Las Vegas. In the late 1970s and early 1980s he opened for Frank Sinatra. Gayle finally won wide recognition when he had a major role (as a panama-hat-wearing aluminum-siding salesman) in the film comedy *Tin Men* (1987).

MORTY GUNTY was a Brooklyn-born nightclub comic and a fixture in the Catskills for many years. He played himself in Woody Allen's film *Broadway Danny Rose* (1984). Gunty died in 1984.

HANABELLE (real name, HANA BELIER) is a remarkably gifted mime and clown. In her show *I'll Be the Circus* she plays the Ringmaster, the Magician, the Tightrope Walker, the Juggler, and many other roles. Her performances are keyed to Judaic themes and holidays.

ROBERT PAUL HIRSCH distinguished himself for many years as a comic actor and mime onstage in Paris at the Comédie-Française.

MARTY INGELS (originally MARTIN INGER-

MAN) became a successful stand-up comedian, played Arch Fenster in the TV sitcom *I'm Dickens—He's Fenster* (1962-63), and appeared in film comedies, such as *If It's Tuesday, This Must Be Belgium* (1969). Later he quit performing to become a theatrical agent and producer.

LOU(IS) JACOBI is an expert performer of comic roles on the stage, in films, and on TV (notably in recurring guest roles as a flamboyant

suitor on *Too Close for Comfort* and as a delicatessen owner on *Barney Miller*).

MILT KAMEN worked as a stand-up comedian in nightclubs and acted in some movie comedies. But he was best known for his appearances on TV programs, such as the game show *To Tell the Truth* and Merv Griffin's talk show, in the latter of which Kamen gave comical film reviews. He died in 1977.

MARVIN KAPLAN, a comedy character actor of owlish appearance, has worked in many films, such as *Angels in the Outfield* (1951) and *The Great Race* (1965). On TV he was in the sitcom *Meet Millie* (1952-56), and in the late 1970s and early 1980s he played Henry, the telephone repairman, in the comedy series *Alice.*

STUBBY KAYE began as a vaudeville comedian and later became successful on Broadway in the musicals *Guys and Dolls* (1950) and *Li'l Abner* (1956). He had a regular role in the TV sitcom *My Sister Eileen* (1960-61). His films have included

Guys and Dolls (1955), *Forty Pounds of Trouble* (1963), and *Who Framed Roger Rabbit* (1988).

SY (originally SEYMOUR) **KLEINMAN,** a lawyer, used humor for many years in his practice and in the classes he taught at the Columbia Law School. In the mid-1970s he began to make weekend and vacation-time appearances as a humorist ("A comedian says funny things; a humorist makes a comment about life with laughter") at colleges, temples, and elsewhere. He donated his fees to the United Jewish Appeal and the Hebrew University in Jerusalem. In the late 1980s illness forced him to stop performing.

PINKY LEE (originally PINCUS LEFT), a wild

☆☆☆☆☆☆☆☆☆☆☆☆☆☆☆☆☆☆☆☆☆

sight-gag performer, began in vaudeville. He reached the peak of his popularity by hosting the children's TV series *The Pinky Lee Show* (1954-56).

PHILIP LOEB, a comedy character actor, won fame as Molly's husband, Jake, in the radio and TV comedy series *The Goldbergs* in the late 1940s and early 1950s. His movies included the Marx Brothers romp *Room Service* (1938) and the Goldberg spinoff *Molly* (1951). Blacklisted during the McCarthy-era witch-hunts, Loeb committed suicide through an overdose of sedatives in 1955.

LOU MASON, one of America's most talented Jewish humorists, has appeared in theaters, in hotels, in nightclubs, in concert halls, on radio, and on TV throughout the United States and Canada. Extemporaneous wit and intelligent observations on Jewish life characterize Mason's programs.

LARRY MILLER is more interested in conveying attitudes than in delivering one-liners. "I am the comic as essayist," he says. "It's a way of looking at the world. It's so much in the Jewish tradition. *Israel* means 'God wrestling.' Jews are unsurpassed for wrestling with the issues." Miller's favorite issue is the lack of merits in his own generation. According to Miller, he and his peers are lazy: "My father held down three jobs and then went to school at night. If I go to the cleaners and back the same day, I need a nap!" They are also pampered ("Can you imagine us lecturing our children, 'Well, I used to have to *drive* to school'?"); selfish (rather than have children, they carry pictures of themselves as children); and distrustful ("Pardon me, but aren't prenuptial agreements like arranging for the divorce before the marriage?"). Twice a month Miller meets with his friends Paul Reiser, Mark Schiff, Jerry Seinfeld, and Lotus Weinstock to study liturgy and the Talmud.

STEVE MITTLEMAN, a young stand-up comedian on the rise, began his career by focusing on self-denigration. Recently he has extended his interest to human flaws in general.

HOWARD MORRIS, a highly skilled comedy character actor, was a regular on the TV variety series *Your Show of Shows* (1950-54) and on the sitcom *The Andy Griffith Show* (1960-68). His films have included *The Nutty Professor* (1963) and *Return to Mayberry* (TV, 1986).

MAXIE ("SLAPSIE MAXIE") ROSENBLOOM, an ex-boxer noted for his slapping technique in the ring, became a familiar comedy character actor in movies, often as a dumb gangster or a punch-drunk fighter. Rosenbloom appeared in *Nothing Scared* (1937), *Hollywood or Bust* (1956), and many other films. He died in 1976.

MARK SCHIFF gained notice in the late 1970s by appearing at New York City comedy clubs, such as Pip's and the Comic Strip. Today he is an admired regular on the comedy circuit. Twice a month he meets with his friends Larry Miller, Paul Reiser, Jerry Seinfeld, and Lotus Weinstock to study liturgy and the Talmud.

ARNOLD STANG, a comedy character actor

known for his hilariously weak chin, was a mainstay on Milton Berle's TV variety series in the 1950s. Stang's films have included *The Wonderful World of the Brothers Grimm* (1962) and *Hercules in New York* (1970).

ROBERT STRAUSS (full name, HENRY ROBERT STRAUSS) was a character actor who often played comic heavies. He is best remembered as the dopey Animal in the movie *Stalag 17* (1953). Among his other films were *The Seven Year Itch* (1955) and *The Family Jewels* (1965). He died in 1975.

MOSHE WALDOKS, a gifted humorist-lecturer, entertains and enlightens audiences with his jokes, stories, commentaries on American-Jewish life, and dramatized excerpts from leading Jewish writers. With William Novak he coedited *The Big Book of Jewish Humor* (1981).

PEARL WILLIAMS (originally PEARL WOLFE) was known for her risqué jokes and her long dialect routines. She retired in 1984, after eighteen years as a regular in Miami.

MEYER ZAREMBA, a former public-school principal, convulses audiences with his jokes, stories, and monologues in both English and Yiddish. He finds humor in every facet of the Jewish experience and simultaneously increases his Jewish listeners' pride in their heritage.

Index

About the Author

Darryl Lyman coedited *Fifty Golden Years of Oscar* (1979), the official history of the Academy of Motion Picture Arts and Sciences. He is coauthor (with Marjorie D. Lewis) of the college textbook *Essential English* (1981) and the author of *The Animal Things We Say* (1983), *Great Jews in Music* (1986), and *Great Jews on Stage and Screen* (1987). His shorter works have appeared in such periodicals as *Newsday* and *Jack and Jill.*